READING

MISCUE

INVENTORY

READING MISCUE INVENTORY

From Evaluation to Instruction

SECOND EDITION

YETTA M. GOODMAN

DOROTHY J. WATSON

CAROLYN L. BURKE

Foreword by Brian Cambourne

Richard C. Owen Publishers, Inc.
Katonah, New York

Library of Congress Cataloging-in-Publication Data

Goodman, Yetta M., 1931–

Reading miscue inventory: from evaluation to instruction / Yetta M. Goodman, Dorothy J. Watson, Carolyn L. Burke.—2nd ed.

p. cm.

Summary: "Describes the theory, purpose, and three procedures for recording and evaluating student reading via miscue analysis. Includes assessment forms and reading strategy lessons"— Provided by publisher.

Includes bibliographical references and index.

ISBN-13: 978-1-57274-737-1 (isbn-13 pbk.)

ISBN-10: 1-57274-737-4 (isbn-10 pbk.)

1. Miscue analysis. 2. Reading. I. Watson, Dorothy J. (Dorothy Jo), 1930- II. Burke, Carolyn L. III. Title.

LB1050.33.G66   2005

428.4—dc22

2005000839

Richard C. Owen Publishers, Inc.
PO Box 585
Katonah, NY 10536
914-232-3903; 914-232-3977 fax
www.RCOwen.com

Acquisitions Editor: Darcy H. Bradley
Production Manager: Amy J. Finney
Index by: Sharon Murphy

Printed in the United States of America

9   8   7   6   5   4   3   2

In Honor and Memory of
BARRY SHERMAN

Contents

PART II: PROCEDURES FOR MISCUE ANALYSIS

Contents

Foreword

Most of us have had those moments of illumination, which perception psychologists call the "ah-ha experience." Sometimes the illumination is slow, like the gradual understanding of the punch line of a joke you don't initially "get." Other times it can be a sudden, "eureka-like" illumination that occurs in a flash, when, like Archimedes in the bath, the solution to a complex problem we've been struggling to resolve suddenly emerges.

While "ah-ha" experiences are merely one of the many forms of learning we can engage in, they're often more memorable and long-lasting than other mundane learning experiences we have in the course of our daily lives. Some of these experiences change our lives to such a degree that we can never go back to thinking, knowing, understanding, or behaving in the ways we did prior to this particular "ah-ha."

I had one of these life-changing "ah-ha's" in 1975 and remember it clearly. I was engaged in postdoctoral work at Harvard, where some of the luminaries of the reading world, including Jeanne Chall, Courtney Cazden, Carole Chomsky, Helen Popp, and others, mentored, guided, and continually challenged me. I also had auditing privileges with MIT, which was two stations away on the MTA. I spent many hours auditing courses in MIT's linguistics department and attending seminars conducted by its psycholinguistic and artificial intelligence research groups. I considered myself to be at the centre of the learning, language, and reading universe. I thought I was in academic heaven.

During one of the many coffee breaks I took at Harvard, the late Jeanne Chall said to me, "Brian, there's this fellow Ken Goodman who's writing a lot about something called miscue analysis. He claims it shows that meaning-based approaches support learning to read better than code-based approaches. Seeing you have more time than the rest of us, why don't you research his claims? Perhaps you could do a paper for the *Harvard Ed. Review,* which we could publish?"

She gave me a rather large red box, which had the words "Reading Miscue Inventory" written on its shiny new exterior. I also noted the authors' names and recall commenting to Jeanne thus: "I thought you said it was 'Ken Goodman' who was responsible for miscue analysis. Only one of these authors is a Goodman, someone named 'Yetta.'"

Jeanne informed me that the authors had worked with Ken on his miscue research and that Yetta was Ken's wife. She then explained how they'd taken the original miscue taxonomy Ken had used in his research and made it more teacher friendly. She finally commented, "A version which has been modified for classroom use might be a good way to 'get into his work.' I took this red box back to my office and opened it. It contained several red booklets, some scoring templates, and some audiotapes. I quickly skimmed the titles of books. The one called *Manual for Using RMI* caught my eye. I opened it and began reading.

Much later, after studying Ken's original research, deconstructing the original full version of the miscue Taxonomy, and after publishing an essay on his work in the *Reading Research Quarterly* (Cambourne 1975–1976) I recognised the brilliance of their work. They'd taken a very complex, multitheoretical taxonomy and turned it into a classroom teacher-friendly tool without "dumbing it down." They'd created a multifaceted educational tool that not only helped teachers understand the reading process, but which helped them identify *all* students' reading strengths and weaknesses and then offered them viable classroom-based strategies that were based on these strengths and weaknesses. In one sense it was a full reading curriculum in a box. It had a solid theoretical base; it could be used as a diagnostic tool; it could be used to quantitatively evaluate, compare, and rank readers in terms of strengths and weaknesses; it could be used to design and justify theoretically valid teaching strategies for each individual member of a class.

From that point my life changed forever. I began a wild, exhilarating, unpredictable, sometimes frightening, intellectual ride, not unlike those I had experienced as a youthful member of the surfboard fraternity in an earlier life. Intellectually it was like pushing oneself over the edge of a huge, slowly breaking wave, feeling it pick you up, thrust you forward with its power, never knowing whether you should stand and cut left, right, or even pull back from the wave before it broke, fearful that if you continued to "go with it" it might suddenly break and "dump" you painfully in the shallows.

As I reflect on that period of my professional growth with the benefit of thirty years' hindsight, it is now obvious that in 1975 I'd been caught up in a Kuhn-ian scientific revolution. According to Strauss (2005), "Scientific revolutions occur when a crisis within the scientific paradigm is resolved by the adoption, within the scientific community, of new, empirically supported principles that redefine what counts as a theoretically significant problem, and the way that problem is solved" (Strauss 2005, 166). Of course, in 1975 I wasn't aware that I was caught up in a Kuhn-ian scientific revolution. I thought I was simply experiencing multiple "ah-ha's" about reading, language, learning, and teaching. One in particular stands out. I clearly remember reading a statement, somewhere in the RMI materials that Jeanne Chall had loaned me, a statement something like this: **"The oral and written forms of language are parallel versions of the same thing—language."**

The implications of this statement struck me with tsunami-like force. Michael Halliday's (1975) *Learning How to Mean* had just been published. When I put Halliday's work and this one particular concept from the RMI together in my head, thoughts started bubbling up and spilling over each other at a frenetic pace; I can still remember the trains of thought that rattled through my head: "If learning to talk is **learning how to mean** using the oral mode of language, then perhaps learning how to read and write is **learning how to mean** using the written form of language. If they're parallel versions of the same thing, then perhaps they can be learned similarly? Perhaps learning how to mean is natural? Perhaps complex meaning making is what the human brain has evolved to do? Perhaps the processes inherent in the complex learning that makes learning to talk possible have some implications for learning to read?"

Those of you who know my work will realise that this one ah-ha pushed me in the direction that I've been travelling for the last thirty years. This long-awaited revised edition of the RMI—a now classic work—will certainly provide fresh insights for both the current and a new generation of educators and scholars. Those familiar with the RMI will revisit Betsy in a new case study, explore on a deeper level the value and use of the Burke Reading Interview, find extensively updated references and new research, and discover several new chapters on differentiated reading instruction. And those new to the RMI will understand readers and reading on an entirely different plane.

I urge you—teachers of children, teachers of adult readers and writers, professors, and graduate students—to use the RMI with real learners reading real texts. I can guarantee that if you do, you too will experience some eureka-like "ah-ha's" that will push you in new professional directions.

Brian Cambourne

References

Cambourne, Brian. 1976-1977. Getting to Goodman: An Analysis of the Goodman Model of Reading with Some Suggestions for Evaluation. *Reading Research Quarterly*. Volume 12, number 4, pp. 605–636.

Halliday, Michael A.K. 1975. *Learning How to Mean: Explorations in the Development of Language* (Explorations in Language Study Series). London: Edward Arnold.

Strauss, Steven L. 2005. *The Linguistics, Neurology, and Politics of Phonics: Silent "E" Speaks Out*. Mahwah, NJ: Lawrence Erlbaum Associates.

Preface

In the original *Reading Miscue Inventory* (RMI), we stated that educators will more readily make changes in their reading curricula if they have a "window on the reading process" that helps them observe and understand their students' reading. This insight remains the major benefit of learning miscue analysis. Knowing miscue analysis helps reading specialists, classroom teachers, special educators, and reading researchers develop an understanding of the reading process that guides everyday decision making in the teaching of reading.

As reading professionals are informed by studying students' miscues (a place where the reader's response does not match the expected response), new questions about the reading process arise and must be addressed. For example, when studying the complexity of third grader Frank's occasional substitution of *for* for *from*, it becomes obvious that he miscues in some grammatical settings, but not others, and that he makes the substitution only when there are certain language relations expressed. Through such analysis, researchers learn about language and how readers use it and how text structures affect the reading process. Teachers begin to understand that simplistic remediation will not help Frank and may even cause further problems. Frank's knowledge and use of the syntactic and semantic complexities of his language become evident through the analysis of his miscues. Rather than attempting to eliminate Frank's "errors," professionals who use miscue analysis understand that miscues may represent strengths that are used to address his needs.

In addition to increasing our understanding of the reading process in general, miscue analysis supplies specific information about a single miscue. John, a fourth-grade student, omits the word *oxygen* each time it appears in a story. During the retelling, as he tries to tell why "the men were getting so sleepy," John shows that he understands the text throughout his reading when he explodes with, "*Oxygen* ... that's the word I didn't get... *oxygen*." The miscue analysis of John's reading shows how he transacts with the text and how his transaction builds his comprehension.

Reading specialists and classroom teachers who analyze such processing are aware that students like John are actively involved in their reading, and beginning with that knowledge they find ways to support the reader's strengths. When Alta reads *then* for *when* throughout a story, but reads *whistle* and *white* without problems, her special education teacher has more to offer than the simple idea that Alta has "a *th/wh* confusion." For example, he helps Alta think about how she uses *then* and *when* in her writing, thus clarifying when each word is appropriately used.

Although miscue analysis is complex and time consuming, its use allows teachers and readers to take charge. Miscue analysis is based on theoretical notions informed by linguistic, psycholinguistic, and sociolinguistic knowledge and by a view of science that empowers educators to ask their own questions, solve their own problems, and consequently come to their own conclusions. Miscue analysis is an open-ended heuristic instrument, that is, a tool that helps teachers and researchers gather information about the reading process, discover supportive information available in the field of literacy learning today, and contribute to that body of knowledge.

Little did we realize when we introduced the ideas behind the RMI to 25 teachers in a school district near San Diego in 1970 that three decades later we would be part of a movement of professional educators and researchers who are committed to understanding why readers do what they do and that what they do reflects their knowledge about language and the world. This is not to imply that miscue analysis alone has been responsible for this historic movement or for teachers taking ownership of their professional responsibilities in the classroom. However, we believe that this tool has played a part in paving the way for teachers and researchers to raise questions about the relationship between learning to read and teaching reading.

Those of you who know us are aware of our enthusiasm for the use of miscue analysis and our conviction that it is the most powerful reading diagnostic tool available. We have been told by teachers and researchers that reading research and the teaching of reading are never the same once one is informed by miscue analysis. We agree.

In the years since the first publication of the *Reading Miscue Inventory*, many colleagues have advised us in our work. To all those who raised questions, criticized, and wondered with us, we want to express our sincere thanks. Let's continue the inquiry for the sake of learning and learners.

Yetta, Dorothy, and Carol

READING MISCUE INVENTORY

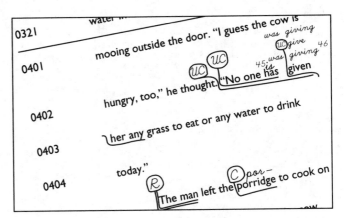

Part I
MISCUE ANALYSIS AND THE READING PROCESS

In Part I we discuss how important it is for teachers and researchers to understand miscue analysis and how it illuminates the process by which we read. In Chapter 1 we talk about miscue analysis for professionals who are seeking answers to their questions about the reading process, reading instruction, and reading research. In addition, we present a historical perspective of the development and use of miscue analysis. The chapter ends with a recommendation for monitoring one's own reading process and an introduction to Betsy, whose oral reading of *The Man Who Kept House* serves as an example throughout the book for teaching miscue analysis. Chapter 2 gives an overview of Kenneth Goodman's holistic model of reading that is informed by miscue research and, in turn, is the basis for theories underlying miscue analysis.

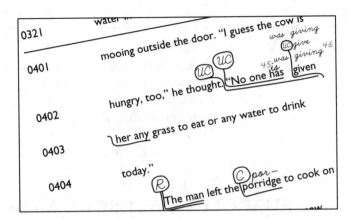

Chapter 1
Observing the Reading Process

Have you ever listened, without interrupting, to a student read an entire story or article? During a reading have you ever asked why readers:

- Substitute *daddy* for *father* or *day* for *morning*?

- Are able to read a word or phrase on Tuesday and unable to read it on Thursday?

- Have difficulty with a word or phrase in one part of the text and no problem with it in another part?

- Read certain segments of a text slowly and deliberately, then move quickly through other segments?

- Omit words or phrases that don't appear to change the author's meaning?

- Omit or substitute one word for another throughout a text and then, when talking about what they've read, use the omitted or substituted word?

- Can read an entire story, even with expression, but not understand what they have read?

- Can make many miscues and appear to struggle, yet understand what they have read?

A *miscue* is a place in which a reader's observed response (OR) does not match the expected response (ER). Miscue analysis is a tool that allows us to investigate such phenomena. Listening to students read, without interruption, provides a "window on the reading process" (Flurkey and Xu 2003; K. Goodman 1973, 5). Those who look through the window, using miscue analysis, have a way of describing, explaining, and evaluating a reader's control of the process.

Miscue analysis not only reveals the reader's proficiency but, just as importantly, provides knowledge about the reading process by including numerous ways of investigating what readers do as they read. Because miscue analysis reveals the strengths of a reader, as well as the strategies used to understand and construct meaning, reading problems also become evident. Teachers with knowledge of miscue analysis are able not only to help their students, but also to help colleagues understand and evaluate reading, the reading process, and reading materials.

PURPOSES OF MISCUE ANALYSIS

The main purpose of miscue analysis is to help teachers and researchers gain insight into the reading process as a *sociopsycholinguistic, transactive model of reading*. Given this understanding, other models, their supporting theories and research, and their resulting classroom usefulness can be contrasted with Kenneth Goodman's theory that *reading is an active search for meaning that requires studying the relationships between the reader's thought processes, language, and sociocultural settings in which both the reader and text are changed during the process* (K. Goodman 1996a; Marek and Edelsky 1999).

Miscue analysis differs significantly from other commonly used diagnostic and evaluative instruments in that the resulting analysis of reading is both qualitative (describing what the reader is doing—the *quality* of the reading) as well as quantitative (providing statistical information—the *quantity* or the frequency of miscues).

When a diagnostic instrument results only in quantitative analysis, all *errors* have equal weight. When exactness is the goal of reading, deviations from the text are considered to be random, by chance, even irrational, and the reader is expected to "attack" written material in a prescribed way (typically by a commercial program). Because quantitative analysis usually examines errors in isolation, strategies such as corrections and repetitions, which are necessary for proficient reading, are often treated as problems. Qualitative analysis, on the other hand, evaluates why miscues are made within a sociocultural context, with readers using the language and thought they bring to written material in an attempt to make the text meaningful.

The analysis of a student's oral reading, including those by students from diverse populations, is another purpose of miscue analysis. Such analysis provides specific information about a student's reading ability, linguistic knowledge, and strategy use, which allows teachers to plan reading programs and instructional strategies that build on a reader's strengths rather than on weaknesses. One should not infer that the needs of readers are disregarded, but rather that instruction begins with and builds on what readers can do, not on what they can not do.

An additional purpose of miscue analysis is to help teachers and researchers evaluate reading material. Miscue analysis helps determine a text's cohesion, coherence and comprehensibility: i.e., how the text unites to make a whole, the complexity of its grammatical structures, and the density of new concepts. Such analysis provides a basis for determining how well the text supports readers and whether it should be used in a reading program.

THE QUEST FOR UNDERSTANDING READING: A HISTORICAL LOOK AT MISCUE ANALYSIS

Miscue analysis was developed by K. Goodman for the purpose of understanding the reading process. After four decades of miscue research, he concludes that there is a single reading process, and it is the same for proficient and nonproficient readers (K. Goodman 1996a; 2004). The difference in these readers' ability to comprehend is influenced by their previous instruction in reading, their concept of reading, the strategies they use, the value they place on reading, the use they make of their language and cultural backgrounds, their opportunities to read, the time given to reading, their purpose and motivation for reading, the situational context of their reading, the supportiveness of the texts they encounter, and the flexibility with which they read the text.

The Goodman Taxonomy of Reading Miscues

The Goodman Model of Reading was developed by analyzing the degree to which miscues change, disrupt, or enhance the meaning of written text. Goodman uses the word *miscue* to eliminate the pejorative connotations of words such as *error* and *mistake* and to underscore the belief that reading is *cued* by a reader's language and personal experience; miscuing is not simply random, uncontrolled behavior. On the basis of his research, Goodman has developed a series of questions called the Goodman Taxonomy of Reading Miscues (Appendix D) to evaluate, categorize, and explain the miscue phenomena he found evident in every reader (K. Goodman 1973; 1982b). The taxonomy, which has gone through a dozen revisions since its original development, evaluates each reader's pattern of consecutive miscues through a series of questions designed to gain the greatest amount of information about the relationship between miscues and their influences on the reader's comprehension. These questions are concerned with the quality of each miscue and with the strategies readers use.

Some of the questions addressed in the taxonomy are:

- Do miscues result in sentences that are semantically and syntactically acceptable?
- Do miscues cause grammatical transformations?
- To what degree do miscues retain the grammatical function of text items?
- To what degree do miscues retain the semantic relationship to the text items?
- To what degree do miscues retain graphic and phonological similarity to text items?
- In what ways do readers use strategies such as self-correcting and predicting?

Goodman, in collaboration with many students and colleagues, has designed and conducted hundreds of miscue studies to answer these and related questions. An extensive number and a broad range of complete stories and articles have been used with readers of different abilities, ethnic backgrounds, physical and learning abilities, languages and English dialects. The Goodman Taxonomy has been used to evaluate the reading of thousands of readers, including first-grade through college students and elderly readers (Brown, K. Goodman and Marek 1996).

Goodman continues testing and adapting his theory and model of the reading process, adjusting the taxonomy to take new findings into account (K. Goodman 1984; 1996a; 2004). The Goodman Taxonomy, with its system of questions, reflects current knowledge and theory in linguistics, psycholinguistics, and sociolinguistics.

While collaborating with Goodman on his early research, Yetta Goodman and Carolyn Burke became interested in bringing miscue analysis to teachers in classrooms and clinics. The analysis used to develop reading curricula for individual students and groups was developed with the help of teachers, special educators, and reading specialists. The original Reading Miscue Inventory (RMI) (Y. Goodman and Burke 1972; Appendix D) included nine questions from the taxonomy that focus on getting information about readers and their language. These questions directly help teachers and were used for years in preservice and in-service classes for the evaluation of students' reading and for research.

MISCUE ANALYSIS PROCEDURES

Through the research and insights of teachers, almost four decades of adaptations have been made to the original RMI. Procedures were modified to save time and to accommodate changes in setting, material, purpose, and audiences. Based on this information, we have refined the procedures into three options for educators and researchers: the **Classroom Procedure**, the **Informal Procedure**, and the **In-Depth Procedure**. Other miscue analysis procedures have been developed by other authors for alternative purposes based on a similar reading model (Davenport 2002; Wilde 2000).

The Classroom Procedure

The **Classroom Procedure** (Chapter 6) is less time-consuming and the knowledge obtained is somewhat more general than that gained in the In-Depth Procedure. The Classroom Procedure evaluates all miscues within one sentence at the same time. Teachers/researchers may code directly on the typescript or on a separate form that can be placed in a student's record-keeping folder. Classroom teachers and reading specialists find that this form gives them information to plan instructional programs with specific strategy lessons.

The Informal Procedure

The **Informal Procedure** (Chapter 6) was developed for individual reading conferences or as the teacher listens for a few minutes to individual students

(Owocki and Y. Goodman 2002). Teachers who become proficient in miscue analysis find themselves using the Informal Procedure intuitively whenever they listen to a reader. Although *comprehension* is always the concern, this procedure is especially focused on the reader's *comprehending* process, that is, the reader's observed responses (OR) while reading. A similar assessment procedure is referred to as "over the shoulder" by Davenport (2002).

The In-Depth Procedure

The **In-Depth Procedure** (Chapter 7), the most complex and time-consuming option, provides the greatest amount of information about the reading process. This procedure allows teachers/researchers to observe how readers use their sampling, predicting, inferring, correcting and integrating strategies since each miscue is analyzed individually within the sentence but in relation to other miscues. Research indicates that simplified analyses do not help teachers develop their own reading model, nor do they highlight and lead to understanding of the issues concerned with the evaluation of individual readers (Long 1985). With the In-Depth Procedure, a reader's strategies are revealed in ways that are not as apparent in other options. Those new to miscue analysis will want to become familiar with concepts concerning the reading process and the influence of miscues on comprehension by learning the more complex In-Depth Procedure as well as the less time-consuming ones.

BUILDING A PERSONAL MODEL OF READING

An important outcome of understanding miscue analysis is the opportunity to build a personal model of the reading process. By learning and using miscue analysis, teachers gain explicit knowledge about language that is important for them to understand as they plan and develop reading instruction and curriculum. Teachers with a well-articulated view of the reading process develop rich opportunities for literacy learning in their classrooms.

When young children come to school, they bring a great deal of sophisticated knowledge about the language spoken in their home communities. For example, English-speaking children know subject-verb-object relationships, without which they could never successfully construct a sentence such as *Leslie helped Joel.* Children know that third person singular verbs end with an *s*, and they know how to construct the past tense by adding *ed*. Without such knowledge, children could not produce sentences such as *He gots my pencil* or *I runned all the way to the fence.* Language scholars are so impressed with the amount of knowledge children as young as two years have that they often characterize them as linguistic geniuses in their ability to use language successfully to get what they want and need.

The reading process described in Chapter 2 shows that all readers of all ages know intuitively, not necessarily consciously, the rules that help them sample, predict, make inferences, self-correct, and construct meaning as they read. Most child and adult readers are not able to articulate these strategies; nevertheless, they use them and are quite likely proficient readers.

Miscue analysis allows teachers/researchers to develop metalinguistic knowledge about the reading process, that is, to become consciously aware of it. Once educators build their own understandings, they come to know that miscues reflect the reader's development, the reader's use of language systems, and the reader's interpretation of the text being read. With such understandings, miscues become a window through which much is discovered about the individual reader as well as about the reading process. If the significance of miscues is not understood, they are likely to be treated as phenomena that must be eliminated (Y. Goodman and Marek 1996).

AUDIENCES FOR MISCUE ANALYSIS

Miscue analysis serves a variety of purposes for a range of educators.

Teachers, Special Educators, and Reading Specialists

For most educators, a major purpose of miscue analysis is to collect information to develop appropriate reading programs for individuals and for both small and large groups. The analysis allows teachers in regular and special education classes and in clinical settings to see the reader's needs; just as importantly, it *provides evidence of the reader's strengths.*

As teachers become aware of what happens during reading, they more easily involve students in developing awareness of the reading process. Thus the reader, too, makes use of miscue analysis for purposes of self-evaluation (Y. Goodman and Marek 1996). Each miscue analysis procedure reveals the strengths and needs of a reader through a series of questions (Appendix A) that focus on the effect of miscues on what is being read. Answers to these questions enable teachers to study the reader's use of available language cues and background information, as well as to examine and evaluate the relationship between the language of the reader and the language of the author. The analysis provides insights into how the reader's thoughts and language are brought to the reading task, how the reader's experiences aid in the interpretation of an author's meaning, and how the reader constructs meaning. Retelling (Chapter 3) is integral to miscue analysis because it adds important information about the reader's search for meaning, helps explain many of the reader's miscues, and helps teachers/researchers evaluate the reader's strengths and needs.

Because miscue analysis examines how the reader's language, thought, and experiences function in reading, it helps teachers:

- Determine the relationship between the miscue and the text.
- Highlight the strength of high-quality miscues.
- Pinpoint specific and repetitive problems.
- Distinguish these problems from difficulties caused by the syntactic complexity or conceptual load of the reading material.

Given these understandings, teachers develop profiles that describe students' knowledge of language, their use of reading strategies, and the patterns of readers' strengths and weaknesses. Comparisons of profiles throughout a school year, as well as from year to year, provide an accurate and continuous picture of students' growth and needs. The information gathered becomes the basis for formulating a reading program that provides readers with supportive materials, supportive instruction, and rich reading and learning experiences (see Part III).

Researchers, Including Teacher Researchers

Miscue analysis is both a methodology and an heuristic tool with possibilities for a range of reading research. It is a quantitative-qualitative procedure for analyzing the reading of a text *as the reading takes place*. Its initial use to investigate reading led to a sociopsycholinguistic model of the reading process that keeps intact the transactional principles underlying the categorization of miscues.

Miscue analysis is quantitative. An analysis of a single reading produces a huge amount of data that can be examined statistically to support the qualitative analysis of a reader's observed responses (OR). Miscue analysis is qualitative in that it requires us to apply professional judgments based on linguistic, psycholinguistic, and sociolinguistic criteria. Because miscue research provides in detail a basis for studying readers' transactions with texts, it is used to test hypotheses and predictions that emerge from different paradigms of reading: Do the readers do what the paradigms predict they will do? Can the patterns of miscues be explained with the principles of the paradigms? Teachers/researchers use the data to analyze their students' current abilities, as well as to consider how their own developing view of reading supports their reading instruction.

Because of its quantitative-qualitative procedures, miscue analysis research methodologies include experimental research designs that serve as a means of contrasting the reading of individuals and groups with different experimental conditions and instructional programs. For example, Fred Gollasch (1980) and Jingguo Xu (1998) used a short story passage embedded with errors to compare how readers of varying ages and abilities perceive such texts. Gollasch studied U.S. students reading texts written in English, while Xu used Chinese readers in Shanghai reading texts written in Mandarin. Other studies use miscue analysis as part of interpretative or naturalistic studies of classrooms. Kathryn Whitmore and Caryl Crowell (1994) used miscue analysis to examine the reading strategies of third graders as part of an ethnographic study of literacy in a bilingual classroom. Many studies use miscue analysis to build greater insights into how a reader's language influences reading comprehension. Yetta and Debra Goodman (2000) examined the dialects of African American students to show how language variation shifts in response to their search for meaning. Ann Freeman (Paulson and Freeman 2003) utilized miscue analysis along with eye movement research to examine bilingual Spanish-English readers. Other studies examine ways in which complex grammatical structures affect oral reading (Flurkey and Xu 2003).

Flurkey (1998) applied miscue research to examine the rate and flexibility with which students read within a text and across texts. His research discerns how readers struggle with new information and unfamiliar grammatical structures. Flurkey contrasts the concept of *flow* with the popular term *fluency*. Eric Paulson (2002) and colleagues (Duckett 2002, 2003; Paulson and Freeman 2003; Paulson and Henry 2002) examine the relationship between eye movements and miscues to understand what readers perceive and comprehend as they fixate on specific linguistic and artistic features of texts. Paulson termed such research Eye Movement Miscue Analysis (EMMA). Y. Goodman, along with a number of researchers and teacher-researchers, used Retrospective Miscue Analysis (Y. Goodman and Marek 1996) to develop ways to involve readers in evaluating their own miscues in order to revalue themselves as readers. No other procedure for analyzing the reading process provides such rich data.

A number of researchers explore the issues of reliability and validity in miscue analysis. Sadoski, Carey, and Page (1999) relate issues of reliability and validity to cloze procedures as well as other measures of reading to examine silent and oral reading relationships. Murphy (1998; 1999) clarifies the validity and reliability of miscue analysis by exploring multiple converging data through miscue analysis research.

A good deal of miscue analysis makes use of the constructs of Lincoln and Guba (1985; Guba 1987; Lincoln 1990) and of Fred Erickson (1986), who describe the characteristics of naturalistic or interpretative research. They suggest that researchers (including teacher-researchers) become familiar with the participants and their culture through in-depth and persistent observations. They make a case for the importance of observation over long periods and of comparisons of data through the use of multiple sources. Miscue analysis lends itself well to careful observation of readers and longitudinal studies. Miscue analysis is also used to explore:

- How a reader's oral language (specific dialect features) affect reading.
- What patterns of miscues are produced at different ages.
- What patterns of miscues are produced in classroom reading, compared to reading in the home.
- What developmental trends are observed in the use of reading strategies and in the control of language cuing systems.
- How miscue patterns change across the reading of the same text.
- How text features affect the patterns of miscue.
- How biliterate readers' production of miscues are the same or different in their first and second languages.
- How miscues of second-language learners reveal mother tongue influences.
- What patterns of miscues a reader produces in the reading of easy material as compared to the reading of difficult material.
- In what ways miscues and retellings differ in silent and oral reading.

- How miscues are affected by specific instructional techniques and commercial reading programs.
- How miscues are affected by illustrated text and how readers' make use of illustrations in their reading.
- How the text font affects miscue patterns and eye movement patterns during reading.
- How miscue analysis informs eye movement studies.

Miscue analysis research provides a rich database from which to respond to a range of sociolinguistic and psycholinguistic issues about how people read.

Material Developers

Miscue analysis is valuable for those involved in developing and publishing reading materials. It supplies a unique basis for determining whether a selection is suitable for specific readers, that is, the degree to which a text supports readers. The advantage of using miscue analysis in readability research is that miscue analysis was developed with the knowledge that both the reader and the text are factors in determining readability (Altwerger and K. Goodman 1981; Flurkey and Y. Goodman 2004; K. Goodman and Bird 2003; K. Goodman and Gespass 1983; Smith and Lindberg 1973).

Teachers become aware of the same or similar miscues that multiple readers make on identical texts. A linguistic analysis of such miscues reveals the vocabulary or structures difficult for readers to predict. For example, a study by Altwerger and K. Goodman (1981) showed that almost 100 ability- and language-different groups of fourth graders, reading the story "Freddie Miller, Scientist" (Moore 1965), miscued most on a rhetorical question in the first paragraph of the story: "What queer experiment was it this time?" Such information leads teachers to develop options for reading instruction. Rather than blame the reader for faulty reading, teachers consider how to help readers respond to unfamiliar structures and concepts, and to anticipate miscuing in the beginning of a text. Miscue analysis also helps authors make decisions about structures they may want to avoid in their writing.

DISCOVERING HOW PEOPLE READ

Everything I know about reading I learned from kids.

Ken Goodman

Both miscue analysis and its underlying theory grew out of listening to people of all ages, abilities, and language backgrounds read and then trying to understand why readers do what they do. In this way, theory is continuously related to reality and reality to theory. The purpose of this book is to help educators use miscue analysis to understand the reading process, value readers rather than blame them, and investigate reading programs and materials.

Soon you will meet Betsy, who helps us learn about the reading process. But before exploring Betsy's reading, please think about your own reading.

Begin by reading the unmarked copy of *The Man Who Kept House* (Appendix C). If you have already read the story, read another complete story or article such as a short chapter from a textbook or a complete article from a newspaper.

After reading silently, write down everything you remember about the text. This experiment works best if at least two or three people read the same text. Then, without looking back at the story, discuss the text with other readers and note responses that are similar and different. During the discussion, consider what might have influenced the similarities and differences. Now compare the responses with the original text. You might want to list generalizations about the processes of reading and retelling on the basis of this experience. As you continue to use this book, refer to your list, and compare your adult responses with Betsy's. Add to or change your developing list of generalizations about the reading process as you study the process through miscue analysis. It is useful to continually reflect on your own reading as you explore the reading of others.

Observing the Reader: Meet Betsy, Our Reader and Teacher

Betsy provides understandings about miscue analysis procedures and the use of the procedures in research and in curriculum development. Betsy is nine years old, lives in Toronto, and is in the second month of third grade. According to standardized tests and other school records, she showed little progress in reading development at the end of first grade and therefore was retained for a year. Betsy's standardized test scores at this time indicate that she is reading at a "second-grade level."

Betsy was selected for miscue analysis because Ms. Blau, her teacher, believed she had untapped potential. Ms. Blau knew that Betsy was bright, alert, and interested in listening to stories, but she was not interested in reading on her own and was moving even further away from active personal involvement with print. Ms. Blau was searching for information that would help her plan a supportive program for Betsy and, in doing so, decided to use miscue analysis as a means of gathering new information.

Ms. Blau asked Betsy to read aloud *The Man Who Kept House* (McInnes 1962) and retell the story when she finished reading. By studying Betsy's reading and retelling, Ms. Blau identified her student's reading challenges and strengths, specifically the language cuing systems she controls and the reading strategies she uses. Such information is used to suggest a reading program for Betsy and other readers (see Part III).

To determine a reader's personal model of reading, many teachers start their analysis with the Burke Reading Interview (BRI). The interview, developed by Carolyn Burke, has proven valuable in understanding a student's beliefs about reading. The BRI is often administered a few minutes before the student is asked to read but can be given a day or two before the reading. The BRI is discussed in detail in Chapter 9. A blank form is in Appendix C, and Betsy's BRI follows (Figure 1.1).

Figure 1.1: Betsy's Reading Interview

Name: _Betsy_   Age: _9_   Date: _11/2_

Interview Setting: _Corner of classroom_

1. When you are reading and you come to something you don't know, what do you do?

    I slow down and sound out the word.

    Do you ever do anything else?

    I get a book out of another basket.

2. Who is a good reader you know?

    You are, and Mom.

3. What makes ___us___ good readers?

    You read a lot and Mom reads the paper. Sophia reads high books.

4. Do you think that _we_ ever come to something ___we___ don't know when reading?

    No, well maybe once in a while.

5. If "Yes," ask: When _____ does come to something he/she doesn't know, what do you think she/he does about it?

    If "No," ask: If _____ came to something she/he didn't know what would she/he do?

    T: What do you think _we_ do when _we_ come to something _we_ don't know?

    I don't know.

    T: What does Sophia do?

    She asks someone – you.

6. How would you help someone having difficulty reading?

    Tell them to slow down and sound each word.

7. What would a teacher do to help that person?

    Get an easier book.

8. How did you learn to read?

    In kindergarten we learned little words and bigger and bigger in grade one.

9. What would you like to do better as a reader?

    Read all the books in the room.

10. Do you think you are a good reader? Why?

    Um . . . well, a medium good reader.

    T: Why?

    I'm just in between good.

Betsy's Reading

This section includes:

- Betsy's and Ms. Blau's conversation that took place after the BRI and before her reading.
- Betsy's typescript, including marked miscues and other notations.
- Her retelling.

The procedure Ms. Blau followed to gather and analyze this information is explained in subsequent chapters.

Directions before Reading

Betsy and Ms. Blau are seated comfortably at a table. They chat informally for a few minutes. Ms. Blau tests the tape recorder to see that it is functioning properly. (The teacher's remarks are marked *T* and Betsy's are marked *B*.)

T: Betsy, this is the story I want you to read. Have you ever read or heard this story before? [*Encourages Betsy to leaf through the story to see how long it is and to be sure she has not read or heard it.*]

B: No.

T: Good. I'd like you to read the story aloud. I'll record your reading. When you're finished I'll ask you to close the book and tell me everything you can remember about the story.

Betsy, when you're reading and come to something you don't know ... anything that gives you trouble ... do whatever you would do if you were reading all by yourself ... as if I weren't here. Do you have any questions?

B: No. [*Betsy reads the story without interruptions from her teacher.*]

Betsy's Marked Typescript

Betsy's In-Depth Procedure marked typescript is shown in Figure 1.2. The organization and marking of typescripts are explained in Chapter 3. Marking and numbering the In-Depth Procedure typescript are discussed in Chapter 7. Read Figure 1.2 before reading Betsy's unaided retelling.

Betsy's Unaided Retelling

T: Betsy, you did a nice job. Thank you. Now, would you close the book and in your own words tell me the story? [*Betsy hands the book to Ms. Blau.*]

B: Um, it was about this woodman, when he ... he thought that he had harder work to do than his wife, so he went home and he told his wife, "What have you been doing all day?" And then his wife told him, and he thought that it was easy work. And so ... so his wife ... so his wife, she said, "Well, so you have to keep ... ." No, the husband says that, "You have to go to the woods and cut ... and have to go out in the forest and cut wood and I'll stay home." (Continued on page 21.)

Figure 1.2: Betsy's Marked Typescript

Name _Betsy_   Date _November 3_
Grade/Age _Grade Three_   Teacher _Ms. Blau_
Reference _The Man Who Kept House_

THE MAN WHO KEPT HOUSE

0101   Once upon a time there was a woodman

0102   who thought that no one worked as hard as

0103   he did. One evening when he came home

0104   from work, he said to his wife, "What do you

0105   do all day while I am away cutting wood?"

0106   "I keep house," replied the wife, "and

0107   keeping house is hard work."

0108   "Hard work!" said the husband. "You don't

0109   know what hard work is! You should try

0110   cutting wood!"

0111   "I'd be glad to," said the wife.

0112   "Why don't you do my work some day? I'll

0113   stay home and keep house," said the woodman.

0114   "If you stay home to do my work, you'll

Figure 1.2: Betsy's Marked Typescript (cont.)

0115   *bread* ⁶ (R) 10 sec (P) have to make butter, ~~carry~~ water from the

0116   well, wash the clothes, clean the house, and

0117   look after the baby," said the wife.

0118   (C) "I can do ~~all~~⁷ that," replied the husband.

0119   *Well,* ⁸ *now* ⁹ (R) "We'll do ~~it~~ tomorrow!"

0201   *day* ¹⁰ So the next morning the wife went off to

0202   the forest. The husband stayed home and

0203   *job* ¹¹ began to do his wife's ~~work~~.

0204   *and* ¹² He began to make some butter. As he put

0205   8 sec (P) ⁻S *shurn.* ¹³ *He* ¹⁴ the cream into the churn, he said, "This is

0206   (C) *a-* / *a-* not going to be hard work. ~~All~~ I have to do

0207   (C) *the* ¹⁵ is sit here and move ~~this~~ stick up and down.

0208   *So* ¹⁶ *buttermilk* ¹⁷ Soon the cream will turn into ~~butter~~."

0209   Just then the woodman heard the baby

0210   (R) crying. He looked around, but he (C) *couldn't* ¹⁸ ~~could not~~

0211   (C) *There is* ¹⁹ ²⁰ (R) see her. She was not ~~in~~ the house. Quickly,

0212   (C) *into* ²¹ (C) *Sh-* he ran ~~outside~~ to look for her. He found the

0213   (C) *forest* ²² *f-* (R) baby at the ~~far~~ end of the garden ~~and~~

0214   *in* ²³ brought her back ~~to~~ the house.

Figure 1.2: Betsy's Marked Typescript (cont.)

0301 In his hurry, the woodman had left the

6. In his hurry
5. In
4. In his
3. In
2. In
1. In the

0302 door open behind him. When he got back to

0303 the house, he saw a big pig inside with its

0304 nose in the churn. "Get out! Get out!"

0305 shouted the woodman at the top of his voice.

0306 The big pig ran around and around the

0307 room. It bumped into the churn, knocking it

0308 over. The cream splashed all over the room.

0309 Out the door went the pig.

0310 "Now I've got more work to do," said the

0311 man. "I'll have to wash everything in this

0312 room. Perhaps keeping house is harder work."

0313 than I thought." He took a bucket and went

3. Then I
2. Then he
1. Then

0314 to the well for some water. When he came

0315 back, the baby was crying.

0316 "Poor baby, you must be hungry," said the

0317 woodman. "I'll make some porridge for you.

0318 I'll light a fire in the fireplace, and the

Figure 1.2: Betsy's Marked Typescript (cont.)

0319   porridge will be ready in a few minutes." ⓒ *flash*[44]

0320   Ⓡ Just as the husband was putting the [15 *sec*]

0321   water into the big pot, he heard the cow

0401   mooing outside the door. "I guess the cow is

0402   hungry, too," he thought. "No one has given
        Ⓤⓒ Ⓤⓒ   Ⓤⓒ *give* *was giving*
        [45] *is* *was giving*[46]

        4. *No one was giving*
        3. *give*
        2. *No one was giving her any*
        1. *No one is*

0403   her any grass to eat or any water to drink

0404   today."

0405   Ⓡ The man left the porridge to cook on the ⓒ *por—*

0406   fire and hurried outside. He gave the cow

0407   some water. *and*[47]

0408   Ⓡ Ⓡ "I haven't time to find any grass for you

0409   now," ⓒ he said to the cow. "I'll put you up [48]

0410   Ⓡ on the roof. Ⓡ You'll find something to eat

0411   up there."

0412   ⓒ *m—* The man put the cow Ⓡ on top of the house.

0413   Then he was afraid ⓒ *the*[49] that she would fall off [50]

0414   Ⓤⓒ *The* Ⓤⓒ *was har—* ⓒ *himself*[51] ⓒ [52]
        the roof and hurt herself. So he put one [21 *sec*]

        3. *The roof and hurt*
        2. *The roof* [21 *sec*]
        1. *The roof was har—*

Figure 1.2: Betsy's Marked Typescript (cont.)

0415   end of a rope around the cow's neck. ⓇHe   *the* 53

0416   dropped the other end down to the chimney.   54 8 sec

0501   Ⓡ Then he climbed down from the roof and

0502   went into the house. He pulled the end of the

0503   Ⓒ*up* rope out of the fireplace and Ⓒ*then* *he* put it around   56   56   57   *2. and he*   *1. then*

0504   his left leg.

0505   "Now I can finish making *the* this porridge,"   58

0506   said the woodman, Ⓡ"and the cow will

0507   Ⓒ*sa-* be safe."

0508   Ⓒ But the man spoke *wood-* Ⓡtoo soon, Ⓡfor just then

0509   the cow fell off the roof. ⓇShe pulled him up

0510   Ⓡthe chimney by Ⓡthe rope. ⒸThere he *is hang* hung,   59   60

0511   Ⓒupside down *never* over the porridge pot. ⓇAs for the   61

0512   cow, she *hang* hung between the roof and the   *rm*   14 sec / 15 sec

0513   ground, and there she had to stay.   *$gorun* 62   *he* 63

0514   It was not very long before the woodman's

0515   wife came home. ⓇAs she came near the

0516   house, Ⓡshe could hear the cow mooing, the

Figure 1.2: Betsy's Marked Typescript (cont.)

0601   baby crying, and her husband shouting for
 cried [64]   *shouted* [65]

0602   help. She hurried up the path. She cut the
 Ⓒ *to* [66] Ⓡ

0603   rope from the cow's neck. As she did so,
 ⒸⒸ *and* [67] *s—*

0604   the cow fell down to the ground, and the
 Ⓡ

0605   husband dropped head first down the chimney.

0606   When the wife went into the house, she

0607   saw her husband with his legs up the
 [68]

0608   chimney and his head in the porridge pot.
 Ⓒ Ⓡ *her* [69]

0609   From that day on, the husband went into

0610   the forest every day to cut wood. The wife
 Ⓡ

0611   stayed home to keep house and to look
 st—
 st—
 Ⓒ *st—*   Ⓡ   *keep* [70]

0612   after their child.
 Ⓞ [71] ⓊⒸ *the* *children* [72] Ⓒ

0613   Never again did the woodman say to his

0614   wife, "What did you do all day?" Never
 Ⓒ *that he* [73]

0615   again did he tell his wife that he would
 Ⓒ *the* [74]

0616   stay home and keep house.
 ⓊⒸ *to keep* [75]

Betsy's Unaided Retelling Continued

And the next day they did that. And the wife left home with a ax. And the husband was sitting down and he poured some buttermilk and um … in the jar. And, he um … heard the baby crying. So he looked all around in the room, and he didn't see the baby. So he went out to … to um … to get the baby. And so he didn't shut the door behind him, and so he, when he came back to, from the baby … he found the baby, then he came back with her.

And then he saw a pig, a big pig. He saw a big pig inside the house. So he told him to get out and the pig started racing around and he um … he … he um … he bumped into the buttermilk and then the buttermilk fell down and then the pig went out. Then the woodman said that he was going to have to clean all the … wash everything in the house.

And then the … the baby started crying again. And then the man said that, "You must be hungry. I'll make some porridge for you." So he lit the fire and he put the porridge on it. And then he heard the cow mooing. And then he went out … he went outside and said, "You must … um nobody, you must … you haven't had any milk or anything like … or anything to eat." So he said, "I'll put you on the roof." So he put the … he put him on the roof and he was … and he was scared that um … he was scared that … that the cow would fall out of the … off into the house from … He was scared that the cow might fall off the roof. So he got a rope and he tied it on the cow's neck. And he put the rope down the chimney and then he climbed down from the roof, and then he went back into the house again and um … and then he tied … then he took the rope and he tied it on his left leg. And then he got the porridge for the baby. And the cow fell over onto the house and the man was upside down, was hanging upside down.

And then his wife was coming down the forest and she heard her husband yelling, "Help." And so then she … so she saw the cow and then she cut the rope from the cow's neck and then … and then she ran inside the house. Then when she went inside the house she saw her husband with one leg up the chimney and his head was in the porridge.

And then from then on the husband did the cutting and he never said, "What have you been doing all day?"

T: Betsy, you remembered so much about the story! What a good job. Is there anything else you want to tell about the story?

B: No.

Betsy's Aided Retelling

T: Now, I'd like to ask you a few questions. You told about a lot of ways the woodman got into trouble. You told about how he had to um … go out and find the baby and that when he went out he forgot to shut the door. Did that cause a problem?

B: Yes, a big pig went inside the house. The woodman told him to get out and the pig started racing around.

T: What happened then ... you know ... when the pig started racing around?

B: He ... he um ... he bumped into the buttermilk and then the buttermilk fell down and then the pig went out. Then the woodman said that he was going to have to clean all the ... wash everything in the house.

T: How did the woodman feel about that?

B: Probably didn't like it much.

T: Betsy, if you were telling a friend what this story was about, what would you say in just a few words?

B: I'd say it was about a woodman who thought he had a harder job than his wife had, and he didn't, and so he stopped saying it.

T: Why do you think the author wanted to write this story?

B: He just wanted to tell a story.

T: About anything in particular?

B: Well, maybe about how people shouldn't brag about all they have to do.

T: What about those people who brag?

B: Well, they get in trouble and other people prove that they work just as hard as they do.

T: Betsy, did you like the story?

B: Yes.

T: What part did you like best?

B: I liked it all.

T: Did you think any part was special?

B: Uh uh [*no*].

T: Did you think any part was funny, or silly, or ...

B: No.

T: Betsy, who did you like best, the woodman or his wife?

B: The wife because she had to work too hard and she had to live with the old man.

T: What do you think that woodman was like?

B: Well, he was grumpy and he griped a lot about everything he had to do.

T: Do you have anything more to say about him?

B: No—yeah. When he said he would take care of the house he really tried to take care of everything—the baby and the water and the cow—everything.

T: Do you think the wife had any trouble with the woodman's job?

B: No—well maybe a little blister, but she did it okay.

For comments on Betsy's use of oral language in her retelling, see "Reading: A Language Process" in Chapter 2.

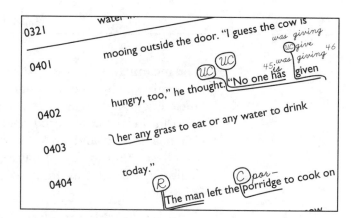

Chapter 2
A Holistic View of Reading: Theoretical Understandings

The theory of reading presented in this book comes from miscue analysis research. It is the basis for a holistic language curriculum that uses authentic reading materials such as fiction and nonfiction books, poems, brochures, magazines, newspapers, and student writings, in order to support a reader's construction of meaning.

THEORETICAL ASSUMPTIONS

In this chapter, we explore four basic assumptions about language, thinking, and learners:

- Reading is an active, meaning-making process.
- Reading is a language process.
- Readers have knowledge about language and their world.
- Authors have knowledge about language and their world.

Reading: An Active, Meaning-Making Process

Going from written language to sound, without comprehension, results in recoding, that is, a change from one code (print) to another code (sound). For our purposes, we use the pyscholinguistic term *recoding* to mean the act of responding to written language without understanding, as differentiated from the term *decoding*, which in some psycholinguistic circles means comprehending or the comprehension of written text (see Harris and Hodges 1995, 55, 215). To avoid confusion over the various meanings of the term *decoding* when we discuss making sense of written language, we use the terms *comprehension* or *comprehending*. The holistic view of reading puts forth the idea that the reader is actively constructing meaning that the author actively and meaningfully constructed. The text (the written material) is the medium through which the reader and the author transact in the attempt to create meaning, that is, to make sense. Without trying to make sense of the text, the act can only be considered recoding. Rosenblatt (1978; 1994) suggests that, when a reader and an author transact, changes take place. Transaction emphasizes the dynamic nature of reading, implying that the reader is as active and creative in the process of reading as the writer was in the process of writing.

Transaction Means That Reading Changes Readers

With supportive, whole, and rich text, readers know more when they finish a piece than when they started, and, although they may not be able to articulate it, they also know more about the reading process. In other words, readers embrace new information that transforms existing knowledge. As part of the transaction, readers engage in problem solving, adjusting their reading strategies to meet the demands of the text.

Transaction Means That the Readers Change the Written Text

This change is reflected in numerous kinds of miscues. Text has the potential for readers to create a parallel text. The degree to which a reader creates a parallel text depends partly on the extent to which the reader taps the text's potential. This parallel text often varies syntactically and semantically from the author's text. Readers construct texts built on their own inferences, schemata (existing knowledge structures), and life experiences, all of which may be parallel with, but not the same as, the author's. The text that readers construct is based on their comprehension of the author's text and is different for each reader (K. Goodman 1994; Folger 2001). There may also be physical changes to the written text, such as underlining, marginal notes, highlighting, self-stick notes, and even turned-down corners of pages, all of which may reflect the construction of meaning.

Text has the potential of being critical in a reader's life. Critical thinking moves the reader to consider new points of view—new ways of thinking—and often nudges readers to action. (Comber and Simpson 2001; Harste, Vasquez, Lewison, Breau, Leland, and Ociepka 2000; Vasquez 2000).

Reading: A Language Process

Too many instructional reading programs, testing materials, and models of reading fail to treat reading as language that is changing and dynamic and as a flexible tool rich with tradition and culture. The authors of such materials and models view language not as a process, but as an object that can be acquired by "scientifically" breaking it into small parts, "mastering" (as opposed to *using*) the smallest parts, then recombining the parts into larger and larger units.

Reading involves the communication of ideas, beliefs, and emotions through shared syntactic, semantic, and pragmatic systems in the same way oral language does. The image of readers having a long-distance conversation with an author brings to mind the features that oral and written language have in common. Their obvious similarity is the use of comparable syntactic and semantic forms to express meaning. For alphabetic languages such as English, a graphophonic relationship exists between the orthographic system of the written language and the phonological system of the oral language. And, in both oral and written language, the users bring common knowledge to the transactional process.

We use Betsy's retelling to show that reading is a language process. For example, if we compare the text of *The Man Who Kept House* with Betsy's retelling, we see similarities between oral and written language. The grammar, for the most part, is similarly structured. In Betsy's retelling, she begins most of her clauses with noun phrases followed by verb phrases, the same structure the author uses. Early in her retelling, Betsy includes *it was, he thought, he went,* and *he told his wife.* The author uses similar constructions: *there was, who thought, he came, he said to his wife.* The overall organization of her retelling is similar to the published text. Betsy tells about the characters and the setting. She knows the story has a beginning, a sequence of events, and an end. Other instances of semantic agreement exist between authors and readers, such as the mutual use of words, idioms, and metaphors. Much of the vocabulary Betsy uses is the same or similar to the author's; Betsy refers to the main character as the *husband* and *woodman*, just as the author does.

However, important differences exist between oral and written language depending on the purpose and use. Oral language serves informal purposes such as talking on the telephone or face-to-face conversations, but can also be used formally, as in structured interviews or lectures. Written language is informal when used for personal letters, notes, and shopping lists; however, written language is formal when used for essays, scientific reports, and historical documents.

In her retelling, Betsy says *um* to connect clauses with *and* or *and then.* She starts a thought and repeats it or changes it to modify an emerging idea. Such utterances are rarely part of written language, even in written dialogue.

In her aided retelling, Betsy uses turn-taking well, waiting until Ms. Blau finishes a question or comment before she responds. Turn-taking, common to oral conversation, is rarely a part of written language unless the author is representing oral dialogue or the text is a play.

The written story, on the other hand, has features that Betsy does not use in oral language. The author uses expressions that convey the style of the folktale genre, such as *keeping house* and *As for the cow, she hung ... and there she had to stay.* Usually only storytellers use such language. Betsy probably would not use these words or phrases in conversation with friends or even in discussions with her teacher.

These differences do not mean that oral language is language and written language is a secondary representation of the oral form. Rather, the many similarities and differences between written and oral language suggest that they are parallel systems, each with unique linguistic forms that adapt to the purpose at hand. Readers use their knowledge of oral language when they transact with the similarities in written language. They expand their language use as they meet the challenge of new linguistic structures in written language.

Readers Have Knowledge about Language and Their World

Children have important knowledge about language by the time they come to school. Although they cannot define grammatical terms (a noun is the name of a person, place, or thing) or make statements about phonology (this is a back vowel and this is a schwa), they have intuitive knowledge about language that is used to produce the sounds, words, and sentences of their language in order to communicate. This ability calls into question the need to teach linguistic aspects prescriptively, such as direct teaching of phonemic awareness, or of grammar rules that the reader already knows. It is, however, helpful to discuss how language is used and organized in the context of real reading and writing.

Oral Language

For the nine years prior to reading *The Man Who Kept House*, Betsy lived in a Canadian English-speaking community where she listened to and spoke in the dialect of her community. Like all children, she knew a great deal about the sounds of her language long before she came to school. When reading *Poor baby* (line 0316), she pronounces *poor* to rhyme with *sir* and not with *pour* as some English speakers might. Betsy uses intonation to show empathy, as she stresses *poor* and elongates the medial vowels.

Children also come to school knowing about the organizational structure of their language, that is, how words, phrases, and sentences are put together. In other words, they know the grammar or syntax of their language. Children as young as 18 months begin to develop a fully functioning and rule-governed system. Even though the rules of children's language do not match those of adult speech, over time their language becomes consistent and systematic, serving as a means for communicating. Betsy's retelling (see Chapter 1) provides evidence of her knowledge and control of English syntax.

As children mature, their language systems become more complex. By school age, their language closely approximates the dialect of the adults in their family and community. Because the adult speech that children hear is structurally close to their own, and because it is learned in functional settings, children find it predictable. Speakers of different dialects usually communicate with each other because the similarities between dialects outweigh the differences. All languages consist of similar, mutually intelligible, but distinct dialects. Every member of a language community is a speaker of a dialect. English language users, when they hear or read *The _____ was chewing on a bone*, know intuitively that only a limited group of nouns, such as *dog, cat, lion,* or *woman* are possible in the blank, either alone or with appropriate adjectives preceding the noun. Because of the speaker's or reader's intuitive knowledge of syntax, words such as *yellow, happen, walking,* or *quickly* are rejected for the noun slot.

0104   from work, he said to his wife, "What do you *I want you*

0105   do all day while I am away cutting wood?" *when always*

On line 0104 of *The Man Who Kept House,* Betsy predicts what a husband might say when he comes home from work; she reads, *He said to his wife, "I want you ... ."* Betsy then slows down considerably as she reads the next three words, *do all day,* which is followed by a long pause. She seems to know that *I want you* is an acceptable structure to follow *he said to his wife,* especially since the word *said* typically cues a declarative sentence rather than an interrogative one. On the other hand, her slower reading and long pause, which lead to rereading from the beginning of the quotation mark in order to self-correct, indicates that she is aware that the structure she produced did not sound quite right. Examination of the syntactic acceptability of Betsy's and other readers' miscues shows how readers bring their knowledge of syntax to their reading.

In addition to knowing the sounds and grammar of their language, children also know how to use language to make sense of the world and to communicate. They know that language helps them get things done, understand the world, and give and gain information. Children have vocabulary to talk about their world, their families, their communities, their values, and their experiences. Children build their vocabulary daily as they interact with adults and peers.

Readers are supported when the language of the written text and the ideas expressed are similar to both their own oral language and their conceptual knowledge. Teachers from the United States are often surprised that Betsy reads the word *porridge* easily. When they learn that many Canadians use the word *porridge* to refer to hot cereal, especially oatmeal, and that Betsy eats hot cereal often and calls it porridge, they understand why she has no problem with the word. On the other hand, Betsy's lack of experience with the activities and language related to making butter in old-fashioned churns, grazing cows on the roofs of sod houses, and *keeping house* help explain some of her difficulty with reading about these concepts.

Vocabulary should be understood as relating to concepts rather than to simple definitions. Readers do not get meaning from words, rather they must bring concepts, sampled from the world they hold in their heads, to words, phrases, sentences, and discourses. If the reader has grown up in a community in which *keeping house* represents the concept of routine household work, then the reader brings that concept to the phrase when constructing meaning. However, if the reader does not have the experience needed to relate the concept of routine household work to *keeping house,* trying to bring the definitions of *keeping* and *house* to the phrase *keeping house* creates a problem the reader must deal with to grasp meaning. If the reader is able to solve the problem, for example, by making sense of the phrase from the context of the story, it becomes easier to predict and construct meaning as the reading continues. Betsy, as do other readers, brings to the text both her prior concepts and the concepts she is constructing as she reads.

Written Language

Readers bring a great deal of social and linguistic information to their reading: knowledge of their language or languages; ideas about written language, such as how it works and why it is used; and their concepts and experiences as individuals, as members of a family, and as members of a community. All such information forms the basis of readers' expectations and beliefs about reading and about what they are reading. These social and linguistic data are well embedded in students' lives and influence their attitudes about reading and learning to read.

Most young children, before they come to school, know about written language. They encounter innumerable forms and functions of written text in the first five years of life. Many have been read to and have handled books, magazines, newspapers, and letters. They know about signs in their environment, labels for food and drinks, advertisements for games, and television programs.

Before school, children often have experience with writing their names and the names of family members. Such experiences with written language help youngsters see themselves as readers and writers, especially when teachers and parents accept their language approximations as a legitimate part of growth in human communication.

As children observe family members reading magazines and newspapers and as they are read to—that is, as they are immersed in reading experiences—they become aware of the importance of reading. At the same time, they begin to feel their control over reading, thus positively influencing their understanding and motivation to read.

Children know that people get information and pleasure from reading. They know that reading takes place at home, on the street, in the markets, at places of worship, and at sports and cultural events. All the functions readers see print used for, all the materials read, and all the places people read influence their reading. As children experience reading, they form attitudes toward reading and learning to read.

Betsy's teacher reads stories to her students daily. Betsy's retelling of *The Man Who Kept House*, in which she retained the author's familiar structure of a story, reflects her experiences of being read to often.

Authors Have Knowledge about Language and Their World

Authors and readers have knowledge in common about their language and their culture, but at the same time each has information not shared by the other. Knowledge and life experiences affect what writers and readers believe about their world, which in turn influences what they write and read. Additionally, authors have beliefs about the abilities of those who read their work and what readers will gain from it. The authority of the author and the reader's beliefs about that authority influence the reader's attitude and how she or he reads.

For authors and readers to communicate, they must share certain conventions, such as how to structure sentences; how to organize fiction and non-fiction pieces, conversations, interviews, poems; and the direction of written language (for example, left to right, top to bottom in English). The more familiar a reader is with the conventions shared and used by an author, the more proficient the reader is in predicting the organization of the text and therefore the less distracted from the main purpose of constructing meaning. In *The Man Who Kept House*, which was taken from a basal reader, the author-chosen conventions are modified by editors and publishers to fit the conventions of a basal reader. The length and organization of the story on the pages represent conventions the publisher decided best match the grade level for which the basal was intended. The publisher also chose three pictures for inclusion in the story.

Written texts are organized in specific genres that have a recognizable organization. Most authors know what readers expect and they use this knowledge as they write. For example, most authors know that readers expect stories to start and end in certain ways that are different from how newspaper articles or letters begin and end. Changes made by publishers who violate the integrity of the text, affecting the writer's and the reader's ability to communicate, are questionable practices. One editor who wanted to simplify the language in *Elizabeth Catches a Fish* (Thomas 1979), a story intended for second-grade readers, changed the word *creel* to *basket*. *Creel* is a regular English word that could enrich a second grader's vocabulary, and many children in urban neighborhoods think a *basket* is a plastic container used to collect the laundry. The editor also changed a term describing the fish scales, *silver discs* to *silver buttons*. Worse yet, according to the author, the editor also changed *great blue heron* to *big blue bird*. This oversimplified language generalizes and is in contrast to authors' advice to use particular, specific language (for example, never write *big blue bird* if you mean *great blue heron*).

In the next section, we present a holistic view of the reading process. Keep in mind that reading is an active language process influenced by the knowledge readers and authors have about their world and their language.

HOLISTIC THEORY OF READING

To understand the reading theory that is the basis of miscue analysis and thus the basis of a holistic curriculum, it is necessary to explore the interrelation of the language cuing systems and the reading strategies that occur as reading takes place.

Language Cuing Systems

Language is systematic. As readers attempt to construct meaning, they use three linguistic cuing systems: graphophonic, syntactic, and semantic. The interrelations of these systems, along with the pragmatic system (that is, the social-cultural context) support the language user.

The Graphophonic System

In alphabetic writing systems, *graphophonics* refer to the orthographic system (conventions of spelling, punctuation, and other print features), the phonological system (the sounds of oral language), and the complex relation between the two (K. Goodman 1993, 65).

Because of its long history and influences from many languages, the English spelling system is complex, often with more than one spelling used for the same sound or different sounds given to the same spelling pattern. For example, Horn (1929) discovered that 50 different sounds are represented by the letter *a*. Although English is spelled more regularly than is commonly believed, the regularities are not simple, and even proficient spellers have difficulty with certain patterns. Examples of the complex aspects of English spelling include the use of double consonants (accommodate, occasion), changes made in words to alter tense or grammatical function (nation, national; site, situate, situation), and multiple ways to represent a single vowel sound (rate, bait, a book). Additionally, the spelling system of English is complicated by conventions of abbreviation and punctuation; consider *Mr.* and *Dr.*, pronounced *mister* and *doctor* even though they appear in abbreviated form.

Proficient spelling is not necessarily the mark of a proficient reader. Many good readers do not spell well. Readers only *sample* the graphophonic system, making predictions and inferences on the basis of their sampling and their past experiences. Both written and oral language are symbol systems that represent thoughts and meanings, but in different ways. Therefore, no written language system can perfectly represent the oral system. Written language has, for example, symbols (letters, words, punctuation marks) that represent objects or ideas about objects. Oral language also has symbols (phonemes, morphemes, intonation) that represent ideas and objects. Such information helps in understanding the imprecise relationship between written symbols and sound symbols.

Each symbolic system—written language, oral language, and thought—represents our perceptions in different ways. Oral expression changes over time, and people who speak and read the same language use variations of the language that represent regional, social class, gender, generational, racial, and ethnic dialect differences. But regardless of how speakers pronounce *out, poor, marry,* or *caught*, the spelling remains the same. Regardless of the differences between the reader's dialect and the author's, both make use of the same spelling system. We can all read English even though we might pronounce it differently. For example, each of the authors of this book pronounces *poor* differently. All of us, however, including Betsy, understand the various concepts of *poor* and realize that *poor baby* in *The Man Who Kept House* does not refer to the financial status of the baby. It is helpful to explore with others the pronunciations of *Mary, merry,* and *marry,* or of *log, dog, bog, tog, hog,* and *jog.* Although the sounds of vowels and consonants change over time, the spelling becomes standardized and often stays the same. For example, at one time the *k* in *knife* and *knot* was pronounced /k/. And in some English dialects, in words such as *often, palm,* and *February,* a consonant phoneme became silent, but the consonant was retained in the spelling. Phonics (the relationship of sounds and symbols) is always evolving and is different for different dialects.

Oral language includes words and phrases that seem, to the listener, to run together, but appear as individual words in written language, for example: *going to* for *gonna, don't you* for *doncha,* and *could have* for *coulduv.* Betsy's oral retelling reveals such words and phrases. In transcribing students' retellings, you may use either conventional spelling or, if you are interested in articulation, spelling that represents the reader's articulation. By examining the reader's pronunciation, teachers gain insight into phonics and spelling systems.

In addition to the relation between the reader's spelling and sound system (phonics), the graphophonic system makes available other information to the reader. Although some apostrophes represent contracted forms such as *don't* for *do not,* other apostrophes represent meaning relation, such as the possessive *s* in *Patty's hat.* Punctuation provides cues that have little relationship to the oral system. Speakers, contrary to popular belief, do not necessarily stop at periods and take breaths at commas. Orthographic markers, such as periods and commas, reflect phrase, clause, and sentence boundaries; however, written language has few orthographic markers to serve as cues for the pitch, stress, and juncture of oral language. Authors find other ways of providing such information, for example, with italics, bold letters, and fonts.

The length and shape of letters and words also provide readers with useful cues. In Betsy's word substitutions, rarely is her observed response (OR) more than one letter longer or shorter than the text word. For example, in line 0102 she substitutes *He threw* for *who thought.* In line 0211 she substitutes *There is* for *She was.*

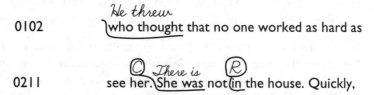

It is important to remember that cues in the graphophonic system operate in concert with the other language cuing systems. Readers use the knowledge, for example, that short words usually are single syllables. At the same time, they know, depending on the context, that such words are often function words, such as prepositions and conjunctions. Proficient readers use cues selectively. The first one or two letters of a word typically are the most important graphic cues for readers. Within context, beginning letters, then final letters and word length, often provide readers with enough information to predict the word. It is important to remember that the proficient and efficient reader is simultaneously making selective and effective use of syntactic and semantic cues. The example in Figure 2.1 indicates how this process operates.

Figure 2.1: Using Syntactic and Semantic Cues

The people followed the minister into the ch_____.

Trudging down the r___d, the group sang to keep up their sp_____.

The sheep j____ed over the f_____.

Proficient readers may resort to a graphophonic analysis of a word when the syntactic, semantic, and pragmatic systems do not provide enough information.

The Syntactic System

The syntactic system of language includes the interrelation of words and sentences within connected text. In English, systematic syntactic relations include word order, tense, number, and gender. The way humans organize words in a sentence or phrase and the relation of sentences to each other, whether for reading, writing, speaking, or listening, is its syntax. Speakers of English know where to place subjects and objects in English sentences, which pronouns to use in relation to the subjects and objects, and where adjectives occur in relation to nouns. Each language and dialect has its own syntax, and writers and readers use this syntactic system in constructing and comprehending texts.

The word *grammar*, often used as a synonym for syntax, refers to the structural rules or conventions of a language. Some people think that the term *grammar* refers to a "correct form" of language as prescribed by a self-styled language maven. When we use *grammar* we refer to it descriptively as linguists do: "a rule ... defined in terms of the usage pattern as found for a group of speakers" (Wolfram 1998, 83). The term *grammar* also refers to how different linguists theorize that a particular language is organized.

We tend to use the term *syntax* to refer to the conventional ways people organize language in their language community. For most English sentences, the typical syntactic organization is a noun phrase (NP) followed by a verb phrase (VP). Once readers perceive the noun phrase, they generally assume that a verb phrase follows.

NP   *VP*

The scared cat / hissed at the dog.

This pattern is so predictable that sentences failing to produce such structures are often those in which miscues occur:

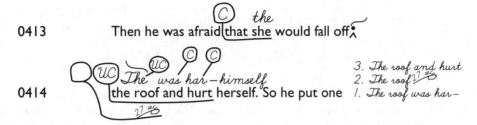

0413   Then he was afraid that she would fall off.

0414   the roof and hurt herself. So he put one

3. The roof and hurt
2. The roof
1. The roof was har—

Betsy anticipates the end of a sentence at the end of line 0413 and produces falling intonation on the word *off*. She then reads *the roof* as if it were the beginning of a new sentence. After reading *The roof* Betsy predicts a verb phrase beginning with *was*. Her miscues are complex and, even though she attempts to self-correct, she doesn't produce the expected response (ER).

0615   again did he tell his wife that he would

Betsy's prediction of *the* for *he* in line 0615 illustrates how she appropriately predicts syntactic structures. Betsy predicts *the woodman* for the author's pronoun *he*. Even proficient readers produce such miscues. Understanding the language's syntax helps us understand the miscues readers make.

When a reference is made to a previously identified character in a story, the author usually chooses to use a pronoun instead of repeating the noun or noun phrase. In such cases, readers make use of the same option. Miscue studies show that pronouns are used to replace the antecedent, unless it helps clarify the story to repeat the noun phrase (K. Goodman and Gespass 1983). However, Betsy, as in the previous example (line 0615), may have decided near the conclusion of the folktale, that the noun phrase, *the woodman*, should be repeated to provide emphasis. She self-corrects before she produces the noun *woodman*.

The Semantic System

Semantics is the study of the meanings of words and phrases, and how they relate to each other. This system of meanings includes the words (vocabulary) known by writers and readers. Knowledge about the world and about language come together to make up the language user's semantic system. Meanings are strongly related to a cultural group, and therefore semantics is influenced by culture and beliefs.

Betsy's knowledge of the common roles of husbands and wives and the chores needed to be done around a house helps her understand a good deal about *The Man Who Kept House*, even though the story is set in a time and place removed from her world. Through reading, Betsy constructs meaning, reshaping personal experiences as she builds concepts, for example, about *keeping house*.

Pragmatics and Sociocultural Context

Pragmatics deals with how and why language occurs in a specific context for communication to take place. Pragmatics influences the semantic system, because it involves the causal and other relations between words, expressions, and symbols and those who use them within cultural norms. Language has different meanings depending on the reason for use, the circumstances in which the language is used, and the ideas writers and readers have about the contextual relations with the language users. For example, what Betsy believes about the roles of men and women influences how she comprehends *The Man Who Kept House*. Her beliefs influence her answer to "Who is right—the husband or the wife?"

Miscues often occur in the sentence, *We'll do it tomorrow* (line 0119). Betsy reads, *Well, you do it tomorrow*, shifting the dialogue to her point of view. Other readers' miscues include, *Well, just do it tomorrow* and *I'll do it tomorrow*. These miscues reflect the readers' views of husband-wife relationships and housekeeping. Context is sometimes thought of as confined to a page or story, that is, to the relation of words in sentences, sentences in paragraphs, and paragraphs in the entire text. Context is much more. In addition to the framework of the written language, context also refers to social and cultural settings in which the text is embedded and in which the writer and reader are involved. The social-cultural context influences the pragmatics of language in use; contexts of place, time, current experiences and even emotions such as national pride influence the ways authors write and readers read. That means, "In pragmatics the important issues concern 'what to say, to whom, when and where'" (Wolfram 1998, 98). (See also Peyton, Griffin, Wolfram, and Fasold 2000.)

The integration of these three linguistic systems depends on the context in which they occur, the relations between the expressions (words, sentences, paragraphs), and the language users (that is, the pragmatics of the situation). The ways we use language to express and understand meanings are complex and relate to how language is systematically and appropriately used in different pragmatic settings. Language cannot exist outside a sociocultural context, which includes the prior knowledge of the language user. Depending on the pragmatics, the speaker and the audience use a functional dialect, one that works within the sociocultural community. Change some degree of pragmatics (perhaps the reason for discussion) and the speaker might switch dialects or use another language. Parents and their children might use some aspects of language differently, and when parents address their own parents, some features may change again. Teachers and their students use some features of language similarly and some differently. And when teachers are in graduate seminars, their language changes to adapt to the new context and to the relations among themselves and the instructor. The knowledge people have about how and when to adapt and change their language to fit the constraints of a social context is not always conscious; nevertheless, speakers respond to pragmatic rules every time they engage in oral interchange.

Pragmatics influence written as well as oral language. Shopping lists, menus, flyers, reports, and plays, for example, are arranged uniquely and are dependent on the message, the intent, the audience, and the context. Fiction and nonfiction have distinct text characteristics that are reflected in vocabulary, syntax, and style. Cartoons are used in both fiction and nonfiction texts, but for different purposes. Students recognize social studies textbooks as different from novels as soon as they see the cover or begin reading. Written language has a complex variety of differences. Understanding these differences becomes apparent when readers experiment with a wide range of written materials.

Understanding the constraints of the pragmatic system on written texts is especially important to those concerned with holistic views of reading. Students respond differently when they read standardized tests, worksheets, and picture storybooks. Tests, especially high-stakes tests that are used for promotion or failure, rewards, or punishment, severely influence the pragmatics of the situation and consequently influence linguistic performance in complex ways.

Providing students with worksheets, controlled vocabulary texts, and drills will not help them understand folk tales, poetry, or scientific writing. While different materials may share common semantic, syntactic, and graphophonic features, each genre has its own organization and each requires certain experiences by the reader. For success with a variety of materials, readers must also consider the pragmatics of the reading, that is, the many relationships among words, phrases, etc., the language users, and the context in which they are reading. Consider the example in Figure 2.2.

Figure 2.2: Bringing Prior Knowledge to Reading

You are handed a drink with a small napkin under the glass. Printed on the napkin is "Thank you to all our _____." The last word is smudged, but can you read it anyway? What do you predict? *Friends, guests, family, neighbors, customers, faculty, staff?*

Many teachers predict *faculty*. One person predicted *classmates*; she had just returned from a class reunion. Now we add pragmatic information—that you are handed the glass by an airline attendant on an airplane. It now becomes easy, if you have been an airline passenger, to read the last word, *passengers*.

There is an important connection between semantics and pragmatics. The questions about semantic acceptability and meaning change must take into account the role of pragmatics, as in the example in Figure 2.2. Let's further consider Betsy's substitution of *bread* for *butter* on line 0115 and *buttermilk* for *butter* on line 0208.

0115   have to make butter, carry water from the

0208   Soon the cream will turn into butter."

Both miscues fit the semantic and pragmatic constraints of the story. Within the story, it is as possible to make bread as it is to make butter, and producing buttermilk is part of the process of turning cream into butter. If Betsy had said *beads* for *butter* in the first instance and *peanut butter* for *butter* (line 0208), we would decide that the substitutions did not result in semantically acceptable sentences. Discussions concerning the semantic acceptability of a miscue often involve pragmatic issues.

Each of the language cuing systems has its function and its place in relation to the other systems and to pragmatics. While the systems can be separated for discussion, research, analysis, or definition, pragmatically they cannot stand alone or be isolated during actual use. If comprehension is to occur, *all the systems of language* must be available for the language user. This view is one of the most important principles of reading.

Reading Strategies

We are actively involved when reading. Our eyes move, a foot or hand is in motion, our heart rate changes, our breathing slows or increases, we cry, we laugh, but above all our brains are busy. In fact, our brains even direct our eyes where to look when reading. In our transaction with the author, our brains choose strategies to create our own meaning, that is, to make sense of what the author offers through the written text.

Proficient readers bring knowledge of their world and their language to the reading experience. In their transaction with authors of varied texts on varied subjects, readers of all ages use the same reading strategies:

- Initiate, sample, and select
- Predict and infer
- Confirm, disconfirm, and correct
- Integrate
- Terminate

These reading process strategies are activated as readers initiate the reading process to make sense of written text. In Figure 2.3, the curves of the lines represent the reading process interrelated strategies used when reading. This figure shows that strategies double back or move forward to be supported by all the available strategies. These strategies are the plans the brain makes as readers use the language cuing systems and their knowledge of the world to make sense of print. In other words, strategies are the problem-solving operations our brain uses to read. The importance of Figure 2.3 is to clarify that reading is not a step-by-step linear process, as might be interpreted from the preceding list of strategies. Rather, reading takes twists and turns, integrating the reading process strategies, all for the purpose of creating meaning.

Initiate, Sample, and Select

Readers activate their reading process strategies as soon as they decide they are going to read. When Betsy was asked to read *The Man Who Kept House*,

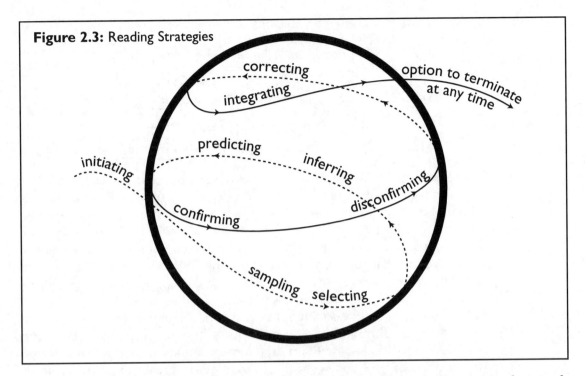

Figure 2.3: Reading Strategies

she knew how and where to begin, that is, she knew how to *initiate* her reading. She read the title of the story, then sampled the first line of print to select the features she needed. When reading, a reader's eyes fixate on only 60–70% of the words in a text (Carpenter and Just 1983; Paulson and Freeman 2003). As Betsy reads, it becomes obvious that she knows that print provides key information, but she also knows that, if she *samples* the pictures, she can get additional information to confirm what she had gotten from the text. In her retelling, Betsy tells about the wife leaving home with an axe; this information was only in an illustration.

Through miscue research and over a hundred years of eye movement research (Paulson 2002; Paulson and K. Goodman 1998), we have learned that, unless students are recoding (going from print to sound, as in handling word flash cards or other lists of nonsense or random words), they do not read word for word. Flurkey's research (1998) shows that reading can move slowly, pick up speed, and slow down again. Readers adapt to the complexities of a text by shifting their strategies. Shifting the flow of reading helps the reader make sense of the text continuously. The silent reading speed of even moderately skilled young readers is so rapid that it negates the idea that the eye focuses on each printed letter and then the mind becomes consciously aware of each word. The speed with which reading is accomplished adds to the evidence that word-for-word reading is a misnomer.

Instead of focusing on individual graphic items such as letters and words, readers *sample and select.* Sampling is not unique to reading; it occurs as part of all perceptual processes (Neisser 1976). Conversation, for example, flows so rapidly that listeners sample and select ideas important to them from the available oral information.

The following reveals Betsy's *sampling* strategies as she reads.

0317   woodman. "I'll make some porridge for you.

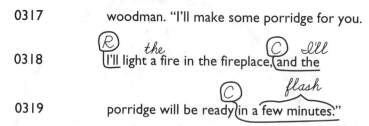

0318   I'll light a fire in the fireplace, and the

0319   porridge will be ready in a few minutes."

Betsy knows from the previous two pages of the story that the woodman now has more work to do because of the mess made by the pig. He has already admitted that keeping house is hard work. She picks up the *I'll* + verb pattern in *I'll make* (line 0317) and *I'll light* (line 0318). She samples the conjunction *and*; she knows that conjunctions often combine two equal clauses, so it is logical that the second clause on line 0318 will start the same way. Based on resampling of the previous syntax and graphophonics, she repeats *I'll* and selects *I'll light*, and then she predicts *I'll* at the end of the line. In line 0319, she samples enough of the end of the sentence, *in a*, to know that a prepositional phrase will occur; she selects the initial consonant *f* in *few* to predict *in a flash*, a phrase that is apparently familiar to her. A more secure reader may not have corrected this miscue, since it results in a semantically acceptable structure. However, Betsy realizes that *in a few minutes* is too long to match her prediction, so she samples the print once again, repeats *in a* and then self-corrects.

To initiate reading, readers make a decision to read. They then begin to sample the print, select important features, make inferences, and predict subsequent structures and meanings. When readers open a morning newspaper, they know that they are not going to read it all. They quickly sample the text (usually the headlines and pictures). When they come to an article they want to read, they continue sampling and selecting from that piece. Within their pragmatic context, which includes their background knowledge, their purpose for reading, and what they care about, readers use selected features of the graphophonic, syntactic, and semantic systems to predict the text. The brain does not process everything that the senses feed into it. It seeks the most useful and important information, directing the eyes where to look and what to look for (K. Goodman 1996a).

William James' discussion of the importance of sampling and selecting based on his concept of selective attention helps explain what occurs during the reading process. James states, "The phenomenon of selective attention ... are ... examples of this choosing activity [being more interested in one part of an object than another] ... But we do far more than emphasize things, unite some, and keep others apart. We actually ignore most of the things before us. ... [W]hat are our very senses themselves but organs of selection. ... [E]ach sense organ picks out those which fall within certain limits of velocity. To these it responds, but ignores the rest as completely as if they did not exist" (James 1892; 1981, 273). Without selectivity of information, the brain would be overloaded; it cannot take in every facet of linguistic information provided in the written text. As you monitor your own reading, consider the idea of selectivity.

Predict and Infer

The concepts of reading strategies are complex because they are entwined, and it isn't clear when one strategy ends and the other begins or if they occur simultaneously. As readers sample and select information, they also predict and infer on the basis of knowledge they already have and information they select from the text.

It is the author's responsibility to write so that readers become actively engaged in the events, experiences, and concepts of the written texts, and to provide information that will help readers relate these to their preexisting knowledge and thus make inferences. Sometimes authors are explicit in their writing, clearly expressing ideas and providing supportive details, while at other times they only imply, suggest, or hint at information or incidences. In either case, readers are responsible for "reading between the lines," that is, engaging in problem solving to know if they should search the text for additional information or if they should search their lives for supportive information, always for the purpose of making sense. In other words, proficient readers are always inferring, reasoning, and evaluating the written text. Inferring leads to predicting (the next word, phrase, concept, idea, or event); predicting leads to more inferring.

By predicting and inferring based on their background knowledge and experiences, proficient readers use written text selectively to comprehend and to develop their own concepts and ideas. Some readers, however, depend too heavily on the written text, believing that the one and only meaning is magically contained in the print and once they have "read" the text, they do not question the author. When readers overrely on the authority of the "external" text, they discount their own understandings. In such cases, readers must adjust their reading strategies to value themselves as learners, and to create meaning for themselves by transacting with the author.

We see how Betsy integrates reading strategies in the following example.

0103   One evening when he came home

0104   from work, he said to his wife, "What do you

0105   do all day while I am away cutting wood?"

As Betsy reads about the woodman, she taps into her semantic and pragmatic knowledge and makes inferences about male and female relationships. She knows that the author uses *he said* (line 0104) before the question in the dialogue. Because of information from her preexisting knowledge of the world and her linguistic knowledge of the syntactic and semantic systems of language, Betsy predicts that the dialogue will be a statement.

Her sampling and selecting of the written text provides graphophonic and syntactic cues, from the beginning of the dialogue, for her to use in predicting a subject-verb-object structure: *I want you.* Sampling the print for the next line of text, she slows her reading down as she begins to think about her prediction, and she carefully selects and then reads *do all day.* A 23-second pause follows as she considers which strategies to use (discussed later under confirming strategies in Chapter 10).

Betsy's predictions of *when* for *while* and *always* for *away* (line 0105) in the last clause of the sentence show:

- Her sampling and selecting of phonic cues (the initial consonants).
- Her use of the syntactic system (the substituted words and the text words serve the same grammatical function).
- Her use of semantic cues that relate concepts of time and place.

Making inferences involves some risk taking, since doing so may result in inappropriate predictions. Nevertheless, *inferencing* is necessary for reading to occur. Betsy shows us that readers infer and predict while utilizing all language cuing systems.

Confirm, Disconfirm, and Self-Correct

By continuously inferring, sampling, and selecting, the reader is able to make predictions. If the prediction is appropriate to the emerging meaning (as in the *when* and *always* substitutions, line 0105), readers *confirm* their predictions and continue to read. However, if readers' predictions are *not confirmed* by the subsequent text, they *disconfirm* and pursue a variety of options to create meaningful text. Readers might also reject their predictions when what they read doesn't make sense in the context of existing knowledge. When Betsy reads *I want you* for *what do you*, she infers that this is what the husband would say on returning home from work. However, as she continues reading, Betsy realizes that *I want you do all day* doesn't sound like an English sentence, nor does it make sense. She therefore *disconfirms* her prediction, samples the text again, and *self-corrects*.

Some readers do not resample the text to gain new information. Readers sometimes decide to stop for a few seconds, think through possibilities, reorganize, modify the meaning of the text being built, and then continue reading. Readers of mysteries know this strategy well. If readers predict that one character is the culprit and later find new clues that point to someone else, they do not usually reread the text. Instead, reconsidering all the possibilities, they adjust their thinking and continue. In other situations, readers decide that, before they can self-correct, they must read on, sampling and selecting the text for more relevant information, searching for clarification. This may have been the situation with Betsy in lines 0312 and 0313.

Here, Betsy disconfirms and attempts to self-correct, but there are too many complexities and her strategies are not working. So she chooses to keep going to maintain the overall meaning of the story rather than worry about this section.

Integrate

The integration of the reader's existing knowledge with information provided by the author in the written text results in the construction of meaning, the goal of reading. The integration of knowledge is evident throughout the reading as the reader predicts, confirms or disconfirms, and corrects. Also, as mentioned, Figure 2.3 illustrates that reading is not a step-by-step linear process; the twists and turns in the figure represent the interweaving and integration of the reading process strategies for the purpose of creating meaning.

Terminate

Readers may choose to stop reading at any time. They may decide that the material is too boring, too simple, or too difficult. However, in instructional settings, terminating reading is seldom an approved option. Only occasionally are students encouraged to stop reading and say, "This is too hard" or "This is boring," even when the text actually is too hard or boring. In some school environments, readers attempt to "read" even when they do not even minimally comprehend. It is helpful to engage readers in considering that there are appropriate times to stop reading.

SUMMARY

The reading strategies and systems of language, along with the pragmatics of language, work together to support the reader. Once the decision to read is made, readers sample, select, predict, infer, confirm or disconfirm, and integrate information as they make use of their language knowledge in a cyclical way, each strategy transacting with the others.

Readers put their perceptual systems to work to process print. The knowledge that the brain uses to direct the eye in informed ways and what starts the process depends on perceptual information, which in turn depends on optical input. The perceptual cycle organizes the material in such a way that the material is recognized as something that can be read. These perceptions activate the semantic system, which is influenced and supported by syntactic information. Each follows the other but at the same time precedes the other, always moving toward constructing a text and making meaning. Each cycle is tentative and partial, melting into the next. Inference and prediction make it possible to leap toward meaning without fully completing the cycles, even though most readers actually believe they see every part of the text. All readers engage in this process (K. Goodman 1996a).

We now move to miscue analysis and the procedures that led to the view of reading presented in this chapter.

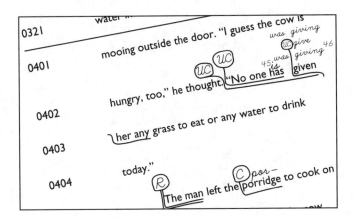

Part II

PROCEDURES FOR MISCUE ANALYSIS

In Part II we present the heart of miscue analysis, that is, the general rationales and guidelines applicable to the three alternative miscue analysis procedures: the **Classroom Procedure**, the **Informal Procedure**, and the **In-Depth Procedure**.

The general information needed to conduct all three procedures are included in Part II. Chapter 3 includes information about selecting students, choosing materials, and marking miscues, along with ways to prepare the environment to collect the reading miscue data. Chapter 4 presents the questions used for miscue analysis, the theoretical and linguistic rationales underlying each question, and the insights about language and reading that inform the analysis. In Chapter 5 we discuss how to analyze miscues.

Chapter 6 presents information specific to the **Classroom** and **Informal Procedures**. Chapter 7 presents information specific to the **In-Depth Procedure**. In these chapters we discuss for each procedure:

- Selecting miscues for coding.
- Miscue questions and how they relate to the procedure.
- Scoring the retelling.
- Forms for miscue coding and retelling.
- Calculating statistical information.
- Specific suggestions for choosing each of the miscue analysis procedures.

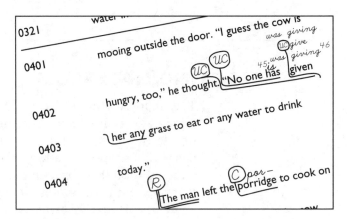

Chapter 3
General Procedures for Data Collection: Readers, Materials, and Retellings

A miscue is an observed response (OR) that does not match the expected response (ER), that is, what the listener expects to hear. The concept of miscue is developed further as the data collection procedures are presented. All miscue procedures include the examination of the oral reading of a complete text, followed by a retelling.

In this chapter and in Chapter 4, we describe the steps and their rationales for preparing and administering the miscue procedures. The rationales provide a basis for understanding the theory that supports the decisions about the reader's strengths and needs. Chapter 3 includes information about selecting readers, selecting and preparing materials, the retelling, and the reading session in general. In Chapter 4 we discuss the typescript marking.

SELECTING READERS

Students' needs, along with teachers' and researchers' interests and instructional goals, guide the selection of readers for miscue study. Teachers often begin their use of miscue analysis with students who have reading needs and for whom information is needed. However, a novice user should not select a reader who produces so many intricate and complex miscues that the teacher/researcher is overwhelmed.

Because other kinds of reading test scores are of minimal help and often misleading, a research instrument is needed to gather data that leads to appropriate instruction. Educators who use miscue analysis as an informative instrument administer the procedure at least twice a year, or whenever they feel additional information about a reader is needed. As teachers become proficient with miscue analysis, they develop "miscue ears" and consequently learn to evaluate students' reading every time they listen to them.

SELECTING MATERIALS

The material chosen for miscue analysis should be a complete text that is unfamiliar to the reader and therefore not practiced. While the selection is new to the reader, it must include familiar concepts and be written in language that supports readers in their understanding of new information. The material should be difficult enough to challenge readers, but not so difficult that they can't continue independently. A selection identified as one grade above the student's assigned reading, along with one or two alternative selections of varying difficulty, should be available to choose from during the session. The recommendation to select a passage one grade above students' reading scores comes from miscue analysis research that suggests the majority of standardized and grade-level reading test scores underrepresent students' abilities to handle authentic reading material.

Select an entire, cohesive, well-written text that is of interest to the student. The choice of the material is based on the goals of the teacher/researcher and may be from any genre: trade books, basal readers, magazines, newspapers, and content-area textbooks. Fiction must have a story line, plot, and recognizable theme. Nonfiction must develop at least one concept thoroughly or fully describe an act or event.

The length of material depends on the age of the reader and the purpose of the analysis. The text for upper elementary and older students should be a minimum of 500 words. Of course, as texts get longer, other aspects of the procedure (preparation of material, data gathering, and analysis) take longer to complete. Instructional materials for young children are typically short; therefore, it is sometimes necessary to ask these children to read two or three selections.

A study by Menosky (1971) indicates that the quality of miscues changes after the reader passes the first 200 words. At about the 200 word point, semantic and syntactic acceptability increases as the graphic and phonemic similarity to expected responses (ER) decreases. Flurkey's (1998) research supports this insight. In other words, as readers become familiar with the text, they produce more miscues that reflect accumulating knowledge of the text, and they correct more miscues that don't make sense. At the same time, readers become more efficient in the selection of phonic cues, sometimes producing a miscue that makes sense in the text, rather than producing a word or nonword that is an exact or nearly exact graphophonic match with the text. Because of such findings, longer passages are encouraged.

Teachers and researchers may want to compare Betsy's (or another reader's) patterns of miscues at the beginning of the text with those at different points in the story to discover how flexibly she uses her strategies. *The Man Who Kept House* (see Chapter 1) has 791 words. The first 200 words, that is the first quarter of the story, ends in line 207; half of the story, 400 words, ends in line 318; and the third quarter ends in line 508.

What about students who defy the usual procedure for selecting materials? Fifth-grader Jermaine was such a student. Jermaine loved to listen to stories but would not pick up a book. He announced, "There ain't anything in those stories I know about." For such readers, as well as for very young readers, it may be necessary to write a text of interest to the student. Because Jermaine's teacher knew her student's interests, she could easily write something that appealed to him, part of which is shown in Figure 3.1. Jermaine couldn't resist reading something about himself. After reading "Jermaine's Story," Jermaine collaborates with his teacher in writing more chapters to make a book of his life.

Figure 3.1: Part of a Text Written by Jermaine's Teacher

Jermaine's Story

My name is Jermaine.

I'm going to tell you some things about me. There are also some things that I probably won't tell you.

I'm going to start by telling you about some things that I like. Then I'm going to tell you about some things that I don't like.

I'm a rodeo fan. I love to ride and I'm pretty good at it. If I feel like it, I may tell you about riding. I might tell you how I got started riding. I might tell you about who taught me to ride. I might tell you where I ride. Maybe I'll write about where I ride. Maybe I'll write about the best rider I know. Maybe I'll write about my very best riding experience. There are a lot of things about riding and the rodeo that I might write about. I might draw pictures about riding and the rodeo. Maybe.

You may have some questions about my riding experiences. You may be wondering if I've ever fallen off a horse. You will have to wait and see if I decide to tell you if I've ever fallen off a horse. You may be wondering if I want to be a rodeo rider when I grow up. You will have to wait and see if I decide to write about what I want to be when I grow up.

If I decide to write about riding, it will be Chapter One of Jermaine's Story.

Compiling a Set of Reading Materials

Many teachers/researchers collect a permanent file of books, magazines, and articles that span a diverse range of materials, difficulty, and interests. Teachers compile a set of materials that have the potential to point up readers' strengths and needs as well as their development over time. Researchers choose materials appropriate for their research questions. Those planning to use a passage extensively may want to test the suitability of the material by presenting it first to a small group of students who are similar to the intended research population.

Materials must have the potential to gain students' attention, as well as contain places for likely miscues. Exclude materials that are too difficult or too easy and that have no interest to students. Over time, the set of texts retained will more closely fit specific needs. Selections used repeatedly for miscue analysis may be removed from the original source and made into booklets. However, if it is possible to keep the original source, the reading environment is more authentic. Note the bibliographic references and comments about the text on the materials.

After preparing typescripts of the texts, duplicate and file several copies for repeated use. Keep materials for students' readings and the typescripts apart from other materials, using them for miscue analysis only; doing so ensures that students have not previously read the pieces. With a large enough set of appropriate materials, it is possible to offer students a choice from three or four reading selections for each miscue collection session. Although the influence of student-selected materials on the production of miscues needs more research, encouraging students to choose their own readings has proven to be successful, especially with the Informal Procedure (see Chapter 6), in which readers often select texts or bring the material they are currently reading to the miscue session.

Text Analysis and Miscue Patterns

Once a set of materials is compiled, repeated use provides information concerning the readability of each piece, that is, how much a text supports a reader in constructing meaning. When the same material is used over time, the places where readers miscue become evident. When a large number of readers, regardless of background and ability, miscue at the same point, the miscue is usually attributed to a unique feature or features of the text. Researchers (Altwerger and K. Goodman 1981; Flurkey 1998; Flurkey and Y. Goodman 2004) have examined miscue points to understand the influence of the text, as well as of the readers' background information, on their reading. Such analysis reveals the complexity of the text as well as the appropriateness of the selection for both miscue analysis and classroom instruction. Texts with potential challenges need not be avoided in selecting material, especially if the piece fits the purpose of the analysis; the idea is not to avoid their use or simplify the text, but rather to know how students respond to different kinds and constructions of texts. Readers need to become flexible in reading a wide variety of materials. Mooney (2001; 2004) provides further information to educators on text selection, as well as text forms and features. Features to consider in selecting material include:

- Support of the language and overall structure of the text.
- Concept load and subject matter.
- Relevance and interest of the material to the reader.

Supportive Text

Supportive text allows readers to use all the systems of language and all the strategies of the reading process.

Language and Structure

Predictability is an important feature of texts and provides support for the reader; the more predictable a text, the easier it is to read. Predictable texts are typically found in song lyrics, nursery rhymes, and children's books with repeated sequences (Rhodes 1981). Steve Bialostok (1992) categorized predictable language books into patterns of words, syntax, concepts, and illustrations. Exemplars for predictable books include *Rap a Tap Tap: Here's Bojangles—Think of That!* (2002) by Leo and Diane Dillon, *Boo to a Goose* (2001) by Mem Fox and illustrated by David Miller, and *If You're Not from the Prairie ...* (1995) by David Bouchard and illustrated by Henry Ripplinger.

A set of carefully selected predictable materials is especially helpful for use with students who doubt their own reading ability. Such texts help them revalue themselves as readers (K. Goodman 1996b). A caution when selecting predictable books: Some materials are almost too predictable in that they never vary sentence patterns, or they consist of a one-line caption-type sentence on each page with a picture. Such materials are often harder for children to read than the book "level" suggests; even very young readers expect cohesive texts.

To determine if a text is supportive, we learn about students' oral language and their experiences with written language. Consider the language of the community (dialect features) and the familiarity students have with the features and conventions of the genre. A few features that might render a text difficult are:

- Unpredictable beginnings.
- Breaks in the traditional sequence of events.
- Information that is irrelevant to the entire text.
- Unusual punctuation or print.
- Unfamiliar language features (including dialect).
- New and unfamiliar information.

These features are not necessarily to be avoided when selecting a text, but the overall piece must be supportive enough to help readers handle difficult spots.

Concepts and Relevance

Supportive text taps the interest, knowledge, cultural and experiential backgrounds of readers, thus encouraging them to make inferences, that is, to read their lives into the text and to read "between the lines." The more known about the students' interests and knowledge, the easier it is to select appropriate materials. Teachers learn about their students by brainstorming social studies and science topics, conducting open-ended discussions, participating in individual conferences, and taking inventories. Such activities reveal the need for materials of different genres and content. Supportive materials can be collected, organized, and labeled with different interests, ages, and ethnic backgrounds of the students in mind.

The relevance requirement is closely related to the issue of concept load. It is important to consider the amount of new knowledge presented to the reader in the selection of material. If the material includes a great deal of new knowledge, the language and format should be familiar so that the reader is supported by known text features (Mooney 2001; 2004). Discovering the factors that make text supportive, including readability (text difficulty) and text relevance, add to miscue researchers' understanding of the reading process.

PREPARING THE TYPESCRIPT

A typescript is prepared for both the **Classroom Procedure** and the **In-Depth Procedure**. The teacher/researcher (observer) uses it to follow along as the student reads, as well as to record miscues, the reader's verbal asides, and any significant nonverbal actions. During the reading, the student may say or do something that raises questions in the observer's mind about the reader's understanding. Observers jot these questions in the margin of the typescript and refer to them during the retelling.

The original text and the typescript should look as much alike as possible, specifically the line length, spelling, punctuation, and other special markings. Given this similarity, the observer makes decisions about the influence of format on the reader. There should be sufficient space between the lines of print (usually triple space) to clearly record miscues. Place a solid horizontal line after the last line of each page of the original passage. Type the subsequent page of the original text on the typescript below the solid line (see *The Man Who Kept House* typescript in Chapter 1). If the original text is printed in two or more columns, use a broken horizontal line to show the separation between the last line of one column and the beginning of the next (see *The Beat of My Heart* typescript in Appendix B).

For repeatedly used materials, type the line and page numbers of the original text in the left margin of the typescript. The first two digits identify the text page, and the second two identify the line of print (as shown in the following excerpt). Such numbering provides an address for the coding sheet and for computer entries. It also facilitates the quick identification of the miscue during coding, analysis, and discussion. An alternative is to number the lines consecutively, starting with number 1.

0101	Once upon a time there was a woodman
0102	who thought that no one worked as hard as
0103	he did. One evening when he came home

(The last line on page 1 of the original text follows.)

0119	"We'll do it tomorrow!"

0201	So the next morning the wife went off to
0202	the forest. The husband stayed home and

Teachers who do not have time to prepare a typescript will sometimes photocopy a text directly from a book. Although it is difficult to mark miscues because of the limited space between the lines, for occasional readings (especially for the Informal Procedure) this "quick typescript" may be suitable. A blank form of *The Man Who Kept House* is provided in Appendix C. All forms may be copied for educational use as needed.

PREPARING THE RETELLING GUIDE

By constructing a retelling guide, we become familiar with the text's features (characterization, setting, events, plot, theme, concepts, organization, and style). Although the guide is carefully constructed, it is important to be flexible with its form and use. The reader does not have to use the exact language of the text in retelling events or specific information, themes, or generalizations. Since we advocate reading as constructing meaning, we also view retellings as parallel stories, often organized in forms and language that differ from the text and with understandings that differ from those of the teacher or researchers (Cambourne and Brown 1990; Y. Goodman 1996; Kalmbach 1986). We hope this is not interpreted as "anything goes"; it is not acceptable to misrepresent an author's text. Just as authors have responsibilities to readers, readers have responsibilities to authors.

In a narrative, attention may focus on characters and characterization, noting physical appearance, attitudes, feelings, behavior, relations to other characters, personality, and morals. Uniquely important aspects of narration, such as setting, inferential information, chain of events, as well as plot and theme statements, are noted on the retelling guides (Appendix C).

In preparing a retelling guide or outline for expository texts (Appendix C), the information is organized around specific information, generalizations, and major concepts. *Specific information* includes facts, events, details, incidents, and conditions. *Generalizations* are drawn from the interrelation of specific information, items, or facts as they relate directly to the topic of the passage. To generalize is to infer a principle, trend, or issue from information that is sometimes meager or insufficient. *Concepts* involve universal views or positions abstracted from generalizations. Concepts may be applied to diverse topics and across fields of study. Some scholars use a hierarchy of categories: subordinate concepts, concepts, and superordinate concepts. After using the retelling guide with a few students, observers might want to reorganize the guide. Students sometimes focus on aspects of the text that adults overlook or consider unimportant.

DATA COLLECTION SESSION

It is helpful for observers to be familiar with the text before taping. This familiarity not only provides content information, but also helps identify potentially difficult syntax, unusual wording, and interesting text features that can be explored with the reader after the reading. Knowing the text also helps ensure easier monitoring of the reader's responses as the material is read and appropriate questioning during retelling.

One way of becoming acquainted with a text is by recording and analyzing one's own retelling, then discussing it with others who have done the same. In Chapter 1 we suggested reading and discussing *The Man Who Kept House* with other readers. At this point you might want to reexamine your retelling of the story and discuss your findings with others.

Figure 3.2: What Observers Need before Taping a Reader

Before the Taping

Observers will need:

- ☐ An audio or video tape recorder in good working condition.
- ☐ A convenient electrical outlet.
- ☐ Suitable reading selections.
- ☐ Typescripts of the selections.
- ☐ Burke Reading Interview (optional).
- ☐ Retelling guides.
- ☐ Pencils (not pens) for marking miscues.
- ☐ A notepad.
- ☐ A comfortable setting with good lighting.

For the **In-Depth** and **Classroom Procedures**, the entire reading experience is preserved on tape to listen and mark the miscues, recheck markings, and transcribe the retelling. Many find it helpful to keep tapes for documenting and sharing a reader's development, as a data base for reporting purposes and longitudinal research, or for use as demonstration protocols with pre-service and in-service teachers.

Before taping, the observer checks the physical requirements, and collects all the materials shown in Figure 3.2. Everything possible should be done to assure a good recording of the reading and retelling; for example, place the microphone on a stand or on a folded cloth with the microphone head toward the reader and away from background noise. Check the recording of the student's voice before taping.

Before and During the Reading

The atmosphere during the data collection session is informal and friendly. The observer chats briefly with the student and possibly administers the Burke Reading Interview (BRI) (Appendix C), in which case copies of the interview are available.

The observer and student sit comfortably, either side by side or across from each other. Marking miscues or writing notes does not distract most students. Usually readers glance once or twice at the observer and then become involved in their reading. If a reader is bothered by marking and note taking, discontinue doing so until the reader is once again involved in the reading and no longer distracted.

It is difficult to mark all miscues as the student reads, especially if the observer is new to miscue procedure. If the student either reads at a fast pace or makes many repetitions and complex miscues, we mark the most relevant miscues to use with the student during the aided retelling.

The observer briefly tells students why they are being asked to read and what is expected of them. We encourage readers to leaf through the text to see how long it is, and ask if they have read or heard the story. Depending on the student and the purpose of the analysis, it is helpful, especially with an insecure student, to tell the title of the story or article: "I'm going to ask you to read a story called *The Man Who Kept House,* or "This article is about a sport I think you enjoy."

The observer asks students to read aloud and, if necessary, reminds them that they are being recorded. Students are encouraged to read as if they were reading alone. We tell readers that they will not be interrupted, that is, they won't receive help or be given suggestions about what to do as they read. Readers need to know before they begin reading that, when finished, they will return the material to the observer and retell the story or article; this lets readers know that they are to focus on meaning, not performance.

Before Betsy began reading, Ms. Blau made sure Betsy had not previously read the story and reminded her of the tape recording, but she didn't go into unnecessary detail. She showed Betsy the length of the story, thus assuring her that the session wouldn't last long. She also reminded Betsy that she was to use her own strategies: "When you come to *something* that gives you trouble, do whatever you would do if you were reading all by yourself, as if I weren't here. I won't interrupt you." The teacher does not indicate the unit (letter, word, phrase, sentence, or paragraph) of language or any concepts that Betsy might have trouble with; rather she tells Betsy that when she comes to *something* she doesn't know, to do as she would do if she were reading silently. Betsy was given an opportunity to ask questions before she began reading.

If students stop reading and look to the observer for help, they are reminded to do whatever they do when reading alone. If they have not moved ahead after 40 seconds, the observer says, "Do whatever you would do if you were reading alone and came to *something* you didn't know." If the reader does not respond, the observer asks, "What are you thinking about?" or "Is something bothering you?" or "Do you need to ask me a question?" Assure readers that any strategy they try is acceptable and encourage them to continue reading.

Reading time usually runs from ten to thirty minutes, depending on the age and proficiency of the reader and the length and complexity of the material. Very young readers may read for a shorter period. When the reading is completed, thank the reader and ask him or her to close the book. Then have the reader begin the oral retelling or an alternate text-suitable presentation, such as making a timeline, following a recipe, or illustrating or writing the retelling.

Stopping the Reader

Once students begin reading, they are stopped under two conditions:

1. *They are not making enough miscues for analysis.* Readers are given challenging material and they are expected to miscue. However, if students don't produce enough miscues for analysis, the data will be insufficient to compile a representative profile of their reading. If readers make very few miscues and the retelling is fairly complete, it may be necessary to provide a more challenging text. If such is the case, tell the readers that they are being given a more challenging piece. Some proficient readers have miscue patterns that are stable across materials. For these students, changing passages may not result in producing more miscues; possibly they need a longer piece or a different genre.

2. *They are unable to continue independently.* If readers appear extremely uncomfortable and are having a very difficult time, they should be asked to stop. Slow, choppy, or hesitant reading is not enough evidence to conclude that readers cannot read independently, and they should not be asked to stop. In fact, the miscue collection procedure often provides the opportunity for such readers to surprise themselves and others with their ability.

In the unlikely event that it is necessary to stop the reader, thank the student, ask for a brief retelling of the material, and then decide if another selection is needed and what the new selection should be. This informal retelling will indicate if the student is gaining meaning from the experience or simply giving an oral performance with little or no understanding. If the reader cannot handle the text independently, and if the retelling reflects the reader's inability to read the text with understanding, choose a more supportive selection.

READERS' RETELLINGS AND PRESENTATIONS

Readers' responses to text provide insights into the depth and breadth of their comprehension. Additionally, responding to a text by retelling, illustrating, dramatizing, setting the story to music or dance, or discussing it in a group provides opportunities for readers to relive, rehearse, modify, and integrate their interpretations of the author's presentation into their own reality. In other words, they have the chance to enhance the construction of meaning.

We conceptualize learning as "coming to know through the symbolic transformation and representation of experience" (K. Goodman, Smith, Meredith, and Y. Goodman 1987). "Coming to know" is the meaning-making process that involves three phases of mental activity: perceiving, ideating, and presenting (Y. Goodman 2003). As a comprehending process, reading involves *perceiving*, becoming aware of new information, and *ideating* on the perceptions of new information and relating it to what is already known. Ideating involves readers' thinking, wondering, and asking questions, whether consciously or intuitively, about what they are reading. This concept suggests the need for readers to have time to reflect on the text. The construction of meaning is enhanced as readers *present* what they perceive and ideate in ways that are interesting to them and compatible with the reading material. The power of *presenting* suggests why retelling is always a part of the miscue analysis procedure. Presenting reflections, concepts, theories, and generalizations to oneself or to others is a way of confirming new knowledge and of testing it against an audience, even if the audience consists of only the reader. Although a variety of presentations are acceptable, an oral retelling is typically used in miscue analysis. The type of presentation depends on the reader, the material, and the purpose of the reading experience.

Oral Retelling Procedures

Retelling a story is an authentic and familiar presentational form in which the reader takes charge. However, as revealing as a retelling is, it never represents a reader's total understanding of the text; readers rarely tell all they know. Retelling scores are always considered along with comprehending patterns and other presentational responses. Even all these factors combined do not reflect total comprehension of the text. *Comprehending* refers to the ongoing consequences of a reader's strategies used *during* the reading, that is, the ongoing sense-making of a text. Comprehension refers to the results of a reader's effort after the reading, that is, the reader's cumulative interpretation of the text.

Unaided Retelling

The retelling is begun on a positive note, regardless of reading performance, for example, "John, thanks for reading. You finished the entire article! Now, will you give me the magazine and tell me what you remember?" After Betsy's reading, Ms. Blau began, "Betsy, you did a nice job. Thank you. Now, would you close the book and in your own words tell me the story?" (See "Betsy's Unaided Retelling" in Chapter 1.)

Once the reader begins retelling, the observer listens carefully, taking notes or checking off items on a retelling outline. Effective observers do not rush. They allow students to reflect, retract, repeat; that is, to respond in any way that makes sense to them. Students are not asked to start at the beginning; rather, they decide where they want to begin and how to proceed. Their decision indicates how they believe a particular text is organized, what they think is the most significant part, or who the most important character is. The observer often asks, after the unaided retelling, why the reader started at a specific point. If the reader begins the retelling somewhere in the middle of the text, we ask what happened before or after that point or ask about the chronology of events. Before asking, however, we give the reader ample opportunity to volunteer such information.

Observers encourage readers by showing interest, but avoid information-giving questions or nodding yes or no. Information-giving questions suggest something to readers they may not know or remember on their own. For example, if the reader does not mention the baby in *The Man Who Kept House* and is asked, "How do you think the baby felt?" the reader gets information from the observer, not from transaction with the text. If the reader appears to be finished and the observer wants to be sure there is nothing more to add, questions that do not give information ("Can you tell me more?" "Is there anything you want to add?" "What else do you remember?") are suitable for both fiction and nonfiction texts. A student's retelling can be surprising; Betsy's is one such example. It seemed that Betsy was finished with her retelling; however, when Ms. Blau invited her to tell more about the story, she did so. (See Chapter 1.)

Occasionally, students have trouble starting their retelling. When this happens, observers are patient and make sure directions are clear. When it is evident that enough wait time is given, it is helpful to ask readers to close their eyes and think about what they read. They may be urged to tell about anything or anyone that is of special interest. Silence is a way to encourage students to continue talking. A pause of 30 or 40 seconds seems uncomfortably long, but often students need thinking time, and after a rather lengthy pause they are able to relate additional information without the interviewer's direct prompting. When readers relate as much as they want to share, we move to the aided retelling.

Aided Retelling

Drawing on information given by the reader during the unaided retelling, which represents the reader's comprehension without an observer's intrusion, observers now ask open-ended questions that encourage continued retelling. The reader's pronunciation of names, places, and events are used in the retelling discussion. For example, if Betsy called the *woodman* the *worker* throughout the story, Ms. Blau would use Betsy's term, *worker*, in the retelling procedure. When readers substitute nonwords for real words, the nonword is used during the retelling. For example, Betsy substitutes *$gorun* for ground. (The symbol *$* is used to designate the spelling of a nonword, such as *$gorun* for *ground*.) Therefore, Ms. Blau uses *$gorun* when any reference to *ground* is made unless Betsy corrects or provides another term for it in her retelling. By using the reader's terms, observers avoid giving readers a sense that their retelling is flawed. Observers may find it easier to avoid using either the student's pronunciation or standard pronunciation of the names, places, and events. In such an event, Ms. Blau might ask questions that are closely related to the *woodman* or to the *ground*, but would not mention them directly by any name.

If important details, characters, or entire segments of the text are omitted in the retelling, observers ask open-ended questions to jog the student's memory. These *cued questions* are asked when it is reasonably certain the student knows the information but for some reason does not include it in the retelling. The following are examples of cued questions:

- You told me about the time Freddie got in trouble because he tinkered with the alarm clock, and the time he turned his sister's doll green. Were there any other reasons he got in trouble with his parents?

- You mentioned Andre, Andre's father, and his grandfather. Were there any other important people in the story? Why were they important?

- You told me how to check your own heartbeat, can you remember how to check the heartbeat of a friend?

Additional Questioning Strategies

Observers selectively use terms such as theme, plot, character, character development, and setting if they think the reader understands them, and if they can do so without providing information. If the reader does not understand questions such as, "What is the setting of the story?" or "Tell me more about the main character," the following might be suitable:

- Tell more about [character named by reader].
- After [event mentioned by reader], what happened? Where were they?
- Why do you think [character mentioned by reader] did that?
- What does this piece tell us about the way people act?

When appropriate, follow the reader's responses with:

- Why do you think so?

- Who/what in the story made you think that?

- Describe [character named by reader] at the beginning of the story and describe [him/her] at the end of the story.

- Did you think [character named by reader] was right or wrong when he/she [action mentioned by reader]?

- Are there other people in the story you haven't mentioned?

- Where did the story take place? Describe that place.

Questions that help readers recount *plot* and *theme* are sometimes difficult to formulate. If students are familiar with terms for the concepts of plot and theme, don't hesitate to use those labels in questioning. If that is not the case, the following questions may be helpful:

- You have told so much about the story; now tell me what the story is about in just a sentence or two.

- If someone stopped you at the most exciting point in the story, what question would you ask about the end of the story?

- What were you wondering about as you read the story?

- Why do you think [event mentioned by reader] happened?

- Why do you think the author wrote this story?

- Do you think the author was trying to teach something in this story?

- Does this story remind you of any other story? In what way?

- What problem was the story concerned with?

To get at *subtleties*, follow up on any aspect of the reading or retelling in which the student appears to be especially interested. For example:

- Was there anything funny or sad?

- Did anything seem strange, unusual, or scary?

- Did anything make you feel uncertain or uneasy?

- Tell about the part of the story that made you laugh or cry.

- Was there anyone or anything that you related (felt close) to?

- Did anyone or anything remind you of yourself or your own experiences?

To encourage readers to *evaluate* and *judge*, consider the following:

- Did you like the story? Why?

- Would you have changed any part of this story?

- Would you have changed the ending?

- If the author writes a sequel, what should it be about?

- Do you think the author is a good writer? Why?

The following questions are directed toward revealing the reader's awareness of *cultural and social relevancy:*

- Did the people in the story act or talk like people you know? In what ways?

- Do you think [mention cultural group] people act or talk like the people in the story? How?
- Do you feel [specific problem or setting] is the way it is described in the story?

Questions that may lead to *critical inquiry* include:

- Who should read this piece? Why?
- Did something in the story make you angry or cause you to feel a sense of injustice?
- Was there an injured or mistreated person or group in the story? Explain.
- Who inflicted pain or injustice on the injured person or group? Explain.
- Were there any people who just stood by and did nothing to help? Explain.
- Was the author accurate and was he/she fair?
- Did you change your mind or attitude about [character, event, topic] as you read this piece?
- Did this article make you want to talk with someone about it?
- Did this piece make you want to find more information?
- Do you want to do something about the topic or cause? What might that be?

Many of the preceding and following questions are suitable for *nonfiction/expository text*, and the following may elicit additional information:

- What did you know about this topic before you read the article that was either confirmed or disconfirmed by the author? What do you think was the author's background? What prepared him/her to write the piece?
- What was the main concept or generalization of the article and was it supported?
- What did the author want you to learn?
- What did you agree and disagree with in the article?
- To whom would you recommend this article? Why?
- Are there questions you would like to ask the author?
- Are there questions you would like to research? What are they?

Questions that provide insight into the *reader's construction of meaning:*

- Was there anything that didn't make sense to you?
- Was this easy or difficult to read? What parts? Why?
- Are there questions you would like to ask other readers of this story/article?
- Are there questions you wish I had asked you?
- Is there anything more you would like to tell me?

Figure 3.3: Retelling Procedure Reminders

- Establish a conversational tone and a comfortable exchange.
- Get to know the reader's interests and background.
- Become familiar with the selected text.
- Avoid giving the reader specific information from the text.
- Mention only information introduced by the reader in questions and comments made during *unaided* retelling.
- Use wait time liberally. Don't rush the reader or yourself. Think through your questions and wait for the reader's reply.
- Make directions and questions clear and avoid giving more than one direction or asking more than one question at a time.
- Avoid accepting, "I don't know" for an answer. Rephrase a question to get information another way. At the same time, don't exhaust the reader with too great a focus on any one topic.
- Let students develop a topic and reach their own conclusions before changing the subject.
- Ask open-ended questions. Questions answered with yes or no or with single words limit the reader's response.
- Retain any nonwords or name changes given by the reader, unless the reader switches to the expected response (ER).
- Ask questions that are particularly relevant to a specific reader or a specific text.
- Take good notes during the unaided retelling. They are needed during the aided retelling.
- Word your comments and questions in a way that is suitable for the student.
- Do not overwhelm the student with questions.

Other Responses and Presentations

Presentations and reading responses can take a variety of forms, even though most research has focused on oral retelling. Retelling is not simply a question-answer session, but rather a conversation to engage students in thinking about what they have read and about the reading process. A contribution could be made to the area of reading comprehension by researching other forms of presentations.

Written Retelling

Some students relate more about their reading in their writing than in their oral retellings. Written retellings give individuals, partners, small groups, or whole classes the opportunity to retell without the teacher being involved at the moment. Teachers make use of a variety of written presentational techniques, avoiding the traditional book report, which tends to stultify students and diminish the experience. Figure 3.4 shows a variety of ways to present written retellings.

Figure 3.4: Presenting Written Retellings

- Journal responses
- Written conversations
- Changing narrative to dialogue, possibly a play
- A letter to a friend about the text
- Extending the story
- Writing and illustrating a book jacket
- Solving a character's or group's problem
- Moving to action by writing an editorial, petition, or plan of action
- Making a bumper sticker
- Creating a poster
- Writing captions for illustrations made by the reader
- Creating content-appropriate pieces such as timelines, tables, or figures

---

Other Symbolic Presentations

Movement across symbol systems—for example, from oral or written language to an art form—allows students to take another perspective and to highlight meanings not explored in an oral retelling. Art, music, drama, and dance all have potential and may be used in combination with oral or written retellings.

Siegel (1999) describes a response activity, Sketch to Stretch, as a way for students to think about what is read, thus exploring their comprehension of the text. Siegel's research was related primarily to the use of Sketch to Stretch with nonfiction materials. The activity is based on the assumption that, when students draw, or make a figure or table (that is, illustrate a response graphically), they bring additional meanings to a conscious level and express a new or deepened perspective. Additionally, in Sketch to Stretch, as in reading, students are encouraged to see the possibility of reading and drawing to gain information (efferent reading), as well as to read or draw in order to live or feel the experience (aesthetic reading) (Rosenblatt 1976; 1978; 1994). Sketch to Stretch brings reading and drawing together as mutually supportive processes.

Fiction and expository materials such as science, math, and social studies lend themselves to various presentational responses. In addition to Sketch to Stretch, making diagrams, charts, and webs are ways to help students think through a process or consider how something is created. When students tell about their sketches or graphics, it is often done in the narrative form. Tierney, Bridge, and Cera (1979) conclude that people frequently retell expository material as narrative, possibly because most readers control the narrative form. For retellings of expository genre, encourage presentations that fit the genre being read. For example, students may:

- Conduct projects or create artifacts in ways that demonstrate their understandings and interpretations.

- Cook or build to show their comprehension of directions.

- Record observations to indicate their understanding of science and math experiments.

- Produce timelines, maps, or graphic designs to show sequences, chronologies, general outlines, and specific details.

Dramatization at all levels provides the opportunity to demonstrate understanding and interpretation of texts. Drama for Vivian Paley (2004), a researcher and teacher of young children, is an essential tool in examining the social and emotional worlds that are the foundations of literacy and learning as well as a window into the construction of meaning that readers and listeners make about the social issues that permeate the lives of children and teachers (Koshewa 1999).

The information presented in this chapter is general and primarily for use with the **In-Depth** and the **Classroom Procedures**, with some information also applicable to the **Informal Procedure**. Information about marking the typescript follows in the next chapter.

Chapter 4
General Procedures: Marking the Typescript

This chapter deals with how the typescript is *marked*. We want to make clear that *marking* the typescript is not the same as *coding* the sentences (as in the **Classroom Procedure**) or *coding* the miscues (as in the **In-Depth Procedure**). The procedures for coding are presented in Chapters 6 and 7.

TYPESCRIPT MARKINGS: MISCUES AND OTHER PHENOMENA

The typescript is a copy of the text on which reading is preserved and the record from which miscues and other markings are analyzed and described. Therefore, all differences between what the observer expects to hear (ER) and the reader's miscues (the observed response [OR]) are recorded on the typescript as accurately as possible.

In the **In-Depth** and **Classroom Procedures** the student reads, while the observer tape records the reading and marks as many miscues as possible on the typescript. Later, the observer listens to the tape as often as needed to verify, revise, and record all miscues. It is advisable to do all markings in pencil; erasing is expected.

To verify miscues, second listeners are helpful. In miscue analysis research, miscues are marked a second time by another researcher, without reference to the original marked typescript, and are arbitrated, whenever necessary, by a third listener. This second marking shows agreement between listeners that validate the occurrence of miscues and their markings. Over time and with experience, reliability between observers is high. In teacher education classes, students are often paired as research partners so that they can corroborate marking and coding. Teachers of secondary students are sometimes paired with primary school teachers. Diverse readers provide miscues (of younger and older students) that teachers can study to investigate their similarities and differences. The research partners are as responsible for their partners' work as they are for their own.

For ease in marking, we recommend using standard symbols and standard marking procedures. Markings that represent phenomena such as repetitions, pauses, and dialect that occur in oral reading are illustrated in the following examples. For purposes of clarity, the examples are sometimes presented as if only a single miscue occurs in the sentence; of course, several miscues can occur in a single sentence.

All the examples used in this book are from Betsy and other real students; none of the miscues are fabricated. Betsy reads *The Man Who Kept House* (Chapter 1) and another student, Gordon, reads *The Beat of My Heart* (Vannier 1967) (Appendix B). When the miscues are from other students reading other stories, no line number precedes the examples. In the examples, the lines from the text are in print and the miscues are written as they would appear on a typescript.

Substitutions

Substitution miscues are written above the appropriate text.

Text Item Substitutions

0210-211   ⓡ ...He looked around, but he *couldn't* could not see her.

There
Where is Sven?

mysterious whispering
I heard a musical whistle near my ear ...

flash
This brought a fresh flood of tears from Anita.

0209   the ⌐heartbeat is *strong* *st–* strongest

In the last example, Gordon pauses and then produces a partial attempt (explained later) of *strongest*, followed by a word substitution.

Substitutions That Are Complex Miscues

In some instances, miscues occur together in such a way that it is not possible to determine word-for-word relationships. When this occurs, the miscue is written over the entire text sequence and a bracket is placed above the sequence to clarify the relation between the OR and the ER. A complex miscue is considered as one miscue. The criteria used to decide what constitutes a complex miscue are discussed later in this chapter.

0107   *and* ⌐keeping house is hard work."

this is the
"No," said the voice.

anything
. . . nothing has any weight in space.

Kitten Jones would not have changed her white
another thing
fur coat for anything.

Substitutions, Often Called Reversals

Two possible markings are used to show the reversal of letters, words, or other linguistic features:

A transpositional symbol that clearly shows what is transposed.

The written OR above the ER.

0710-0711
ways
. . . but the two best ones are the easiest to do.

best two ways
. . . but the two best ones are the easiest to do.

down looking
I sat looking down at Andrew.

Where can I see this baby brother of yours?

Was something wrong with Papa?

Substitutions Involving Bound Morphemes

Insertions or omissions of bound morphemes (i.e., prefixes or suffixes attached to words) are always coded as word-for-word substitutions. However, they may be marked in different ways. Inserted bound morphemes are added after the word above a caret (^), or the entire word substitution is written above the ER. Deleted bound morphemes are circled, or the word substitution is written above the ER.

0113
ing
. . . and keep house   or   *keeping*
. . . and keep house . . .

0109
. . . heart beating   or   *beat*
. . . heart beating.

0220
. . . friends heart.   or   *friend*
friend's heart.

0324   . . . a minute*y* or . . . a minute. *(minutes)*

0505   on the (in)side . . . or on the inside *(side)* . . .

Omissions

Omissions are indicated by circling the text item. It is not necessary to draw a line through the omitted word as it often hides the ER.

0726-727 On and on your heart beats year (in) and year out.

0613   Never again did the woodman say to his

0614   wife (,)(") *that he* "What did you do all day?"

     He worked (at home) every afternoon.

     With these (reservations) out of the way *re –* . . .

On lines 0613–0614, Betsy reads *...his wife that he "What did you...* . Before correcting her miscue, Betsy reads the section as if there is no comma or quotation mark after *wife* and she substitutes *that he* for *What did*. The omission of the comma and first quotation mark are circled.

In the preceding example, the student reads *With these re- out of the way*. The partial *re-* is not corrected; therefore, *reservations* is circled as an omission. Partials are considered omissions when they are not self-corrected since the observer is not able to determine the reader's linguistic intent. Partial words are determined primarily by the reader's intonation. The student reads *re-* with a rising intonation, as if expecting to produce the next syllable. If the student reads *re* with a level or falling intonation and if it sounds like a complete English word, the miscue is marked as a nonword substitution.

Insertions

An insertion mark or caret (^) indicates the point of insertion, with the OR written above the caret.

0415-416 He dropped the other end down ^ the chimney. *to*

0321   First listen ^

0718   The other way

0719   _^*is* to take care of your heart

When the chair rocked the ^fell^ *boy* *off*

Repetitions

The term *repetition* in miscue analysis means the rereading of a portion of the text. To mark repetitions, a line is drawn from where the reader begins to repeat, to the left under the text portion repeated, and up in front of the first word that is repeated, culminating in a circle. The letter code written inside the circle reflects the strategy the reader uses, such as R for repetition, C for correction, UC for unsuccessful attempt to correct, and AC for abandons correct response. Each time the reader repeats, an additional line is added under the repeated text. The number of lines under a repeated text item will be one less than the number of times the reader actually reads the item because the last reading is not repeated.

Repetitions are not miscues. However, they provide evidence of the strategies readers use to solve their problems. Many repetitions show that the reader is anticipating a problem in the text, usually to the right of where he or she is reading, and reflecting on which strategies to use.

0112   Ⓡ "Why don't you do my work Ⓒ *so* some day?

0509   . . . Ⓡ She pulled him up

0510   Ⓡ the chimney by Ⓡ the rope . . .

Some repetitions extend beyond a single line:

0106   "I keep house," replied the wife, Ⓡ "and

0107   *and* keeping house is hard work."

Betsy reads: *... and keeping ... and keeping house ... and ... work,* then continues reading.

Repeating and Correcting the Miscue

0301 Ⓡ Ⓒ feels
      Blood feeds

0302 Ⓒ c – Ⓒ oranges
      all the cells and organs

Gordon corrects each of the preceding miscues immediately.

0301 Ⓡ Ⓒ Ⓡ the
      In his hurry, the woodman had left the . . .

Betsy reads: *In the … In … In … In his … In … In …*, then continues reading.

Repeating and Abandoning a Correct Form

ⓐⓒ in
She ran into the store.

The student reads: *She ran into … .* He then abandons the correct response, and reads *in the store.*

ⓐⓒ complaining
She was always comparing.

The student reads: *She was always comparing …* He then abandons the correct response and reads *… complaining.*

ⓐⓒ future
He left home to make his fortune.

The student reads: *He left home to make his fortune …* She then abandons the correct response and reads *his future.*

Repeating and Unsuccessfully Attempting to Correct

ⓤⓒ That
      Then
0508 This is called your pulse.

Gordon reads *Then … That is called your pulse.*

He reads *Then* for *This,* and unsuccessfully attempts to correct by reading *That.*

ⓤⓒ frog
The fish swam . . .

The student reads *The frog … the frog … the frog swam … .* The reader repeats twice but does not correct the miscue.

The\fro̶g swam . . .

The student reads *The fern ... Fred swam.* His attempt to correct is unsuccessful.

hid
head
He had\heard a lot.

The student reads *He had head ... hid a lot.* His attempt to correct is unsuccessful.

Clarida
Clarence
Her name was Clarible.

The student reads *Her name was Clarence ... Her name was Clarida.* Her attempt to correct is unsuccessful.

Repetitions That Affect More Than One Miscue

A circle without a mark in it at the end of the repetition line indicates that two or more things happened during the repetition.

0408-9   . . . the heart is a sensitive machine.

Gordon reads *the heart is sense ... is a sense machine.*

Gordon corrects the omission of *a* but does not correct *sense* for *sensitive.* Therefore, we leave the circle empty and make individual marks in a circle at the point of each miscue.

0313   *Then he*
              than I thought

Betsy reads *Then ... Then he ... Then I thought ... .*

The first **UC** is marked because Betsy does not correct *Then* for *than* when she makes her first one-word repetition. After she reads *Then he,* she makes a two-word repetition. Again, she does not correct *Then* for *than,* but she does correct *he* for *I.*

0114   *start house*
              "If you stay home to do my work, . . .

Betsy reads *if you start house to do ... If you start home to ...* then continues reading. In her rereading, Betsy does not correct *start* for *stay,* but corrects *house* for *home.*

Additional Markings

Partial Attempts

When a reader attempts to produce an entire word but does not do so, the partial attempt is written above the ER, followed with a dash (–). The reader's rising intonation identifies a partial. The readers in the following examples correct their partial attempts. We mark the partials as corrected, with a circled C.

0206   *C a–*
                  a–
                 ...All I have to do

0405   The man left the *C por–*
                 porridge...

0609   *C Ex–*
                 Exercise helps your heart

0218   or a *C roll–*
                 rolled-up piece...

Although *roll* (line 0218) is a word, Gordon reads it with a rising, abrupt intonation that indicates a partial rendition of a word. It is therefore marked with a dash. If *roll-* is not corrected, it is marked as an omission. If *roll* is read with an intonation indicating a complete word, it is marked a substitution. If a reader's intonation is not indicative of a partial, that is, if the student reads *por* for *porridge* (with no rise in intonation), as in a complete word, the OR is marked without a dash and is a nonword substitution.

Nonword Substitutions

When a reader produces a miscue that is not recognizable as a known word, the miscue is identified as a nonword. The dollar sign indicates that the observer invented a spelling to reflect the reader's pronunciation. In marking nonwords, we retain as much of the original spelling of the ER as possible. For example, if a nonword that sounds like *fu-hon-ma* is substituted for the word *phenomena*, we write the OR above the ER and spell it as *$phuhonma*. This provides information about the graphophonic cues the reader is using. If there is any doubt about how to read the nonword, we make a notation in the margin of the typescript about its pronunciation.

0512-513   ...between the roof and the *$gorun*
                 ground...

0310   *$liver*
                 to your liver...   (*Rhymes with diver.*)

                 Her usually restless tail hung straight down, not

                 $twigching
                 twitching at all.

                 $distroubles
                 If it bothers you to think of it as baby sitting...

Dialect and Other Language Variations

Students' dialects are reflected phonologically, syntactically, and semantically in their reading (see Chapter 2). While syntactic and semantic reflections of dialect are always marked and coded, a reader's phonological variations are marked *only if there is a particular interest in the phenomenon*. Phonological dialect is sometimes marked on the transcript to help the teacher consider the supportive role of a reader's dialect in making sense of the text. When English is a second language, the student's first language phonology is often apparent in his or her reading. If a teacher/researcher wants to record this phenomenon, it is marked as a dialect form. In marking dialect miscues, spell the variation as closely to how it sounds as possible, and retain as much of the ER spelling as possible (for example, *mus* for *must*, *aks* for *ask*, *vant* for *want*, and *broblem* for *problem*). ORs reflecting dialect are indicated with a ⓓ.

like ⓓ
. . . just about everybody likes babies.

How ⓓ
How're you doing?

headlights ⓓ
I switched off the headlamps of the car . . .

done ⓓ
He did this experiment.

Misarticulations

Misarticulations are unconventional pronunciations of words, and include child language forms that usually diminish with age. Adult readers produce misarticulations of words such as *tachistoscope* and *strategy*. Misarticulations are spelled to reflect the readers' pronunciation and are marked with a circled ⓐ.

$pecific ⓐ
He had a specific place in mind.

$pasghetti ⓐ
The spaghetti was delicious.

Intonation Shifts

Intonation shifts at the clause or sentence level are marked only if the shift changes meaning or changes the grammatical structure of the ER. We note intonation shifts within the word with an accent mark over the stressed syllable. We note intonation shifts at the clause level above the ER and in the margin if clarification is necessary. Shifts within and between sentences are indicated by the insertion, substitution, or omission markings of punctuation and capitalization, and are noted in the margin of the typescript for clarification, if necessary.

récord
He will record her voice.

contented
That is one contented cow!

project
We want the project to succeed.

he cut   *(The noun "cut"*
After the cut in his allowance. *is changed to*
                                the verb "cut.")

0413   . . . she would fall off.
                                        ∧

0414   *The*
                  the roof and hurt herself . . .

                                      anyway. The
Dog was almost right. Anyway,   the fall had . . .

The student reads the last example as if it were punctuated: *Dog was almost right, anyway. The fall had ...*

Split Syllables

When a reader separates words into identifiable syllables, resulting in unnatural pronunciation, the shifts are indicated with a slash. These split syllables are not considered miscues, but provide information about the reader's sounding-out or pronunciation strategies.

0109-10   You should try cut/ting wood!

                           The lit/tle girl yelled her head off.

Pauses

Pauses (usually for more than five seconds) are indicated as shown. It is often useful to note the length of the pause.

0204-05   As he put the cream into the/churn . . .

0320   Just as the/husband . . .

Complex Miscues

If the miscue involves phrases, clauses, and sentences in such a way that it is not possible to determine word-for-word relations, the entire sequence is marked as one complex miscue. To determine if a miscue is complex, we compare individual observed responses (ORs) to the expected responses (ERs) on a word-for-word level. If this can be done easily, each miscue is marked separately; they do not constitute a complex miscue. We designate a complex miscue with a bracket.

0211   . . . her. Ⓒ *There is* / She was not . . .

They are / He is going to

Complex miscues are marked as a single miscue to show that the ER and the OR relate in complex ways. This complexity often involves syntactic shifts or transformations.

0104   . . . he said to his wife, Ⓒ *I want you* / "What do you

0105   do all day . . .

Betsy substitutes the entire clause *I want you* for the entire text clause *What do you*. She predicts a declarative sentence instead of an interrogative one. We cannot say that Betsy substitutes *I* for *What* or *want* for either *do* or *what*. In fact, Betsy's *you* is the object of the clause she predicts, instead of the subject, as it is in the text. Because it is not possible to separate the miscues, the substitution of one clause for another is treated as a single complex miscue.

0204   . . . make some butter○ *and* / As he put

0205   the cream into the churn, • *He* / he said, "This is

By substituting *and* for both the *period* and *As*, Betsy joins two sentences with two independent clauses rather than starting the second sentence as a dependent clause. This substitution of one word for both a period and a word is a complex miscue. This miscue is a factor in Betsy's producing another miscue, the substitution of the *period* for the *comma* after the word *churn*. Her intonation indicates that she not only ends the sentence, but she begins a new sentence with *He said*. Often insertions or omissions with related substitution miscues are considered complex.

He could *have stayed* / stay at home.

The insertion of *have* and the substitution of *stayed* for *stay* are inseparable and therefore marked and coded as one complex miscue; the reader's prediction of a shift of tense required the substitution.

... never been a rule against pets in

space stations

ⓐ space station.

When omissions and insertions occur within a noun or verb phrase, the miscue is often complex.

In the preceding example, the omission of the determiner *a* and insertion of *s* on *station* indicate that the reader has substituted a plural noun phrase for a singular one.

The reversal of sequential words (see above) and the omission of two or three sequential words or lines in the text are also treated as complex.

Laura wanted to eat

dinner. She went out

with her good friends.

If readers omit a line, the omitted line is treated as a single complex miscue.

The student reads *Laura wanted to eat with her good friends.* The OR is read using the reader's intonation to decide if the resulting transformation is semantically and syntactically acceptable. In this case, the reader's intonation indicates that she moved from one line to the next without interrupting the pattern of the sentence.

Complexity of ORs and ERs

Occasionally, even though we can find a word-for-word relationship between the OR and the ER, they may also be related in complex ways linguistically. If so, we cannot mark word-for-word relationships separately without losing information about the entire miscue. In this case, we treat the miscue as complex.

seven pets

In no time at all, Sven's pet *were* was everybody's pet.

The omission of the *comma* (evident when listening to the reader's intonation) is considered a separate miscue because it could have occurred whether the following cluster of miscues occurred or not. However, the cluster of miscues, *seven pets were*, needs more consideration to determine the number of miscues involved. *seven pets* for *Sven's pet* is one complex miscue, not simply because of the relationship of the syntactic cues of plurality (*pets*), but also because of the possessive graphophonic cue (*Sven's*). Deciding if the substitution of *were* for *was* is part of the complex miscue is a borderline call. We mark it separately because it involves a point at which the reader could have corrected rather than making the form of *to be* (*were* for *was*) consistent with the subject.

Additional miscues often result when readers attempt to accommodate text to prior miscues. If these are all treated as complex miscues, we lose important insights into the reader's strategies.

the passes
The rest of us passed around the oxygen bottle.

The complex syntactic and semantic meaning changes influenced by the substitution of a noun phrase, *the passes*, for an object of the preposition, plus a verb, makes this miscue too interrelated to mark separately. It is sometimes hard to clearly distinguish word-for-word substitutions from complex miscues. Experience with miscue analysis builds consistent rationales and aids in decision making.

Repeated Miscues

There are a number of types of repeated miscues. They are marked on the typescript as all other miscues are marked; however, the second and subsequent identical miscues are identified as *RM*.

0304   . . . nose in the churn. "Get . . .   *cream*

0307   . . . bumped into the churn, knocking . . .   *jumped* *cream RM*

Repeated miscues occur when content words such as nouns, verbs, adjectives, and adverbs are substituted across the text for an identical expected response. When there is an omission of an identical expected response and the omission is repeated across the text, the omissions are repeated miscues. We mark the second and subsequent omissions as follows:

0101   Lub-dup . . .   *Lu-bump*

0102   Lub-dup . . .   *Lu-bump RM*

0103   Lub-dup . . .   *Lu-bump RM*

Repeated miscues are discussed in detail in Chapters 6 and 7.

Multiple Miscues

Readers occasionally produce two or more observed responses for one word in one place in the text. When multiple attempts occur, we list them sequentially above the text item, starting with the first attempt placed closest to the text.

0308   . . . The cream splashed all over the room.   *shadow* *shout*

Betsy reads *The cream shout, shadow, splashed all ...* . Betsy makes two attempts on *splashed* and then corrects.

Poor Freddie was in trouble again.

The reader reads *Poor Freddie was in t-, $troub, time again*. The reader makes three unsuccessful attempts on *trouble*.

This chapter includes the procedures for marking the miscues on the typescript. A summary of miscue markings is available in a condensed form in Appendix A. In the following chapters we present the three alternative miscue procedures.

Chapter 5
General Procedures: Analyzing Miscues

Inquiry is at the heart of miscue analysis. Questions are asked about miscues, patterns of miscues, the relationship of those patterns to each other, and how miscues affect the remainder of the written text. Such questioning evaluates the relationships discussed in previous chapters between the:

- Linguistic systems of the text and the reader.
- Languages of the reader and the author.
- Concepts understood by the reader and the author.
- Reader's strategies for initiating, sampling, selecting, predicting, inferring, correcting, confirming, and integrating.

Everyone brings his or her own language, concepts, and knowledge about language and thinking to the interpretation and evaluation of miscues. This individuality is demonstrated by an example involving dialect features. A reader might say something for the word *picture* that sounds like *pitcher*. If you use this pronunciation for both a container that holds liquid and for a piece of art, you will probably consider *pitcher* an acceptable response for both words. However, those who say something closer to *pick-chure* for a piece of art and *pitcher* for a container might consider *pitcher* for *picture* a miscue.

The specific questions asked in the Classroom and In-Depth Procedures depend on the issue and purposes of those conducting the analysis. One observer might want to know if a student is self-correcting appropriately, while another might want to discover which linguistic structures students are most likely to correct.

QUESTIONS TO EVALUATE READING

The questions selected for evaluating reading evolved from the Goodman Taxonomy (Appendix D) and from the original Reading Miscue Inventory (Appendix D). These questions are considered the most significant for reader evaluation, reading research, understanding the reading process, and classroom instruction. The questions come from the miscue analysis of thousands of readers for over forty years of research. The questions focus on:

- Syntactic acceptability.
- Semantic acceptability.
- Meaning change.
- Correction.
- Graphic similarity.
- Sound similarity.

Questions are framed in such a way that the interaction of all the language cuing systems and reading strategies are taken into consideration. Such interrelations are involved in most miscues; rarely does a miscue involve only one system of language or a single reading strategy. The examination of a reader's language and strategies helps us determine how proficiently reading strategies and language systems are used and for what purpose they are used.

Because numerous miscue examples in this and following chapters are taken from Betsy's reading of *The Man Who Kept House*, it is helpful to make a copy of her reading (Chapter 1 for the In-Depth Procedure and Chapter 6 for the Classroom Procedure), and keep it available when the miscues are discussed.

Syntactic Acceptability and Semantic Acceptability

The two questions related to syntactic and semantic acceptability are the most important ones in miscue analysis because they focus on the major purpose of the reading process, that is, to produce a meaningful text that sounds like language. These questions provide the greatest insight into a reader's proficiency. (The In-Depth Procedure questions follow. The Classroom Procedure questions are in Chapter 6.)

- *Syntactic acceptability:* Does the miscue occur in a structure that is syntactically acceptable in the reader's dialect?
- *Semantic acceptability:* Does the miscue occur in a structure that is semantically acceptable in the reader's dialect?

Answers to these questions reveal the proficiency of a reader's use of the strategies of predicting, inferring, and confirming. Although all readers produce miscues, the degree to which their miscues result in structures that sound like language (syntactic acceptability) and make sense within the context of the story (semantic acceptability) reveals reading proficiency.

For the most part, proficient readers produce miscues that are semantically and syntactically acceptable within the entire text. When they produce unacceptable miscues, they make use of their confirming and correcting strategies. This means that proficient readers who are monitoring their reading tend to self-correct miscues that disrupt meaning. Less proficient readers are not as consistent in their patterns of strategy use, and they may produce acceptable sentences less than half the time (Flurkey and Xu 2003; K. Goodman and Burke 1973). The ability to produce semantically and syntactically acceptable structures or, if the structures are unacceptable, the ability to self-correct provides evidence of a reader's predicting, inferring, and confirming strategies.

The term *structure,* used in the two questions, refers to a sentence. However, depending on your purpose, other text units might be examined. For instance, in the Goodman Taxonomy, the main clause and all its dependent clauses, or the minimal terminable unit (T-unit) (Hunt 1965), is the linguistic *structure* analyzed for acceptability. Because the concept of the sentence in written language is more easily understood than the clause or T-unit, the sentence is considered the primary linguistic unit in current miscue analysis procedures.

After examining the acceptability of portions of sentences or entire sentences, the overall question of acceptability is ultimately considered within the complete text. Partial acceptability is considered for the **In-Depth Procedure** and is discussed in Chapter 7. Relating acceptability to self-correction is the best way to observe a reader's use of prediction strategies.

Syntactic Acceptability

Words in a sentence have both syntactic and semantic organization. Although linguists have varying concepts for the two, we use *syntax* and *grammar* synonymously in this book. However, because many people think of grammar as a set of prescriptive rules about "correct" language, the word *syntax* is used predominately. To determine syntactic acceptability, the following In-Depth Procedure question is asked. (The Classroom Procedure question is in Chapter 6.)

- Does the miscue occur in a structure that is syntactically acceptable in the reader's dialect?

A sentence can have an acceptable syntactic structure without having acceptable meaning; for example, *The plants ate the ripe grapes* is syntactically acceptable because the sentence has a subject, verb, and object in the appropriate English order. In addition, the determiner *the* (rather than *a*) is used because the nouns, *plants* and *grapes,* are plural. The sentence is considered semantically acceptable only if the author is telling a science-fiction story. Even nonsense sentences can assume syntactic acceptability, as in *The flugs glatted the slusy eberts.* The structure of the sentence makes it obvious that *the flugs* are things (a plural noun phrase serving as the subject of the clause) that did something called *glatted* (serving as the verb of the clause) to something called *the slusy eberts* (another plural noun phrase serving as the object of the clause). Another way to test that this sentence is syntactically acceptable is to ask a speaker of the language questions such as, *Who glatted the slusy eberts?* or *What did the flugs do to the slusy eberts?* Even though readers construct nonsense words and parts of sentences, nonsense sentences are seldom produced.

The syntactic structure of the declarative sentence above is described as:

determiner, noun + plural marker, verb + past tense,
determiner, adjective, noun + plural marker

and can be used to produce any number of semantically acceptable sentences, such as:

- The cars hit the rusty barrels.
- The men moved some heavy tractors.
- The magicians tricked the surprised children.

Answers to the syntactic acceptability question reveal the degree to which the sentences sound like language. Answers indicate the success with which the reader controls the structure of sentences as well as the relation of the sentences to the structure of the entire text. Miscues can result in syntactically acceptable sentences that are structurally different from the text, but still retain acceptability within the entire text. For example, in the last sentence of *The Man Who Kept House*, Betsy changes the conjoined verb phrases *stay home and keep house* to a verb phrase followed by an infinitive, *stay home to keep house*. Although Betsy changes the syntax of the sentence, she still produces a sentence that is syntactically acceptable in the story.

Semantic Acceptability

The semantic acceptability question focuses on the success with which the reader produces meaningful text. To determine semantic acceptability, the following In-Depth Procedure question is asked. (The Classroom Procedure question is in Chapter 6.)

- Does the miscue occur in a structure that is semantically acceptable in the reader's dialect?

Just as readers have an intuitive feel for the structure of language, they have a sense for meaning relations. The semantic system of language is significant because it cues meaning associations within a text. Miscues can result in semantically acceptable sentences that differ from the ER but that are still acceptable within the story. For example, Betsy reads *he took the basket and went to the well for some water* for *he took a bucket and went ...* (line 0313). Although basket and bucket mean different things to many readers, some types of baskets can hold water; therefore, this miscue actually produces a semantically acceptable sentence in the context of this story.

Syntactic structures create a frame with appropriately ordered words, phrases, and clauses; this frame or pattern supports meaning. Once a sentence is considered to be syntactically acceptable, its semantic acceptability is then evaluated. Semantic acceptability is dependent on and limited by syntactic acceptability. For this reason, for the purposes of miscue analysis, semantic acceptability is judged after syntactic acceptability. A sentence is always considered to be semantically unacceptable if it is syntactically unacceptable.

Readers sometimes produce sentences that are acceptable on the sentence level but not acceptable within the context of the entire story or article. For example, in reading *The Man Who Kept House*, a reader produces the following sentence: *So the next month the wife went off to the forest* for *So the next morning the wife went off to the forest* (lines 0201–0202). The miscue of *month* for *morning* (the substitution of a noun for a noun) produces a sentence that is syntactically acceptable within the entire story. However, because of the previous sentence (*We'll do it tomorrow!*), the miscue is semantically acceptable only at the sentence level, not in the context of the entire story. To be fully acceptable in the entire text, the sentence must fit the pragmatic considerations, that is, have acceptability within the total social context of the story. Betsy produces a fully acceptable miscue in a sentence that is also semantically acceptable in the entire text when she reads, *So the next day the wife went off to the forest,* substituting *day* for *morning,* which is considered synonymous in the context of this story.

Issues Relating to Syntactic and Semantic Acceptability

There are a number of issues to consider when evaluating readers in relation to sentence acceptability.

Bilingual Readers

Bilingual students may have a greater understanding of what they read in their second language than is immediately evident as they are reading. Although semantic acceptability is considered dependent on syntactic acceptability (that is, semantic acceptability is not considered acceptable if the miscue is not syntactically acceptable), we carefully consider the linguistic knowledge of bilingual speakers when responding to the questions concerning syntactic and semantic acceptability. This same judgment applies to deaf and hearing-impaired students who sign. American Sign Language (ASL) signers are bilingual (Ewoldt 1981; Ewoldt and Mason 1996) and therefore receive the same consideration that all bilingual readers are given.

Readers who are more proficient in a language other than English (including ASL) may be translating meanings they gain while reading into their native or dominant language, even though they produce English sentences that are syntactically unacceptable. Teachers gain information about the developing proficiency of second language learners when, for example, they substitute the determiner *a* for *the.* This substitution indicates that readers are gaining control over, in this case, English syntax and may comprehend more than is revealed by their miscues. Discussions with bilingual readers following their retelling give insights into this issue. We also gain information by asking readers to retell in their native language before retelling in English.

Intonation

Readers' observed response (OR) intonation patterns sometime result in pitch, pause, or stress that differ from the observer's expectations (ER). Such changes may occur in combination with other miscues within words, phrases, or sentences. Intonation is a significant clue to a reader's understanding of language units and knowledge of the syntactic structure. Syntactic or semantic miscues involving intonation are often influenced by the reader's anticipation of a different structure or being unfamiliar with the author's structures.

There is no simple one-to-one correspondence between written punctuation and oral intonation. Speakers do not always stop or pause where periods and commas occur. Punctuation in English is placed at the end of a phrase, clause, or sentence to help the reader segment linguistic structures into meaningful language. Proficient readers predict appropriate intonation before the beginning of the linguistic unit. For example, in a declarative sentence the heaviest stress usually falls on the subject of the sentence, while in an interrogative sentence the heaviest stress is often on the initial question marker (for example, *wh* markers, such as *what, why, when*).

In line 0104 of *A Man Who Kept House*, Betsy makes an intonation decision.

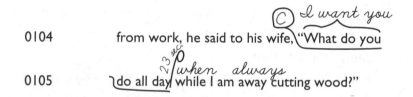

0104   from work, he said to his wife, "What do you

0105   do all day while I am away cutting wood?"

In predicting a declarative sentence, she places heavy stress on the pronoun *I*. Betsy corrects and adjusts her intonation appropriately. Had she predicted a question, her stress pattern would have changed. By listening to the contour of the entire linguistic unit, especially at the beginning of clauses and sentences, we are better judges of the appropriateness of the intonation. Contrary to popular belief, readers do not always pause at punctuation, use falling intonation at the end of declarative sentences, or use rising intonation at the end of questions. It is the intonation contour of the entire sentence—the degree of stress and pitch that flows from the beginning to the end and from one phrase to another—that is significant in determining acceptable intonation structures.

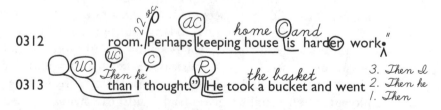

0312   room. Perhaps keeping house is harder work."

0313   than I thought." He took a bucket and went

After carefully listening to Betsy read lines 0312 and 0313, we see that she ends her sentence after *hard work* and that she reads *Then I thought* as a dialogue carrier for the next sentence.

The major difference between *then* and *than* (line 0313) is not in the sound of the vowel, which most English speakers pronounce the same; rather, the intonation signals whether the word is the beginning of a clause as a connective or as a comparative. The former gets a good deal more stress.

Intonation shifts (pitch, stress, and pause) are considered miscues only when they change or disrupt the meaning or the syntax of a sentence. As observers develop their listening ability, it becomes possible, for example, to know whether a reader means *to*, *two*, or *too*, or whether *can* is a question marker (*Can you do this?*), a noun (*Put this in the trash can.*), or a verb (*We will can tomatoes today.*) In time, listeners become proficient at verifying whether readers are producing a change in either syntax or meaning, if they are substituting an acceptable alternate intonation, or if the intonation is optional. Intonation is considered when answering the questions concerning syntactic and semantic acceptability.

Meaning Change

Answers to the question concerning meaning change examine how much miscues retain what the observer believes to be the author's intended meaning. To determine meaning, the **In-Depth Procedure** question is:

- Does the miscue change the meaning of the entire text?

This question helps evaluate the extent of change the reader appears to have made in the text. No one knows exactly the author's meaning, unless the author is present to provide such information. (Interestingly, authors have been known to say that they don't remember what they intended at the time they wrote the piece; they can say only what it currently means to them.) Readers construct their personal texts based on their interpretations of what they are reading. Because of personal interpretation, the greatest amount of variation between two or more people observing the same reading occurs when the *meaning change* question is considered. Such variations are especially true for those just beginning to use miscue analysis.

However, as observers work together, they develop similar criteria for evaluating meaning change, that is, they build shared understandings about the meanings of texts. Betsy's substitution of *basket* for *bucket* (line 0313) helps clarify this point. As discussed earlier, many think that a basket cannot hold water and therefore decide that Betsy's substitution is a major change in the meaning of the story. However, those who know that baskets can be watertight argue that it is possible to get water from a well with a basket; so this miscue causes only a minimal change. If Betsy had substituted *pail* for *bucket*, most observers would agree that there is no change in meaning, as bucket and pail usually refer to the same object. The more miscue analysis is used and discussed, the more consistent the decisions become for evaluating meaning change, and a high level of agreement results.

The question of degree of meaning change is extremely difficult to answer for syntactically and semantically unacceptable structures. Therefore, *meaning change* is evaluated only for sentences that are fully syntactically and semantically acceptable.

The question concerning meaning change is easier to answer when the significance of the miscue is judged in light of the entire story. We judge the extent of meaning change as no change, partial change, or extensive change. Examples of meaning change follow.

There is *no change* of meaning in the following example because *I'll* for *I'd* is a tense change only. The meaning is not affected.

                              I'll
0111   "I'd be glad to," said the wife.

There is a *partial change* of meaning in the following example. Partial change indicates a change of, inconsistency of, or loss to *minor* facts, concepts, incidents, characters, or sequences. For example, Betsy's OR, *Well, you do it* makes only a minor change in the context of the entire story. Both the woodcutter and the wife retain their activity in the story even though the person talking has changed.

                        Well, you Ⓡ
0119   "We'll do it tomorrow!"

There can also be a change of, inconsistency of, or loss to *major* facts, concepts, incidents, characters, or sequences. In the following, a student omits *spirit*, resulting in a syntactically and semantically acceptable sentence that is acceptable within the story, but the meaning change in this context is a major one. The mountain did not make the change; the *mountain spirit* made the change.

              So the mountain (spirit) made the change again.

Dialect

If language "sounds right" to a listener, it usually falls within the range of the listener's community language. Variation in language resulting from geography, social status, or cultural influence is known as *dialect*. The acceptability of a reader's miscue is based on what the listener expects the reader to say and how he or she expects it to be said. By examining dialect in relation to questions concerning meaning change, we decide whether the reader's or the author's dialect interferes with the attempt to make sense.

The syntactic and semantic acceptability questions are answered with the *reader's* dialect in mind, not with a dialect approved by the school, teacher, or text. In reading, the purpose is to gain information and construct meaning, not to use an approved dialect. Often judgments about oral reading are based on what listeners believe to be appropriate, according to the standards of their social rank and culture, rather than on the language that readers use to communicate and understand their world.

In miscue analysis, dialect is considered when there is a difference between the author's dialect and the reader's dialect. Because what observers consider to be dialect depends on their own dialect and its variations from that of the reader's, we have to know the language of students well enough to recognize variations between our own language and that of our students. Knowledge of the dialect variation in the school community is critical in the understanding of students' language and learning (Christian and Wolfram 1989; Christian, Adger, and Wolfram 1999).

Miscue analysis is concerned with how much readers comprehend, not with the resolution of issues surrounding standard English usage. Evidence about a reader's comprehension is provided when dialect is examined. When reading results in sentences that are syntactically and semantically acceptable in the reader's dialect, readers are obviously translating the written language of the author into their own language variation.

There is a great deal of discussion among educators and researchers concerning the effect of dialect on learning to read. Researchers (K. Goodman 1982a; K. Goodman and Buck 1982; Y. Goodman and D. Goodman 2000; Sims 1972) using miscue analysis have studied many aspects of dialect

Figure 5.1: Categories and Examples of Dialect Variations

Reader*	Text
Sound Variations	
pitchur	picture
idear	idea
lot bub	light bulb
wif	with
amond	almond
cot	caught
wof	wolf
dere	there
Vocabulary Variations	
goed	went
headlights	headlamps
bag	sack
greens	salad
pop	soda
Syntactic Variations	
he don't	he doesn't
John be going	John was going
stand on line	stand in line
everybody pet	everybody's pet
everyone get in their seat	everyone get in his seat.
two boy	two boys
that ain't no cup	that isn't a cup
none of us never	none of us ever
do it quickly!	do it quick!

*Spellings are representations of readers' pronunciation

features in reading and have provided documentation that proficiency in reading is not constrained by a readers' dialect. Speakers of all variations of English can be proficient readers and writers of English. Despite this knowledge, readers, including second language speakers, are often made to feel self-conscious about their oral language, hindering their development as proficient readers.

Dialect miscues occur as variations of sounds, syntax, vocabulary, and meaning, as shown in Figure 5.1.

Dialect-related miscues are marked on the typescript with a circled *ⓓ*. Phonological dialect variations are marked but are not considered to be miscues. Since most speakers produce phonological variations for specific sounds, depending on the surrounding phonological context, knowledge about phonology and dialect are required to evaluate the variations. For example, language such as *dat* for *that* or *walkin'* for *walking* involves no change in syntax, semantics, or meaning.

Phonological features are considered only when there are research or instructional reasons for analyzing the relations between oral and written characteristics. Teachers/researchers, for example, may want to examine phonological dialect features to gain insight into dialect variations in a community. If the reader is a speaker of languages other than English or is a signer of language, the dialect question is easily expanded to include pertinent language variations.

Syntactic and vocabulary dialect variations are examined as a part of miscue analysis, with dialect examined as part of the syntactic and semantic acceptability questions:

- Is the miscue syntactically and semantically acceptable *in the reader's dialect?*

Correction

Over the years, we have discovered that readers use a range of correction patterns. Proficient and less proficient readers often self-correct differently. Self-correction depends on the reader's view of reading. If readers believe that reading must precisely match what appears in the text, their correction patterns differ from those who believe that the purpose of reading is to make sense of the text. To consider self-correction in the In-Depth Procedure, the question is:

- Is the miscue corrected?

This question is asked separately in the **In-Depth Procedure** (Chapter 7) to help the observer examine the relation between correction and predictability. In the **Classroom** and **Informal Procedures** (Chapter 6), correction is considered when asking the syntactic and semantic acceptability questions. When readers correct their syntactically unacceptable miscues, they are concerned with linguistic structure and they want their reading to sound like language. When they correct miscues that are both syntactically and semantically unacceptable, they are concerned that their reading makes sense.

Miscue corrections, or the lack of them, provide information about a reader's confirming strategies. When readers become aware that they have miscued, some immediately attempt to correct either silently or orally. Others continue reading without correcting, but make appropriate alterations, either silently or orally, to the overall meaning as they move along in the text, integrating the information with their prior knowledge. By examining corrections along with syntactic and semantic acceptability across the text, we discover a reader's judgments about which miscues should be corrected and their success in doing so.

Readers need not correct all miscues. Self-correction is considered in relation to the quality of the miscue produced. Readers are considered *efficient* when they do not correct miscues that are semantically and syntactically acceptable. A decision not to correct in this instance shows that the reader predicts appropriately and, while confirming, decides there is no reason to correct, since their response is meaningful and acceptable. *Proficient* readers may not consider the miscue significant to their development of meaning; in fact, readers are often unaware of making high-quality miscues and therefore seldom correct them. Proficient readers correct their miscues selectively, indicating they know what aspects of text are important.

Many readers, even proficient readers, tend not to correct if there are too many low-quality miscues (miscues that disrupt syntax and meaning) clustered in the same phrase or clause. Such a situation results in the reader "short-circuiting"; that is, the reader produces a structure that he or she does not know how to unravel or does not choose to take time to sort out. Even proficient readers, especially when they have insufficient background knowledge for the text, short-circuit, and as a result they can produce an oral rendition that sounds as if they understand, even if they don't. Less proficient readers may sound out and produce a series of nonwords (K. Goodman 1996b). However, many readers rethink the problem as they continue reading, gather new information, construct new meanings, and correct orally or silently. Such evidence is available by examining how readers handle the same words or phrases across the entire text.

In general, proficient readers correct a higher percentage of low-quality miscues (those that result in unacceptable sentences) than less proficient readers do. Of course, proficient readers don't produce as many miscues that result in unacceptable sentences. Less proficient readers often show little concern that their reading makes sense and that it sounds like language. They do not appear to be monitoring their reading, thus failing to correct unacceptable miscues. They continue reading despite disruptive miscues and lack of meaning making.

Even though readers might leave highly disruptive miscues uncorrected during the reading of the entire text, when they retell, they sometimes demonstrate that silent correction has occurred and that acceptable meaning has been constructed. Therefore, to make appropriate judgments about a reader's proficiency, we examine correction patterns and compare the patterns with the retelling.

Betsy has problems with the structures *stay home, keeping house,* and *keep house.* Although she has a tendency to correct often, on line 0113 she leaves the miscues *I'll start house* for *I'll stay home* and *keeping house* for *keep house,* with no attempt to correct.

0112   Ⓡ   Ⓒ *so*
                    "Why don't you do my work⟍some day? I'll

0113   *start house   keeping*
                stay home and keep house," said the woodman.

Examination of Betsy's strategies each time she reads *stay home and keep house, stay home,* and *keep house* indicates she is aware of a problem and is continuing to work on it. Betsy's retelling adds evidence that she built an understanding of the phrases as she read the story. Analyzing how readers handle the same word or phrase across text is so important that there is a special section of the Reader Profile (Appendix C) for the collection and evaluation of such data.

Some readers correct high-quality miscues even though the miscues make little or no change to the text meaning. When this occurs, the reader is paying unnecessarily close attention to graphic information. These careful readers might anticipate a contraction as they come to the phrase *could not* (as Betsy did in line 0210), read aloud *couldn't,* and then self-correct. Most proficient readers continue without self-correction at such places.

As stated, proficient readers, confident of their construction of meaning, do not always self-correct. The range of self-correction among all readers is 10–40 percent. As the percentage of correction *by itself* provides no insight into a reader's proficiency (Flurkey and Xu 2003), self-correction is always considered along with the syntactic and semantic acceptability of miscues. The correction procedure, in relation to partial miscues, also adds to our understanding of reading proficiency.

Correction and Partials

Partial miscues occur when a reader produces a sound, even an initial syllable or two, but doesn't provide enough information to determine grammatical function or word meaning. Partials are detected by listening for a rising intonation and abrupt conclusion of the OR. The partial is marked with a dash following the OR, for example, *haz-* for *hazard.* Sometimes the OR is read as a complete spoken word although it is only a part of the ER. Such miscues are marked without a dash and are considered substitutions, for example *haz* for *hazard.* In this case *haz* (without a dash) is a nonword substitution and marked *$haz.*

The vast majority of partials are corrected, but, when they are not, they are treated as omissions of the text items. Corrected partials are not miscues because the reader does not provide enough information to answer the miscue analysis questions. However, all partials are marked on the typescript to better understand the reader's strategies. Corrected partials, in one miscue study, were counted to evaluate their influence on miscue frequency. The researchers (K. Goodman and Burke 1973) found that proficient readers produce more immediately corrected partials than less proficient readers. Although proficient readers make fewer miscues than less proficient readers, when corrected partials are added to the number of miscues made by proficient readers, the number of miscues per 100 words is about the same as it is for all readers. This finding suggests that proficient readers start to produce as many miscues as less proficient readers, but their effective use of confirmation strategies allows more immediate and efficient self-correction. Observing and analyzing a reader's confirmation strategies through self-correction provide information about the reader's comprehending strategies.

Correction and Repetition

Self-correction is a strategy that takes the form of repetition. When this occurs, the repetition is not considered a miscue; however, sometimes readers repeat to correct and in doing so produce another miscue. Sometimes the reader produces the ER and then abandons it in favor of a miscue. (See marking examples in Chapter 4.)

Self-correction indicates the amount of problem solving the reader engages in. The amount of text repeated or reread is shown on the typescript by the length of the line under the text reread. Repetition, with or without correction, is marked on the typescript to show the size of the language unit involved, the number of times it is repeated, and the possible reasons for the repetitions. These repetitions are identified by a letter or letters placed in a circle at the beginning of the repetition line. (See examples in Chapter 4.)

Graphic Similarity and Sound Similarity

The graphophonic system includes graphic cues (the orthography or print), the sound cues (the phonology or oral language), and the relationship between the two (the phonic system) (K. Goodman 1993). Only word-for-word substitutions are analyzed for graphic and sound similarity. Answers to questions concerning graphic and sound similarity provide evidence about how much readers make use of the graphophonic system.

- How much does the miscue (OR) *look* like the text word (ER)?
- How much does the miscue (OR) *sound* like the expected response (ER)?

In addition to using the semantic and syntactic systems to predict words and phrases, readers anticipate a word either by relating its physical characteristics to known or similar patterns or by assigning possible sounds to its various letters and letter combinations. The two related systems, graphic and sound, are evaluated separately in miscue analysis to document how readers systematically use orthographic cues as well as phonological cues. The graphic and sound systems of English and their relationship to each other are complex. There is no simple one-to-one correspondence between letters and sounds. Miscues show that readers are aware of the complexities of these systems (K. Goodman 1993).

Readers do not use all the available graphophonic information in a text. Betsy's miscues of *when* for *while* and *always* for *away* in line 0105 (*while I am away cutting wood*) are examples of a reader sampling only enough information to predict language and meaning. Here Betsy begins to understand that the husband is complaining about his wife, so all she needs is enough graphic information to predict that a time-related clause marker, *when*, might occur, introducing a clause in which another time-related adverb, *always*, might occur.

Readers use the graphophonic system along with their predicting and confirming strategies. Beginning on line 0318 (*I'll light a fire in the fireplace, and the porridge will* ...) Betsy uses both syntactic and semantic information to predict that the second clause in the sentence should begin with *I'll*, and she therefore reads *and I'll*. But *I'll* does not fit with the subsequent text, so Betsy gathers additional graphophonic information and self-corrects. A similar phenomenon occurs at the end of the sentence (line 0319) when she predicts *in a flash* for *in a few minutes*.

Proficient readers do not use the graphic and sound systems to a high degree at all times. In fact, studies show that about half of proficient readers' substitution miscues have only some degree of graphophonic similarity to the text item. On the other hand, nonproficient readers often overuse graphophonic information and consequently have higher scores on graphic and sound similarity than more proficient readers (Brown, K. Goodman, and Marek 1996; K. Goodman 1993).

Results of miscue analysis research indicate that graphic similarity scores are usually higher than sound similarity scores for all groups of readers. This evidence suggests that the way a word looks and the patterns related to the visual organization of a word provide more important information than the way the word sounds (Brown, K. Goodman, and Marek 1996).

Evaluating the sound and graphic systems separately provides a great deal of information about how the graphophonic system works in English. Such evaluation also reveals the reader's sophistication in using the graphophonic system.

Graphic Similarity

When judging graphic similarity, we examine the sequence and shape of the written miscue and the text word with no concern for pronunciation. To determine graphic similarity, ask:

- How much does the miscue (OR) look like the text word (ER)?

The OR and ER are compared visually to determine the degree of likeness. When marking graphic similarity, especially for phonological dialect, remember that there are often varieties of pronunciation for the same graphic item. Many observers do not mark phonological dialect because these ORs are not miscues. Regardless of whether a speaker says *offen* or *ofTen*, the word is always spelled *often*. Speakers use varying pronunciations for certain words depending on their dialect and on the phonological features of the words in the surrounding context. In the following examples, the variations of *and* illustrate this point:

- Richard an' Doug will be the ones picked.
- Ham 'n' cheese sandwiches are delicious.
- And let me tell you one more thing.

No matter how speakers say or read variations of *and*, when they write the word, they spell it *and*. Therefore all the sound variations are considered graphically identical to the written word.

Word-level substitutions are evaluated for their graphic similarity by dividing both the OR and the ER into three parts for comparison purposes: beginning, middle, and end.

Graphic Similarity Examples

*High Graphic Similarity (**H**)*. Two or more parts of the OR look like two or more parts of the ER and appear in the same location.

always	*house*	*heard*	*$soud*
away	home	had	sound
I'll	*first*	*start*	*$shurn*
I'd	fist	stay	churn
philosophical	*Well*	*Then*	*friend's*
physical	will	than	friend
jumped	*she*	*he*	
bumped	the	the	

Nonwords, such as *$soud* for *sound*, *$shurn* for *churn*, and *$cornpan* for *cornucopia*, are spelled as phonemically close to the reader's OR as possible. When readers substitute a nonword that is spelled just like the ER, as in *$līver* (long *ī*) for *liver*, use phonological markings and/or indicate something that will make the pronunciation clear, such as writing *"rhymes with diver"* near the miscue or in the margin. If a reader substitutes the noun *dove* for *dome*, the note *"a bird"* in the margin prevents confusion with the verb *dove*.

*Some Graphic Similarity (**S**)*. One part of the OR looks like one part of the ER and appears in the same location, or there is the same general configuration of the OR and ER and a letter in common.

threw	*There*	*shout*	*forest*
thought	She	splashed	far
pinch	*bread*	*up*	*keep*
watch	butter	out	look
when	*is*	*and*	*the*
while	was	in	his
job			
work			

*No Graphic Similarity (**N**)*. No degree of graphic similarity exists between the OR and the ER.

to	*the*	*the*	*yet*
and	your	a	now
And	*in*	*bang*	*day*
as	for	shot	morning
he			
did			

Graphic Similarity Complexities

Sometimes the OR and the ER cannot be conveniently divided into three parts (beginning, middle, and end) for evaluation. When this happens, consider other reasonable visual information: similar letters (no matter where they appear), word length, word configuration, and whether the letters are uppercase or lowercase.

Following are guidelines for interpreting miscues that do not clearly fall into the stated categories.

*High Graphic Similarity (**H**).* The entire OR is found in the entire ER, or the entire ER is in the OR, but with the letters possibly not in the same order.

top	*was*	*no*	*stop*
pot	saw	on	post
press	*buttermilk*	*so*	*he*
pressure	butter	soon	she
the	*as*	*children*	*here*
their	a	child	he
into	*on*	*tile*	*little*
to	or	list	tile
he	*she*	*$cornpan*	
the	he	cornucopia	

*Some Graphic Similarity (**S**).* The OR and ER have a letter or letters in common, but they do not appear in the same position (beginning, middle, end), or they have similar length and configuration:

the	*then*	*and*	*up*
his	and	in	out
was	*the*	*you*	*keep*
and	his	to	look

When a graphic substitution does not clearly fall into a category, develop a rationale for the interpretation that is most in keeping with linguistic knowledge, remaining consistent with any further coding of that substitution. It is helpful to keep a list of such coding to maintain consistency.

Sound Similarity

When judging sound similarity, the graphic shape or sequence of letters is not considered. The focus of consideration is on the reader's pronunciation, not on the written form. To determine the sound similarity between the miscue and the text, ask:

- How much does the miscue (OR) sound like the expected response (ER)?

To consider sound similarity, the OR and ER are contrasted by dividing each into three parts: the beginning, the middle, and the ending sounds or syllables. It is important to keep the reader's dialect in mind when evaluating sound similarity.

Sound Similarity Examples

High Sound Similarity (H). Two parts of the OR sound like two parts of the ER and are heard in the same location (beginning, middle, or end).

ways	*feels*	*fat*	*bump*
ones	feeds	fit	pump
philosophical	*buttermilk*	*water*	*$liver (diver)*
physical	butter	wander	liver
heard	*Well*	*Then*	*funny*
had	We'll	than	phony
first	*light*	*bite*	
fist	least	blight	

Some Sound Similarity (S). One part of the OR sounds like one part of the ER and is heard in the same location in both words.

start	*children*	*when*	*house*
stay	child	while	home
that	*triangle*	*feet*	*is*
what	tripod	beam	was
for	*so*	*as*	
from	soon	and	
rate	*singing*		
pace	lounging		

No Sound Similarity (N). There is no degree of sound similarity between the miscue and the text.

job	*and*	*on*	*away*
work	is	to	any
the	*a*	*drum*	*river*
she	in	bass	lake
There	*to*	*then*	*on*
She	she	three	or
up			
out			

Sound Similarity Complexities

Just as words are not always easily divided into three parts for graphic similarity evaluation, they also are not always easily divided into three distinct sound groupings. In this case, make use of all sound information, such as the similarity of the phonemes, where they are heard in the words, and the length of the utterance. The following guidelines help interpret miscues that do not easily fall into the stated categories.

*High Sound Similarity (**H**)*. The entire OR is heard in 50% of the ER, or the entire ER is heard in 50% of the OR.

some	*inside*	*percent*	*person*
something	in	percentage	perspiration
that	*into*	*the*	*inside*
at	to	a	side
he	*I'll*	*you*	*he*
who	I'd	to	she
tire			
entire			

When Graphic and Sound Similarities Are Not Evaluated

Omissions, insertions, repeated miscues, intonation shifts, complex miscues, and punctuation are not coded for graphic and sound similarity. For example, if the miscue involves only punctuation or intonation variations, graphic similarity cannot be evaluated and these questions are not asked, as when Betsy combines two sentences by omitting the period and inserting *and* (or substituting *and* for the period). The period and the first word in the next sentence, *As*, are bracketed.

0204   He began to make some butter⌢As he put
                                                    and

If it is not possible to determine which word is substituted for the text item, the miscue is complex and considered an insertion or omission. In the following, Betsy appears to substitute *flash* for *few minutes*, thus making it too speculative to conclude that she substitutes *flash* for either *few* or *minutes*.

0319   porridge will be ready in a few minutes."
                                                          flash

ADDITIONAL RESEARCH QUESTIONS TO EVALUATE READING

Miscue analysis is easily expanded and adapted to specific concerns and questions. Researchers may be interested in knowing how much miscues change the syntax of a passage, the kinds of grammatical transformations that occur, or the effect of pragmatic changes on reading. To gain information about a student's understandings of concepts and vocabulary, teachers may want to study the semantic relation between substituted words and the text. In such situations, teachers/researchers develop appropriate miscue analysis questions to meet their needs. When questions are added or modified (for example, inquiry concerning grammatical function similarity or peripheral vision), an appropriate rationale for the inquiry should be developed and tied to the questions and to the beliefs about the reading process. Appendix D shows previous miscue analysis formats. Although the categories in these formats are not used in the procedures presented in this book, researchers and teachers have found them useful in answering their research questions, thus adding to understandings of the reading process and the insights into a reader's knowledge about language.

Research in miscue analysis continues to grow. A number of researchers are currently integrating miscue analysis with eye movement studies to deepen understanding of readers' use of perception as they read. This research brings an added awareness of readers' use of peripheral information (Paulson and K. Goodman 1998; Paulson and Freeman 2003).

In this chapter, we presented the questions asked about readers' miscues that are supported by the theoretical rationale driving miscue analysis. Teachers and researchers use this heuristic tool to seek answers to their own questions about the nature of reading, the reading process, and reading instruction. The following two chapters explain the three miscue procedures: **Classroom**, **Informal**, and **In-Depth**.

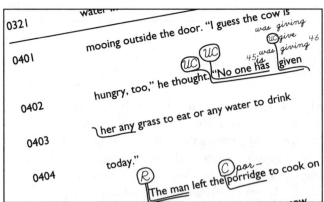

Chapter 6
The Classroom Procedure and the Informal Procedure

Chapters 6 and 7 explain three different miscue analysis procedures for analyzing the reading process by answering specific questions about students' reading. The **Classroom Procedure** and the **Informal Procedure** are discussed in this chapter. The **In-Depth Procedure**, which involves more complex analysis and is more time-consuming, is explained in Chapter 7.

The procedures differ in their examination of the reader's observed responses (OR) and in how the results are used. The **Classroom Procedure** investigates the influence of the reader's miscues on the sentence in the context of the entire story or article. The result of the analysis leads to instructional strategies and classroom experiences. The **Informal Procedure** examines the acceptability of miscues at the text, paragraph, and sentence levels. This procedure is conducted in a more casual setting, such as a reading conference, and is not always tape recorded; the results are immediately applicable within the conference setting.

In previous chapters we explained the *marking* of miscues on a typescript. It is now time to introduce the *coding* procedures. After judgments are made, in terms of answering questions about readers' observed responses, answers are *coded* (recorded) on the typescript or on the Classroom Procedure Coding Form (see Appendix C).

THE CLASSROOM PROCEDURE

Teachers/researchers select students and materials and mark the typescript, following the general procedures described in Chapters 3 and 4. Teachers often administer miscue analysis at the beginning and end of the year and when additional information is needed. If time is limited, teachers begin miscue analysis with students for whom they have little information or who exhibit obvious reading challenges.

One difference between the Classroom Procedure and the other procedures is that the *typescript* is used for analyzing the sentences as well as for marking and coding the miscues. However, for permanent record keeping, a Classroom Procedure Coding Form is available in Appendix C. Betsy's Classroom Procedure Coding Form is in this chapter.

Preparing the Typescript for Marking and Coding

The top of the first page of the typescript is labeled with the reader's name, date, the reader's grade or age, the teacher's/researcher's name, and the text read. Some observers add a word or two about the text's genre and content. Because the linguistic focus of the **Classroom Procedure** is on the sentence, each sentence is numbered (in color if possible) and, if the coding is done on the typescript, a short line is drawn in the right-hand margin at the end of each sentence. Coding results are written on the line (see Betsy's typescript, Figure 6.1). The statistical results of the coding are computed at the end of the typescript. (See Chapter 3.)

Coding the Classroom Procedure Typescript

The linguistic unit for analysis in the Classroom Procedure is the sentence within the entire text. To determine acceptability, each sentence is read by the observer as the reader finally produces it. All sentences must be coded, whether or not they include miscues. To code sentences that include miscues (substitutions, omissions, insertions, repeated miscues, multiple miscues, complex miscues, intonation, and punctuation shifts) the observer reads them as finally read by the reader.

We first discuss the Classroom Procedure, in which the coding is recorded in the right-hand margin of the typescript. Later in this chapter, the Classroom Procedure using the Coding Form (Figure 6.9) is presented. If the text is unusually long, consider coding the first 75 sentences. If the text is short, use two stories or articles. We recommend that the written material include at least 500 words. (See Chapter 3 for information on selecting materials.)

Classroom Procedure Questions

The questions in Figure 6.2 are asked for the Classroom Procedure.

The examples following Figure 6.2 help the observer to explore some miscues of two readers (Betsy and Gordon), to code acceptability of their miscues at the sentence level and within the entire text, and to code the graphic and sound similarity of word-level substitutions. To begin the coding of each sentence, the observer reads the first sentence and asks Questions 1, 2, and 3: syntactic acceptability, semantic acceptability, and meaning change. The patterns following the Classroom Procedure questions result from the answers.

Figure 6.1: Betsy's Marked Transcript

Name *Betsy*   Date *November 3*
Grade/Age *Grade Three*   Teacher *Ms. Blau*
Reference *The Man Who Kept House*

THE MAN WHO KEPT HOUSE

0101   ① Once upon a time there was a woodman ⌃ Ⓒ

0102   *He threw* who thought that no one worked as hard as

0103   he did. One evening ② when he came home Ⓡ   ① 𝓎 𝓎 𝓃

0104   from work, he said to his wife, "What do you Ⓒ *I want you*

0105   do all day while I am away cutting wood?" *when always*   ② 𝓎 𝓎 𝓃

0106   ③ "I keep house," replied the wife, "and Ⓡ Ⓡ

0107   keeping house is hard work." *and*   ③ 𝓃 𝓃 –

0108   ④ "Hard work!" said the husband. "You don't Ⓒ H– ⑤   ④ 𝓎 𝓎 𝓃

0109   know what hard work is! You should try Ⓒ H– ⑥   ⑤ 𝓎 𝓎 𝓃

0110   cutting wood!"   ⑥ 𝓎 𝓎 𝓃

0111   ⑦ "I'd be glad to," said the wife. *Ill*   ⑦ 𝓎 𝓎 𝓃

0112   ⑧ "Why don't you do my work some day? I'll Ⓡ Ⓒ *so* ⑨   ⑧ 𝓎 𝓎 𝓃

0113   *start house keeping* stay home and keep house, said the woodman.   ⑨ 𝓃 𝓃 –

0114   ⑩ "If you stay home to do my work, you'll ⓊⒸ RM RM Ⓒ *start house* *well,*

0115   have to make butter, carry water from the *bread* Ⓡ

Figure 6.1: Betsy's Marked Transcript (cont.)

0115   have to make butter, carry water from the

0116   well, wash the clothes, clean the house, and

0117   look after the baby," said the wife.   ⑩ y n –

0118   "I can do all that," replied the husband.   ⑪ y y n

0119   "We'll do it tomorrow!"   ⑫ y y P

0201   So the next morning the wife went off to

0202   the forest. The husband stayed home and   ⑬ y y n

0203   began to do his wife's work.   ⑭ y y n

0204   He began to make some butter. As he put   ⑮ y n –

0205   the cream into the churn, he said, "This is

0206   not going to be hard work. All I have to do   ⑯ y n –

0207   is sit here and move this stick up and down.   ⑰ y y n

0208   Soon the cream will turn into butter."   ⑱ y y P

0209   Just then the woodman heard the baby

0210   crying. He looked around, but he could not   ⑲ y y n

0211   see her. She was not in the house. Quickly,   ⑳ y y n
                                                                     ㉑ y y n

0212   he ran outside to look for her. He found the   ㉒ y y n

0213   baby at the far end of the garden and

0214   brought her back to the house.   ㉓ y y n

Figure 6.1: Betsy's Marked Transcript (cont.)

0301   In his hurry, the woodman had left the

0302   door open behind him. When he got back to

0303   the house, he saw a big pig inside with its

0304   nose in the churn. "Get out! Get out!"

0305   shouted the woodman at the top of his voice.

0306   The big pig ran around and around the

0307   room. It bumped into the churn, knocking it

0308   over. The cream splashed all over the room.

0309   Out the door went the pig.

0310   "Now I've got more work to do," said the

0311   man. "I'll have to wash everything in this

0312   room. Perhaps keeping house is harder work."

0313   than I thought." He took a bucket and went

0314   to the well for some water. When he came

0315   back, the baby was crying.

0316   "Poor baby, you must be hungry," said the

0317   woodman. "I'll make some porridge for you.

0318   I'll light a fire in the fireplace, and the

Figure 6.1: Betsy's Marked Transcript (cont.)

0319   porridge will be ready in a few minutes." — Ⓒ *flash* — ㊴ *y y n*

0320   Just as the husband was putting the — ㊵Ⓡ *15 sec* 0

0321   water into the big pot, he heard the cow

0401   mooing outside the door. "I guess the cow is — ㊶ — ㊵ *y y n*

0402   hungry, too," he thought. "No one has given — ⓊⒸ ⓊⒸ ㊷ *was giving / give / was giving* — ㊶ *y y n*

4. No one was giving
3. give
2. No one was giving her any
1. No one is

0403   her any grass to eat or any water to drink

0404   today." — ㊷ *y y n*

0405   The man left the porridge to cook on the — ㊸Ⓡ Ⓒ *por–*

0406   fire and hurried outside. He gave the cow — ㊹ — ㊸ *y y n*

0407   some water. *and* — ㊹ *n n –*

0408   "I haven't time to find any grass for you — Ⓡ Ⓡ ㊺

0409   now," he said to the cow. "I'll put you up — Ⓒ ㊻ — ㊺ *y y n*

0410   on the roof. You'll find something to eat — Ⓡ Ⓡ ㊼ — ㊻ *y y n*

0411   up there." — ㊼ *y y n*

0412   The man put the cow on top of the house. — ㊽Ⓒ *m–* Ⓡ — ㊽ *y y n*

0413   Then he was afraid that she would fall off. — ㊾ Ⓒ *the* H

0414   the roof and hurt herself. So he put one — ⓊⒸ Ⓒ Ⓒ *The was har– himself* ㊿ — 3. The roof and hurt / 2. The roof / 1. The roof was har– — ㊾ *n n –*

0415   end of a rope around the cow's neck. He — *the* n — 51 Ⓡ — ㊿ *y y n*

0416   dropped the other end down the chimney. — *to* — 51 *y y P*

Figure 6.1: Betsy's Marked Transcript (cont.)

0501   ®52 Then he climbed down from the roof and

0502   went into the house. 53 He pulled the end of the   52 *y y n*

0503   ©*up* rope out of the fireplace ©*then* and *he* put it around   *2. and he* / *1. then*

0504   his left leg.   53 *y y n*

0505   54 "Now I can finish making *the* this porridge,"

0506   said the woodman, ® "and the cow will

0507   ©*sa–* be safe."   54 *y y n*

0508   © 55 *wood–* But the man spoke ® too soon, ® for just then   55 *y y n*

0509   the cow fell off the roof. ® 56 She pulled him up   55 *y y n*

0510   ® the chimney by ® the rope. © 57 There he hung, *n H* *is hang*   56 *y y n*

0511   © *H never* upside down over the porridge pot. ® 58 As for the   57 *n n –*

0512   *RM hang 2* cow, she hung between the roof and the *14 sec. 5 sec.*

0513   *H $gorun* *H he* ground, and there she had to stay.   58 *n n –*

0514   59 It was not very long before the woodman's

0515   wife came home. ® 60 As she came near the   59 *y y n*

0516   house, ® she could hear the cow mooing, the

0601   *H cried* baby crying, and her husband *H shouted* shouting for

0602   help. 61 She hurried © *to* up the path. ® 62 She cut the   60 *n n –* / 61 *y y n*

0603   rope from the cow's neck. ©© 63 *and* *s–* As she did so,   62 *y y n*

Figure 6.1: Betsy's Marked Transcript (cont.)

0604   the cow fell down to the ground, and the

0605   husband dropped head first down the chimney.   63 y y n

0606   (64) When the wife went into the house, she

0607   saw her husband with his legs up the

0608   chimney and his head in the porridge pot.   64 y y n

0609   (65) From that day on, the husband went into

0610   the forest every day to cut wood. The wife   65 y y n

0611   stayed home to keep house and to look

0612   after their child.   66 y y n

0613   (67) Never again did the woodman say to his

0614   wife, "What did you do all day?" Never   67 y y n

0615   again did he tell his wife that he would

0616   stay home and keep house.   68 y y n

1: y 60 88%;   n   8 12%;   68 Sentences
2: y 57 84%;   n 11 17%;   68 Sentences
3: n 53 93%;   P   4   7%;   y   0   0%   57 Sent.
4: H 36 55%;   S 19 29%;   n 10 15%   75 Miscues

Figure 6.2: Classroom Procedure Questions

QUESTION 1: *Syntactic Acceptability*

Is the sentence syntactically acceptable in the reader's dialect and within the context of the entire text?

Y The sentence, as finally produced by the reader, is syntactically acceptable.

N The sentence, as finally produced by the reader, is not syntactically acceptable.

QUESTION 2: *Semantic Acceptability*

Is the sentence semantically acceptable in the reader's dialect and within the context of the entire text? (Question 2 is coded **N** if question 1 is coded **N**.)

Y The sentence, as finally produced by the reader, is semantically acceptable.

N The sentence, as finally produced by the reader, is not semantically acceptable.

QUESTION 3: *Meaning Change* (Question 3 is coded only if questions 1 and 2 are coded **YY**.)

Does the sentence, as finally produced by the reader, change the meaning of the entire text?

N There is no change in the meaning.

P There is inconsistency, loss, or change of a *minor* idea, incident, character, fact, sequence, or concept.

Y There is inconsistency, loss, or change of a *major* idea, incident, character, fact, sequence, or concept.

QUESTION 4: *Graphic Similarity*

How much does the miscue (OR) look like the text word (ER)?

H A high degree of graphic similarity exists between the miscue (OR) and the text word (ER).

S Some degree of graphic similarity exists between the miscue (OR) and the text word (ER).

N No degree of graphic similarity exists between the miscue (OR) and the text word (ER).

QUESTION 5: *Sound Similarity* (optional)*

How much does the miscue (OR) sound like the expected response (ER)?

H A high degree of sound similarity exists between the miscue (OR) and the expected response (ER).

S Some degree of sound similarity exists between the miscue (OR) and the expected response (ER).

N No degree of sound similarity exists between the miscue (OR) and the expected response (ER).

---

*Miscue analysis research shows that Sound Similarity is similar (lower in High and Some) to Graphic Similarity; therefore, coding Sound Similarity is optional in this procedure.

YYN   Syntactically acceptable, Semantically acceptable, No meaning change

YYP   Syntactically acceptable, Semantically acceptable, Partial or minor meaning change

YYY   Syntactically acceptable, Semantically acceptable, Major meaning change

YN–   Syntactically acceptable, Semantically unacceptable (meaning change not coded)

NN–   Syntactically unacceptable, Semantically unacceptable (meaning change not coded)

Betsy's Miscue Patterns

Betsy's examples include sentences with variations of miscues and correction patterns.

YYN

The following examples result in the **YYN** pattern.

0101   ① Once upon a time there was a woodman ⟨C⟩

0102   *He threw* ⟩who thought that no one worked as hard as

0103   he did.   ① *y y n*

READER: *Once upon a time there was a woodman. He threw who thought that no one worked as hard as he did.*

READ FOR CODING: *Once upon a time there was a woodman who thought that no one worked as hard as he did.*

Because Betsy corrected all her miscues, the sentence is coded syntactically and semantically acceptable, and there is no meaning change.

0103   ② One evening ⟨when he⟩ ⟨R⟩ came home

0104   from work, he said to his wife, ⟨C⟩ *I want you* "What do you

0105   23 ⟩ *when always* ⟩do all day while I am away cutting wood?"   ② *y y n*

READER: *One evening when he when he came home from work, he said to his wife, "I want you do all day (pause) What do you do all day when I am always cutting wood?"*

READ FOR CODING: *One evening when he came home from work, he said to his wife, "What do you do all day when I am always cutting wood?"*

This sentence has three miscues. (The repetition of *when he* is not a miscue.) I *want you* is a complex miscue that is self-corrected, and the remaining miscues (*when* for *while* and *always* for *away*) are syntactically and semantically acceptable in the sentence and the story. The sentence is coded syntactically and semantically acceptable with no meaning change.

0108   "Hard work!" said the husband. "You don't   ④ 𝒴 𝒴 𝓃

READER: *"H- Hard work!" said the (pause) husband...*

READ FOR CODING: *"Hard work!" said the husband...*

The partial *H–* is not a miscue, as it is corrected. Partials are not miscues. The sentence is syntactically and semantically acceptable, and there is no meaning change.

YYP

The following examples result in the **YYP** pattern.

0208   Soon the cream will turn into butter."   ⑱ 𝒴 𝒴 P

READER: *So the cream will turn into buttermilk."*

READ FOR CODING: *So the cream will turn into buttermilk."*

The two miscues, *So* for *Soon* and *buttermilk* for *butter*, do not disrupt the syntax or semantics of the sentence. The substitution of *buttermilk* for *butter* constitutes a minor meaning change. The sentence is syntactically and semantically acceptable with minor meaning change.

0313   He took a bucket and went

0314   to the well for some water.   ㉟ 𝒴 𝒴 P

READER: *He He He took the basket and went to the well for some water.*

READ FOR CODING: *He took the basket and went to the well for some water.*

The substitutions of *basket* for *bucket* and *the* for *a* result in a syntactically and semantically acceptable sentence. *Basket* for *bucket* is considered a minor meaning change and is coded **YYP**. (For a more complete discussion of *basket* and *bucket*, see Chapter 5.)

0415-16   He dropped the other end down the chimney.   ㊾ 𝒴 𝒴 P

READER: *He He dropped the other end down (pause) to the chimney.*

READ FOR CODING: *He dropped the other end down to the chimney.*

The insertion of *to* results in a syntactically and semantically acceptable sentence with a minor change in meaning.

YYY

Betsy and Gordon have no observed responses that result in sentences that are syntactically and semantically acceptable with major meaning changes. See below for **YYY** examples from other readers.

YN–

The following examples result in the **YN–** pattern.

Meaning Change is coded only if the sentence is syntactically and semantically acceptable, **YY**. To indicate that Meaning Change is not coded, a dash is placed after **YN** or **NN** (the coding for syntactic and semantic acceptability).

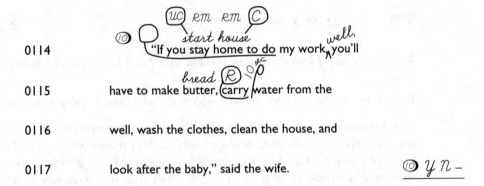

0114	"If you stay home to do my work, you'll
0115	have to make butter, carry water from the
0116	well, wash the clothes, clean the house, and
0117	look after the baby," said the wife.

READER: *"If you start house to do If you start home to do my work, well, you'll have to make bread, carry carry (pause) water from the well, wash the clothes, clean the house, and look after the baby," said the wife.*

READ FOR CODING: *"If you start home to do my work, well, you'll have to make bread, carry water from the well, wash the clothes, clean the house, and look after the baby," said the wife.*

The sentence is syntactically acceptable, but the substitution of *start* for *stay* results in a sentence that is semantically unacceptable in this story. The **YN** pattern is not coded for meaning change; a dash is placed after **YN** to indicate that meaning change is not coded.

0204	He began to make some butter. As he put
0205	the cream into the churn, he said, "This is
0206	not going to be hard work.

READER: *He began to make some butter and he put the cream into the (pause) $shurn. He said, "This is not going to be hard work."*

READ FOR CODING: *He began to make some butter and he put the cream into the $shurn. He said, "This is not going to be hard work."*

Betsy combines two sentences by substituting *and* for the period and *As*. Despite this miscue, both sentences result in syntactically acceptable sentences. However, her substitution of the nonword *$shurn* for *churn* results in both the sentences being semantically unacceptable. The dash indicates that meaning change is not coded for **YN** patterns.

NN–

The following examples result in the **NN–** pattern.

READER: *"I keep I keep house," replied the wife, "and keeping and keeping house and work."*

READ FOR CODING: *"I keep house," replied the wife, and keeping house and work."*

This sentence has one complex miscue (*and* is substituted for *is hard*), resulting in a syntactically and semantically unacceptable sentence. The repetitions of *I keep* and *and keeping house* are reading strategies and not coded as miscues. Meaning change is not coded because the sentence is syntactically and semantically unacceptable.

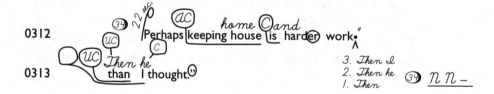

READER: *(pause) Perhaps keeping house keeping home and is hard work. Then Then he Then I thought.*

READ FOR CODING: *Perhaps keeping home is hard work." Then I thought.*

This sentence has six miscues that result in two sentences rather than the one text sentence. The text sentence is the unit of analysis, and, if the text sentence is not fully syntactically acceptable, it is coded **N**. This is an example of a sentence in which the unacceptability is apparent when the coder reads the entire paragraph. Semantic acceptability is coded **N** because syntactic acceptability is **N**. Meaning change is not coded because the sentence is both syntactically and semantically unacceptable.

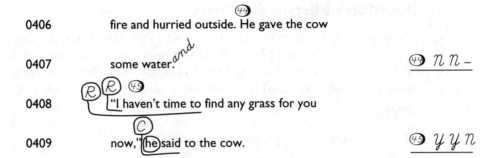

0406   fire and hurried outside. He gave the cow

0407   some water.

0408   "I haven't time to find any grass for you

0409   now," he said to the cow.

READER: *He gave the cow some water and "I I haven't time to I haven't time to find any grass for you now, said he said to the cow."*

READ FOR CODING: *He gave the cow some water and "I haven't time to find any grass for you now, he said to the cow."*

Betsy left sentence 44 with one miscue, the substitution of *and* for the period at the end of the sentence. Betsy's intonation indicates that she expects another clause to follow; however, when she reads sentence 45, she treats it as a new sentence, and therefore it is not affected by the previous sentence. Sentence 44 is coded **NN−**. Sentence 45 is coded **YYN**; the omission of *he* is self-corrected.

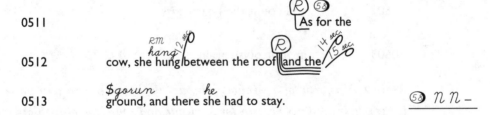

0511   As for the

0512   cow, she hung between the roof and the

0513   ground, and there she had to stay.

READER: *As as for the cow, she hang (pause) between the roof and the and the(pause) and the (pause) and the $gorun, and there he had to stay.*

READ FOR CODING: *As for the cow, she hang between the roof and the $gorun, and there he had to stay.*

This sentence is not syntactically acceptable because of the inappropriate tense substitution of *hang* for *hung*. The sentence is coded **N** for semantic acceptability since it is not syntactically acceptable. Additionally, it is not semantically acceptable because of the nonword substitution *$gorun* for *ground*. (Nonwords are semantically unacceptable except in fictional name substitutions.) The substitution of *he* for *she* would be syntactically acceptable if it had been the only miscue in the sentence. However, the substitution of *he* is a reference to the woodman, who in this story cannot be hanging from the roof, resulting in a semantically unacceptable miscue. Although Betsy read *and the* four times there are only three repetition lines under the words; the last time she read *and the* she continued the sentence and did not repeat. Repetitions are indicative of the reader's strategies and not coded as miscues.

Gordon's Miscue Patterns

Nine-year-old Gordon read an expository text, *The Beat of My Heart* (Vannier 1967). Gordon's examples include sentences with variations of miscues and correction patterns. His marked **In-Depth Procedure** typescript, unaided and aided retelling, and his Retelling Guide are in Appendix B.

YYN

The following examples result in the **YYN** pattern.

0328   ㉒ *the beat*
            Then listen to his heart again.   ㉒ 𝓎 𝓎 𝓃

READER: *Then listen to the beat again.*

READ FOR CODING: *Then listen to the beat again.*

The sentence is syntactically acceptable, and because *beat* is a suitable meaning substitution for *heart* (in this sentence and in this story), the sentence is semantically acceptable and there is no meaning change.

0601   ㉛
            Now, run for a minute

0602   and count the heartbeats

0603   in your pulse again.   ㉛ 𝓎 𝓎 𝓃

READER: *Now, run for a minute and count the heart beats in your pulse again.*

READ FOR CODING: *Now, run for a minute and count the heart beats in your pulse again.*

There are no miscues in the sentence. Sentences without miscues are coded **YYN**.

0223   ⑭ *bump*
            When it goes dup,

0224   it is pushing blood out

0225   *RM* / *your*
            to all parts of the body.   ⑭ 𝓎 𝓎 𝓃

READER: *When it goes bump, it is pushing blood out to all parts of your body.*

READ FOR CODING: *When it goes bump, it is pushing blood out to all parts of your body.*

This nonfiction article is written in the second person, so the substitution of *your* for *the* fits. The sentence is syntactically and semantically acceptable, and there is no meaning change.

YYP

The following example results in the **YYP** pattern.

0712	㊹ One is to get lots of exercise *a lot*
0713	by playing (vigorous) games
0714	out of doors. *Y Y* P

READER: *One is to get a lot of exercise by playing (pause) games out of doors.*

READ FOR CODING: *One is to get a lot of exercise by playing games out of doors.*

The sentence is syntactically and semantically acceptable. The omission of *vigorous* is a minor meaning change in this article.

YN–

The following examples result in the **YN–** pattern.

0301	⑯ Ⓡ Ⓒ *feels* Blood feeds
0302	all the cells and organs Ⓒ c– Ⓒ *oranges*
0303	of your body
0304	so that they can do
0305	their own special work Ⓒ *sp– sp–*
0306	to keep you (physically) fit. *fat* ⑯ *Y n–*

READER: *Blood blood feels feeds all the c- cells and oranges organs of your body so that they can do their own sp- sp- special work to keep you (pause) fat.*

READ FOR CODING: *Blood feeds all the cells and organs of your body so that they can do their own special work to keep you fat.*

The sentence is syntactically acceptable, but semantically unacceptable. The observed responses of *feel* and *oranges* are corrected; *fat* for *fit* is not. The sentence is syntactically acceptable because the substitutions retain the same grammatical functions. Although *fat* for *fit* produces a sentence that sounds like language, it does not make sense in this piece about physical fitness. Since the sentence is not fully acceptable both semantically and syntactically, it is not coded for meaning change.

NN–

The following examples result in the **NN–** pattern.

0615   ㊱ It rests for 1/6 of a *one-six minute* second

0616   between every beat.   ㊱ *n n –*

READER: *It rests for one-six of a minute between every beat.*

READ FOR CODING: *It rests for one-six of a minute between every beat.*

The observed response is not syntactically nor semantically unacceptable due to the substitutions of *one-sixth* for *1/6* and *minute* for *second*.

0104   ② This/strange (sound) *8 sec 0*

0105   is the sound *$soud*

0106   of a/wonderful (machine)   © *m – / m –* *8 sec 0*

0107   inside your body.   ② *n n –*

READER: *This (pause) strange is the $soud of a (pause) wonderful m- m- machine inside your body.*

READ FOR CODING: *This strange is the $soud of a wonderful machine inside your body.*

The sentence is read without a subject and therefore is neither syntactically nor semantically acceptable. Meaning change is not marked.

0620   ㊳ This rest gives your heart

0621   © *chan –* a chance to keep

0622   *a* © in/good work(ing)(condition) © *con –*

0623   as well as to grow *you*

0624   (bigger) and (stronger)   ㊳ *n n –*

READER: *This rest gives your heart a chan- a chance to keep a good work good working con- condition as well as you grow big and strong.*

READ FOR CODING: *This rest gives your heart a chance to keep a good working condition as well as you grow big and strong.*

Gordon's grammatical transformation *to keep a good working condition as well as you grow big and strong* results in a sentence that is syntactically unacceptable. The substitution of the pronoun *you* disrupts the conjoined infinitive forms *to keep* and *to grow*. Since the meaning is coded **N** as syntactically unacceptable, it is also semantically unacceptable, **N**. Meaning change is not coded.

YYY

The following example result in the **YYY** pattern.

Rarely do miscues result in a sentence that is syntactically and semantically acceptable with a major change in meaning. (Betsy and Gordon have no **YYY** pattern in their readings.) Two other readers made the following miscues that result in a **YYY** pattern.

0415   "Let's have a look at her,"

0416   said Jock Duncan, *Jack* (AC) *"I'll call the* our cook and

0417   doctor."   *Y Y Y*

READER: *"Let's have a look at her," said Jack Duncan, our cook and doctor. "I'll call the doctor."*

READ FOR CODING: *"Let's have a look at her," said Jack Duncan, "I'll call the doctor."*

The student reads the expected response but then abandons the correct response (AC) for *"I'll call the doctor."* It is evident that the reader couldn't imagine that someone could be a cook and a doctor. This substitution is coded **Y** for semantic and syntactic acceptability and **Y** for a major meaning change. Since Jock Duncan is a doctor, it is not necessary for him to call a doctor. Although this miscue is plausible in the story and fully acceptable, the meaning change is a major one.

                      made
The signs are not mixed up now.   *Y Y Y*

READER: *The signs are not made up now.*

READ FOR CODING: *The signs are not made up now.*

The substitution of *made* for *mixed* is syntactically and semantically acceptable in the story; however, in this story there is a major difference between *making* up the signs and *mixing* up the signs.

Graphic Similarity and Sound Similarity

Each word-for-word substitution miscue, whether corrected or not, is evaluated to determine graphic and sound similarity, and is coded using the criteria presented in Chapter 5. If there are multiple substitutions for the same text word, the first complete word or nonword is coded. To code for graphic and sound similarity, place **H** (High), **S** (Some), or **N** (None) above word-for-word substitutions. Omissions, insertions, repeated miscues, intonation shifts, complex miscues, and punctuation are not coded for graphic and sound similarity.

Following are some of Gordon's miscues coded for graphic similarity. In the Classroom Procedure, in which the typescript is used for coding, sound similarity is optional. Miscue Analysis Research indicates that the total of Sound Similarity percentages are usually slightly lower than Graphic Similarity percentages; therefore, Sound Similarity is optional for this procedure.

The questions concerning graphic and sound similarity of word-level substitutions are:

QUESTION 4: How much does the miscue (OR) *look like* the text word (ER)?

H A high degree of graphic similarity exists between the miscue and the text word.

S Some degree of graphic similarity exists between the miscue and the text word.

N No degree of graphic similarity exists between the miscue and the text word.

QUESTION 5 (optional): How much does the miscue (OR) *sound like* the expected response (ER)?

H A high degree of sound similarity exists between the miscue and the expected response.

S Some degree of sound similarity exists between the miscue and the expected response.

N No degree of sound similarity exists between the miscue and the expected response.

You will find the coding of Betsy's Graphic Similarity on the Classroom Procedure *typescript* (Figure 6.1) and the coding for both Graphic and Sound Similarity on her Classroom Procedure Coding Form (Figure 6.5) later in this chapter.

Following are examples of Gordon's miscues that are coded for both Graphic and Sound Similarity. Graphic Similarity is coded on the left, followed by the Sound Similarity (optional) on the right as in the examples below. See Chapter 5 for a discussion concerning Graphic and Sound Similarity coding.

SN   HS
the beat

0328   Then listen to his heart again.

GRAPHIC SIMILARITY: *the* for *his* is coded **S**, and *beat* for *heart* is coded **H**. *The* and *his* have one segment in common, and *beat* and *heart* have two segments in common, the *ea* pattern and the *t*.

SOUND SIMILARITY: *the* for *his* is coded **N**, and *beat* for *heart is coded* **S**. *The* and *his* have no sounds in common. *beat* and *heart* have the final sound in common.

㉚   *SS*
              find   b—
0506   You will feel the beat

              of your heart

GRAPHIC SIMILARITY: *find* for *feel* is coded **S** because the initial consonants are the same.

SOUND SIMILARITY: *find* for *feel* is coded **S** because the initial sounds are the same.

㉕   *HH*
        Now
0329-30   How many times a minute.
                    nn
                    yet
              is his heart beating now?

GRAPHIC SIMILARITY: *Now* for *How* is coded **H** because two of the three letters are the same. *Yet* for *now* is coded **N** as there are no letters in common.

SOUND SIMILARITY: *Now* for *How* is coded **H** because 50 percent of the ER is heard in 50 percent of the OR. *yet* for *now* is coded **N** *because no sounds are similar.*

Classroom Procedure Statistical Summary

The statistical summary in Figure 6.3 is compiled on a separate page or at the bottom of the last page of the typescript (see Betsy's typescript and statistical summary earlier in this chapter, Figure 6.1).

To compute Syntactic Acceptability, count the number of sentences coded **Y** (syntactically acceptable) and the number of sentences marked **N** (syntactically unacceptable). Place the numbers on the appropriate lines at the

---

Figure 6.3: Classroom Procedure Statistical Summary

Ques 1   Syntactic Acceptability   Y___ ___% N___ ___%   No. Sentences Coded _____

Ques 2   Semantic Acceptability   Y___ ___% N___ ___%   No. Sentences Coded _____

Ques 3   Meaning Change   N___ ___% P___ ___% Y___ ___% No. Sentences Coded _____

Ques 4   Graphic Similarity   H___ ___% S___ ___% N___ ___% No. Miscues Coded _____

Comments:

Optional: Total No. Miscues_____   No. Words Read _____

                MPHW (miscues per hundred words) _____ Time _____

bottom of the typescript. Divide each number by the total number of coded sentences and write the result on the appropriate percentage line.

To compute Semantic Acceptability, count the number of sentences coded **Y** (semantically acceptable) and the number of sentences marked **N** (semantically unacceptable). Place the numbers on the appropriate lines. Divide each number by the total number of coded sentences, and write the result on the appropriate percentage line.

To compute Meaning Change, count the number of **N** (no meaning change), **P** (partial or minor meaning change), and **Y** (major meaning change) coded. Determine the percentages of each by dividing each number by the number of sentences coded for meaning change. Sentences not coded for meaning change (marked with a dash) are not counted.

To compute Graphic Similarity, count the number of miscues coded **H** (high graphic similarity), **S** (some graphic similarity), and **N** (no graphic similarity). Determine the percentages by dividing **H**, **S**, and **N** by the number of coded word-level substitutions.

To compute Sound Similarity, count the number coded **H** (high sound similarity), **S** (some sound similarity), and **N** (no sound similarity). Determine percentages by dividing each **H**, **S**, and **N** by the number of coded word-level substitutions.

Computation of miscues per hundred words (MPHW), counting the number of words read, and timing the reading are all optional. To compute MPHW, count the total number of miscues coded, divide by the number of words read, and multiply by 100. Some observers time the reading.

Comments concerning retelling may be added to the Classroom Procedure Statistical Summary (Figure 6.3) or placed on the Retelling Summary (Appendix C). Betsy's Classroom Procedure Retelling Summary (Figure 6.7) is at the end of the chapter. (Betsy's Retelling is in Chapter 1.)

Checklist for the Classroom Procedure: Using the Typescript

Figure 6.4 is a checklist for completing the Classroom Procedure: Using the Typescript.

The Classroom Procedure Coding and Reader Profile Forms

Rather than coding the Classroom Procedure in the margin of the typescript, the observer may choose to use the Classroom Procedure Coding Form and the Classroom Procedure Reader Profile Form (Appendix C). These forms facilitate recordkeeping, are useful in planning strategy lessons, and are convenient for use in conferences with students, parents, other teachers, and Individual Education Plans (IEP). Betsy's Coding Form (Figure 6.5) and her Reader Profile Form (Figure 6.6) follow.

Figure 6.4: Classroom Procedure Checklist: Using the Typescript

- ☐ Select student.
- ☐ Select material.
- ☐ Prepare typescript.
    - ☐ Number sentences and draw marginal lines.
- ☐ Prepare retelling guide.
- ☐ Prepare tape recorder and setting.

Collect data:

- ☐ Oral reading and miscue marking.
- ☐ Retelling.
- ☐ Listen to recording and verify miscue marking.
- ☐ Complete Retelling Summary.

Code:

- ☐ Code sentences for questions 1–3 in the margin of the typescript.
- ☐ Code word-for-word substitutions for graphic similarity, question 4.
- ☐ Code word-for-word substitutions for sound similarity, question 5 (optional).
- ☐ Prepare Reader Profile Form (optional).

The Classroom Procedure Coding Form

The Classroom Procedure Coding Form (Appendix C, Figure 6.5) is divided into two sections, **Language Sense** and **Word Substitution in Context**. The *Language Sense* section documents the syntactic and semantic acceptability of miscues and the reader's concern for constructing meaning. All sentences are coded, whether they include miscues or not, following the procedures for coding presented earlier in this chapter. Coding all sentences gives a picture of the influence of the reader's strategies on the entire story, not just on the sentences that include miscues. The *Word Substitution in Context* section is used to record word substitutions and their graphic and sound similarity to the expected response (ER), and reveals the reader's knowledge of the phonological, the orthographic, and the phonics systems.

Language Sense

The Language Sense section of the Coding Form indicates the reader's ability to produce sentences that make sense and sound like language. This section also reflects how proficiently the reader uses strategies involving sampling, predicting, inferring, confirming, correcting, and integrating meaning. The questions (Figure 6.2) are the same as those for the Classroom Procedure in which the typescript is used for coding, except that the answers are coded on the Classroom Procedure Coding Form.

Figure 6.5: Betsy's Miscue Analysis Classroom Procedure Coding Form

READER: Betsy
TEACHER: Ms. Blau
SELECTION: The Man Who Kept House
AGE/GRADE: 3
DATE: November 3
SCHOOL: York Elem.

Language Sense (per sentence)

Sentence No./Line No.	No. Miscues in Sentence	1. Syntactic Acceptability	2. Semantic Acceptability	3. Meaning Change	Pattern
1	3	Y	Y	N	Strength (YYN)
2	3	Y	Y	N	Strength (YYN)
3	1	N	N	—	Weakness (NN-)
4	0	Y	Y	N	Strength (YYN)
5	0	Y	Y	N	Strength (YYN)
6	0	Y	Y	N	Strength (YYN)
7	1	Y	Y	N	Strength (YYN)
8	1	Y	Y	N	Strength (YYN)
9	3	N	N	—	Weakness (NN-)
10	2*	Y	N	—	Weakness (YN-)
11	2	Y	Y	N	Strength (YYN)
12	2	Y	Y	P	Partial Strength (YYP)
13	1	Y	Y	N	Strength (YYN)
14	1	Y	Y	N	Strength (YYN)
15	1	Y	N	—	Weakness (YN-)
16	2	Y	N	—	Weakness (YN-)
17	2	Y	Y	N	Strength (YYN)
18	2	Y	Y	P	Partial Strength (YYP)
19	0	Y	Y	N	Strength (YYN)
20	1	Y	Y	N	Strength (YYN)
21	2	Y	Y	N	Strength (YYN)
22	1	Y	Y	N	Strength (YYN)
23	2	Y	Y	N	Strength (YYN)
24	2	Y	Y	N	Strength (YYN)
25	1	Y	Y	N	Strength (YYN)

COLUMN TOTAL / PATTERN — Strength: 18   Partial Strength: 2   Weakness: 5

Word Substitution in Context

Dialect (d)

Reader	Text	Line/Sentence No.	Graphic (4) H/S/N	Sound (5) H/S/N
he	who	1 / 1	H	H
threw	thought	1	H, S	H, S
when	while	2 / 2	H, S	H, S
always	away	2 / 2	H	S
I'll	I'd	7	H	H, S
so	some	8	H	S
start	stay	9	H, S	H, S
house	home	9	H	S
keeping	keep	9	H, S	H, S
bread	butter	10	H	H
Well	we'll	12	H	H, S
day	morning	13	N	N
job	work	14	H, S	S, N
$churn	churn	16	H, S	H, S
the	this	17	H	
So	Loom	18	H	
buttermilk	butter	18	H, S	S
There	the	21	H, S	H
is	was	21	H	S
into	to	22	H	S
forest	far	23	H	S
in	to	23	N	N
the	his	24	H	H, N
head	had	24	H	H, N
cream	churn	25	H	N

COLUMN TOTAL / TOTAL MISCUES

a. TOTAL MISCUES _____
b. TOTAL WORDS _____

*Not counting RM's

Goodman, Watson, Burke

118

Figure 6.5: Betsy's Miscue Analysis Classroom Procedure Coding Form (cont.)

READER Betsy
TEACHER Ms. Blau   AGE/GRADE 3
SELECTION The Man Who Kept House
DATE November 3
SCHOOL York Elem.

WORD SUBSTITUTION IN CONTEXT

SENTENCE NO.	LINE NO.	READER	TEXT (Dialect ⓓ)	GRAPHIC 4 H	GRAPHIC 4 S	GRAPHIC 4 N	SOUND 5 H	SOUND 5 S	SOUND 5 N
27	shout	shout	shouted	✓			✓		
28	big	big	pig	✓	✓		✓		
28	and	and	the			✓			✓
29	jumped	jumped	bumped	✓	✓		✓		
30	shout	shout	splashed	✓	✓		✓	✓	
32	I'll	I'll	I've	✓			✓	✓	✓
33	and	and	in						
34	home	home	house	✓		✓			
34	and	and	is						
34	hard	hard	harder	✓	✓		✓		
34	Then	Then	than	✓		✓	✓		
34	he	he	I			✓			✓
35	the	the	a						✓
35	basket	basket	bucket	✓		✓	✓	✓	
39	the	the	a						✓
39	I'll	I'll	the						
42	is	is	has	✓	✓		✓		
42	giving	giving	given	✓	✓		✓		
49	the	the	she	✓	✓		✓		✓
49	was	was	and		✓	✓	✓		
49	himself	himself	herself			✓	✓		
50	the	the	a		✓				✓
53	up	up	out	✓	✓		✓	✓	
53	then	then	and	✓	✓			✓	
54	the	the	this	✓				✓	

LANGUAGE SENSE

SENTENCE NO./LINE NO.	NO. MISCUES IN SENTENCE	1 SYNTACTIC ACCEPTABILITY	2 SEMANTIC ACCEPTABILITY	3 MEANING CHANGE	PATTERN Strength (YYN)	PATTERN Partial Strength (YYY/YYP)	PATTERN Weakness (NN-/YN-)
26	0	Y	Y	N			
27	1	Y	Y	N	✓		
28	2	Y	Y	N	✓		
29	1*	Y	Y	N	✓		
30	1	Y	Y	N	✓		
31	0	Y	Y	N	✓		
32	1	Y	Y	N	✓		
33	1	Y	Y	N	✓		
34	6	N	N	P			✓
35	2	Y	Y	N	✓	✓	
36	0	Y	Y	N	✓		
37	0	Y	Y	N	✓		
38	0	Y	Y	N	✓		
39	3	Y	Y	N	✓		
40	0	Y	Y	N	✓		
41	0	Y	Y	N	✓		
42	2	Y	Y	N	✓		
43	0	Y	Y	N	✓		
44	1	N	N	—			✓
45	1	Y	Y	N	✓		
46	0	Y	Y	N	✓		
47	0	Y	Y	N	✓		
48	0	Y	Y	N	✓		
49	4	N	N	—			✓
50	1	Y	Y	N	✓		

COLUMN TOTAL / PATTERN TOTAL PERCENTAGE: Strength 21 | Partial Strength 1 | Weakness 3

a. TOTAL MISCUES _____
b. TOTAL WORDS _____
a ÷ b × 100 = MPHW _____

*Not counting RM's

COLUMN TOTAL / TOTAL MISCUES / PERCENTAGE

Goodman, Watson, Burke

119

Figure 6.5: Betsy's Miscue Analysis Classroom Procedure Coding Form (cont.)

READER **Betsy** TEACHER **Ms. Blau** AGE/GRADE **3** SELECTION **The Man Who Kept House** DATE **November 3** SCHOOL **York Elem.**

LANGUAGE SENSE

SENTENCE NO./LINE NO.	NO. MISCUES IN SENTENCE	1 SYNTACTIC ACCEPTABILITY	2 SEMANTIC ACCEPTABILITY	3 MEANING CHANGE	PATTERN Strength YYN	PATTERN Partial Strength YYY/YYP	PATTERN Weakness NN-/YN-
51	1	Y	Y	P		✓	
52	0	Y	Y	N	✓		
53	3	Y	Y	N	✓		
54	1	Y	Y	N	✓		
55	0	Y	Y	N	✓		
56	0			—			
57	3	N	N	—			✓
58	2*	N	N	—			
59	0	Y	Y	N	✓		
60	2	N	N	—			✓
61	0	Y	Y	N	✓		
62	0	Y	Y	N	✓		
63	1	Y	Y	N	✓		
64	2	Y	Y	N	✓		
65	0	Y	Y	N	✓		
66	3	Y	Y	N	✓		
67	1	Y	Y	N	✓		
68		Y			✓		
Totals for sentences 51–68					14	1	3
" 26–50					21	1	3
" 1–25					18	2	5
COLUMN TOTAL PATTERN TOTAL				68	53	4	11
PERCENTAGE			78%		78%	6%	16%

WORD SUBSTITUTION IN CONTEXT

SENTENCE NO.	LINE NO.	READER (Dialect ⓓ)	TEXT	4 GRAPHIC H	S	N	5 SOUND H	S	N
57		is	he			✓			✓
57		hang	hung	✓			✓		
57		never	over	✓			✓		
58		fgorun	ground	✓	✓		✓		
58		he	she	✓			✓		
60		cried	crying	✓				✓	✓
60		shouted	shouting					✓	
61		to	the					✓	
63		and	As	✓	✓			✓	
64		leg	legs		✓			✓	
64		her	his	✓					
66		keep	look	✓	✓				
66		the	their	✓					
66		children	child	✓					✓
68		the	he						✓
COLUMN TOTAL / TOTAL MISCUES 65				36	19	10	28	21	16
PERCENTAGE				55%	29%	15%	43%	32%	25%

a. TOTAL MISCUES **75**
b. TOTAL WORDS **791**
a ÷ b × 100 = MPHW **9.46**

*Not counting RM's

Goodman, Watson, Burke

Sentence Numbering

In preparation for coding, each text sentence is numbered with a colored pencil. In the Language Sense section of the Coding Form, the sentence numbers or the line numbers are written under the column headed Sentence/ Line No. The second column indicates the number of miscues in the sentence, excluding the miscues marked RM on the typescript. (On Betsy's Classroom Procedure Coding Form, an asterisk is placed after the number of miscues in the sentence to indicate the sentences that include Repeated Miscues. This is an optional notation.) Complex miscues are counted as one miscue. If there are no miscues in the sentence, 0 is written in the column. With this information miscues per hundred words (MPHW) can be computed.

To answer Questions 1–3, read each sentence as the reader resolves it. In other words, *all corrected miscues, repeated miscues, and attempts at correction are read as finally produced by the reader.* See the Classroom Procedure Questions (Figure 6.2) earlier in this chapter and in Appendix A.

QUESTION 1: Is the sentence syntactically acceptable in the reader's dialect and within the context of the entire text?

QUESTION 2: Is the sentence semantically acceptable in the reader's dialect and within the context of the entire text? (Question 2 is coded **N** if Question 1 is coded **N**.)

QUESTION 3: Does the sentence, as finally produced by the reader, change the meaning of the entire text? (Question 3 is asked only if questions 1 and 2 are **YY**, that is, if the sentence is syntactically and semantically acceptable.) The answer to this question gives information about how much miscues and corrections change the intended meaning of the story, according to the observer's interpretation.

The Language Sense patterns (Strength, Partial Strength, and Weakness) are checked on the Coding Form by matching them with the patterns coded in columns 1, 2, and 3. These three columns are computed for statistical information.

Word Substitution in Context and Graphic and Sound Similarity

In this section of the Coding Form, word-for-word substitutions are evaluated to determine the degree that graphic and sound cues influence readers. The questions concerning graphic and sound similarity of word-level substitutions are:

QUESTION 4: How much does the miscue (OR) *look like* the text word (ER)?

QUESTION 5 (optional): How much does the miscue (OR) *sound like* the expected response (ER)? See the Classroom Procedure Questions at the beginning of this chapter.

In preparation for coding, write the sentence number in the first column of the Word Substitution in Context section. Line numbers (second column) are helpful but optional. In the column marked Reader, write the miscue

(OR). Write the expected response (ER) in the column marked Text. Each substitution miscue is evaluated using questions 4–5. If the reader's dialect has influenced the miscue, mark ⓓ after the miscue. If the miscue is a repeated identical substitution, mark RM but do not code the miscue; only the first attempt is coded. (See the discussion of Repeated Miscues that follows.)

The Classroom Procedure Reader Profile Form

The Reader Profile form (Appendix C) summarizes information taken from the Coding Form (under Language Sense and Word Substitution in Context). The Reader Profile form provides a place for Repeated Miscues Across Text and for comments concerning those miscues. Betsy's Classroom Reader Profile Form is Figure 6.6 and Gordon's In-Depth Profile Form is in Appendix B.

Repeated Miscues

Over the years, we have become aware of the importance of studying readers' responses to the same text item across single and multiple texts. As discussed earlier, written continuous text offers the reader multiple encounters with identical words and phrases. These places provide a map of the strategies readers use as they transact with these same words, phrases, and concepts in different contexts. The analysis shows the development of readers' comprehending strategies and vocabulary development as they learn from their transaction with the text (Meek 1988).

There are three types of repeated miscues. One type includes miscues that are *repeated identical substitutions or omissions* for the same text item, and it is recorded as follows:

- *Marking:* If the OR and ER are the same in pronunciation, meaning, and grammatical function, these attempts are *repeated miscues.* All repeated miscues are marked on the typescript as other miscues are marked. However, the second and subsequent identical miscues are identified ⓡⓜ on the typescript.

- *Coding:* To avoid inflation of statistical data, only the first repeated identical miscue is coded on the Coding Form under Word Substitution in Context.

- *Reader Profile Form:* The first miscue and all subsequent identical miscues are coded under Repeated Miscues Across Text on the Reader Profile. A place is provided to jot comments.

The second type of repeated miscues includes instances of *varied responses* for the same word or phrase, and it is recorded as follows:

- *Marking:* Each different substitution is marked on the typescript.

- *Coding:* Each different substitution is coded on the Coding Form under Word Substitution in Context.

- *Reader Profile Form:* Each different substitution is recorded under Repeated Miscues Across Text. A place is provided to jot comments.

Figure 6.6: Betsy's Miscue Analysis Classroom Procedure Reader Profile

DATE November 3

SCHOOL York Elem.

READER Betsy

TEACHER Ms. Blau AGE/GRADE 3

SELECTION The Man Who Kept House

	%	%	PERCENT
LANGUAGE SENSE			
Strength	78		⎫
Partial Strength	6	84	⎬
Weakness	16		⎭
WORD SUBSTITUTION IN CONTEXT			
Graphic			
High	55		⎫
Some	29	84	⎬
None	15		⎭
Sound			
High	43		⎫
Some	32	75	⎬
None	25		⎭
RETELLING			
Holistic Score			

Comments Very complete unaided retelling. Doesn't always seem to understand concept of cow on roof of sod house. Uses pictures to aid retelling. Tone toward story always serious.

REPEATED MISCUES ACROSS TEXT

LINE	READER	TEXT	COMMENTS (place in text, correction, etc.)
113	start	stay	first occurence of stay
114	start	stay	start home for stay home 2 times; gets stayed (202): stay (513) (616)
113	house	home	no miscue on first occurrence (103)
114	house	home	no miscue on home 4 out of 6 times
			miscues home for house (312) but no
			miscue on house 13 times
205	$shurn	churn	never produces ER
304	cream	churn	syn. & sem. acceptable
307	cream	churn	syn. & sem. acceptable
207	the	this	In the majority of cases, she gets
508	the	this	the and this appropriately. Her
			substitutions of function words are
			either semantically acceptable or
			corrected.
510	hang	hung	Only two occurences of the OR;
512	hang	hung	irregular verb form

COMMENTS For the most part Betsy uses predicting and confirming strategies proficiently. She may be overattending to surface features of text.

Goodman, Watson, Burke

The third type of repeated miscues includes substitutions and omissions of *function words* such as determiners, verb markers, conjunctions, prepositions and is recorded as follows:

- *Marking:* Substitutions and omissions of function words that are repeated miscues are marked on the typescript.

- *Coding:* Substitutions and omissions of function words that are repeated miscues are coded on the Coding Form each time they occur, since they often reflect different language relations in each text occurrence.

- *Reader Profile Form:* Substitutions and omissions of function words that are repeated miscues are recorded under Repeated Miscues Across Text. A place is provided to jot comments.

Repeated Miscues Across Text on the Reader Profile Form

Because Repeated Miscues (RM) reveal a great deal about readers' concept development and their reading strategies, the RMs are grouped and listed along with comments about them, on the Classroom Procedure Reader Profile Form. The analysis of these RMs provides evidence that readers use text information to adapt their reading strategies to develop meaning. Following is an example of identical Repeated Miscues across text.

0101	*Lu-bump* / Lub-dup . . . *(Lu sounds like initial sounds in love.)*
0102	*RM* / *Lu-bump* / Lub-dup . . .
0103	*RM* / *Lu-bump* / Lub-dup . . .

In *The Beat of My Heart, Lub-dup* occurs six times, for which Gordon substitutes *Lu-bump* each time (see Appendix B). The first substitution (line 0101) is coded on the Classroom Procedure Coding Form. All the subsequent identical substitutions (lines 0102 ,0103, 0728, 0729, and 0730) are marked RM and are grouped and listed on the Classroom Procedure Reader Profile form.

Following are *varied responses* on the same text item (ER) across text.

0205	the cream into the͏ *Sshurn. He* churn, he said . . .
0304	. . . nose in the *cream* churn. "Get . . .
0307	. . . bumped into the *RM cream* churn, knocking . . .

In *The Man Who Kept House, churn* occurs three times. Betsy substitutes a non-word $shurn for the first occurrence of *churn* (line 0205). On the second occurrence of *churn* (line 0304), she substitutes a different word, *cream*. On the third occurrence of *churn* (line 0307), she again substitutes *cream*; therefore, *this identical miscue* is marked RM on the typescript. The first two substitutions are coded on the coding form. All three miscues are recorded on Betsy's Classroom Reader Profile form, Figure 6.6.

When the *grammatical function of the ER changes*, miscues that occur on that word are coded and recorded on the Reader Profile. For example, if *pat* is substituted for *pet* (a noun), and later *pat* is substituted for *pet* (a verb), these are not identical miscues; both, therefore, are listed on the Classroom Coding Form and the Classroom Reader Profile.

Following is an example of Repeated Miscues on the same *function word* across text.

0207   (17) is sit here and move ⓒ the [this] stick up and down

0505   (54) "Now I can finish making the this porridge,"

Betsy substitutes *the* for *this* on two occasions in reading *The Man Who Kept House*. All miscues that are repeated on the same text item (ER) involving function words are coded each time and recorded on the Reader Profile.

Comments in the Repeated Miscue section of the Reader Profile provide insights about the reader's strategies that the teacher and student may want to explore, such as:

- How readers modify their reading strategies in response to the language cuing systems.
- How particular word sequences influence repeated miscues.
- Where in the text the same ER does not generate miscues.
- How the context and the language systems continue to influence miscues throughout the text.
- When it is necessary to correct.
- How the author's use of identical words and identical or similar concepts across text support the reader's learning.

With this information, the teacher plans instructional experiences with the student.

Retelling

The Retelling Summary (Appendix C and Betsy's Retelling Summary, Figure 6.7) includes places to write information about the reader's retelling of the plot, theme, inferences, and misconceptions. *Misconceptions* are unexpected responses that reflect inferences students make, based on what they construct from the text and their prior knowledge. The retelling may be

Figure 6.7: Betsy's Classroom Procedure Retelling Summary

READER _Betsy_

DATE _November 3_

SELECTION _The Man Who Kept House_

Holistic Retelling Score (optional): _____

Plot Statements   It was about a woodman who thought he had a harder job than his wife had and he didn't so he stopped saying it.

Theme Statements   Maybe about how people shouldn't brag about all they have to do. They get in trouble and other people prove they work as hard as they do.

Inferences
— wife got blister
— wife left home with ax (in picture)
— discusses personality traits of major characters

Misconceptions
— poured buttermilk in the jar
— cow fell over the house
— calls cow "he"
— cow drinks milk

Comments   Very complete unaided retelling. Doesn't always seem to understand concept of cow on roof (sod house). Uses pictures to aid retelling. Tone toward story always serious.

(Goodman, Watson, Burke)

contrasted with other students' retellings of the same text or with retellings of other texts by the same reader. The Retelling Summary is a framework, not a step-by-step verification of the contents of the original text. The teacher's comments are about the student's comprehension, retelling strategies, and possible future reading experiences. For nonfiction texts, the Retelling Summary includes specific information, generalizations, and major concepts rather than plot and theme statements. (See Gordon's Retelling Summary in Appendix B.)

If a score is required, holistic scoring (Irwin and Mitchell 1983) provides a broad estimation of the retelling by considering its overall substance. The holistic score may involve an even-numbered scale (e.g., 1–4), so that there is no average, or it may be an odd-numbered scale (1–5) to provide a midpoint.

Checklist for the Classroom Procedure: Using the Coding Form

Figure 6.8 is a checklist for administering the Classroom Procedure when using the Coding Form and Reader Profile.

Figure 6.8: Classroom Procedure Checklist: Using the Coding Form

- ☐ Select student.
- ☐ Select material.
- ☐ Prepare typescript.
  - ☐ Number sentences.
- ☐ Prepare retelling guide.
- ☐ Prepare tape recorder and setting.

Collect data:
  - ☐ Oral reading and miscue marking.
  - ☐ Retelling.
- ☐ Listen to recording and verify miscue marking.
- ☐ Complete Retelling Summary.

Code miscues on Classroom Procedure Coding Form:
  - ☐ Code sentences for questions 1–3.
  - ☐ Code patterns.
  - ☐ Code word-for-word substitutions for graphic similarity, question 4.
  - ☐ Code word-for-word substitutions for sound similarity, question 5 (optional).
- ☐ Compute statistics for Coding Form.
- ☐ Transfer statistics from Coding Form to Reader Profile.
- ☐ List repeated miscues.
- ☐ Add comments.

THE INFORMAL PROCEDURE

The **Informal Procedure** allows those who are familiar with miscue analysis to make a relatively quick evaluation of a student's reading. The procedure is especially helpful for the classroom teacher as part of a reading conference, as well as for an initial evaluation by a reading specialist or special education teacher.

The Informal Procedure focuses on the most important aspect of miscue analysis: the connection between semantic acceptability and self-correction. As discussed earlier, the significance of the interrelations between these two phenomena is documented by miscue analysis research. The evaluation of these interrelations results in a *comprehending score*. Betsy's Informal Procedure Conference Form (Figure 6.9) follows.

The Informal Procedure does not require tape recording or use of a typescript. Rather, the teacher listens to the student and keeps a tally of the acceptability of each sentence within the entire text by asking:

- ■ Does the sentence, as the reader resolved it, make sense within the context of the entire text?

- **Y** Sentences that are fully semantically acceptable (assuming total syntactic acceptability) within the context of the entire story or article and those acceptable or unacceptable but corrected are tallied Yes.

- **N** Those that are partially acceptable or unacceptable within the entire text and not corrected are tallied No.

The material read is, in most cases, the student's choice. The student is asked to read from the point in the story or article that he or she stopped reading before the conference. Beginning at this point assures that the reader is reading new material but has some background. As the student reads, the teacher tallies each completed sentence.

Informal Procedure Conference Form

This form (Betsy's Form Figure 6.9 and a blank form in Appendix C) provides direction for computing the comprehending score, determined by dividing the total number of sentences read into the total number of sentences tallied Yes. The quality of the retelling is noted under Retelling Information.

As part of the conference, engage the reader in a discussion about what he or she has just read and about successes and problems. Note comments and anecdotes on the Informal Procedure Conference Form, especially information from the reader or your new understandings that will help with reading instruction. Such information includes what and how much the student is reading, the student's current interests, projects the student is working on, resources being used, reading strategies the student is using successfully and unsuccessfully, and retelling information related to the reader's strengths and needs.

Figure 6.9: Betsy's Informal Procedure Conference Form

READER _Betsy_   DATE _November 3_

TEACHER _Mrs. Blau_   AGE/GRADE _Grade Three_

SELECTION _The Man Who Kept House_

Does the sentence, as the reader resolved it, make sense within the context of the entire text?

Yes _//// //// //// //// ////   //// //// //// //// //// //// //_   Total _57_

No _//// //// /_   Total _11_

Number of Sentences Read _68_   Comprehending Score _84%_

Divide total Yes by Total number of sentences for Comprehending Score _57 ÷ 68 = .84_

Retelling Information   _Very complete retelling. Doesn't always seem to understand concept of cow on roof (sod house). Uses pictures to aid retelling. Tone towards story always serious._

Comments   _For the most part Betsy uses predicting and confirming strategies proficiently. She may be overattending to surface features of text._

Involve Betsy in reading a variety of material. Help her choose her own reading. Perhaps suggest some humorous reading such as Robert Munsch. Concepts about churns and sod roofs may be extended as appropriate.

Checklist for the Informal Procedure

The overview in Figure 6.10 is a checklist for the **Informal Procedure**.

Figure 6.10: Informal Procedure Checklist

☐ Select student.

☐ Select material (usually selected by student, but may be by teacher).

☐ Oral reading.

☐ Tally sentences on the Informal Procedure Conference Form (Appendix C) as the student reads.

☐ Retelling.

☐ Student-teacher discussion.

☐ Enter comments concerning the retelling on the Informal Procedure Conference Form.

☐ Compute comprehending score (optional).

Chapter 7 discusses the **In-Depth Procedure**, which involves the examination of individual miscues within the sentence and the sentence within the entire text, in order to study the reader's attempt to construct meaning. The **In-Depth Procedure** also provides information for a broad range of research investigations.

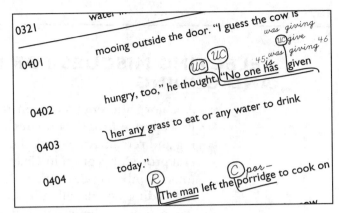

Chapter 7
The In-Depth Procedure

Miscue analysis examines readers' control and use of the language cuing systems and reading strategies while reading orally. The **In-Depth Procedure** provides for the study of each reading miscue in relation to other miscues within the sentence and within the entire text, evaluating how the text and the reader's prior knowledge influence the reading. Because of its potential for extensive investigation, the **In-Depth Procedure** is recommended for reading specialists and researchers who are concerned with developing detailed knowledge about students' reading. It is also recommended for graduate study, reading diagnosis courses, and other courses in which the reading process and readers' control of the process is investigated. For the **In-Depth Procedure**, teachers/researchers follow the general procedures presented in Chapters 3–5 to select students, choose the reading material, prepare the typescript, mark and analyze miscues.

NUMBERING MISCUES

In the In-Depth Procedure, observers decide where to begin numbering the miscues. Numbering can begin at the very beginning of the text or after the first paragraph or two, when the reader has "settled into reading." If the text is lengthy, the teacher/researcher (observer) chooses a section within the larger selection and begins numbering and coding miscues at the beginning of the selected section. In Betsy's case (see Chapter 1), because the text structures of *stay home* and *keep house* influenced her reading strategies, coding begins for the In-Depth Procedure on line 0112; her first coded miscue is the substitution of *so* for *some*. Betsy's familiarity with the style, concept density, and the predictability of the structures enter into the decision about where to begin coding (Menosky 1971). We recommend 25–50 consecutive miscues be coded to arrive at the patterns of readers' strategies and to understand their knowledge of language. Very young readers may not produce 25 miscues because of the short length of the text. In which case, we use the consecutive miscues available by combining two short texts.

SELECTING MISCUES FOR NUMBERING AND CODING

A major difference between the two other procedures and the In-Depth Procedure is how the miscues are coded. After recording the student's reading and retelling, we mark the miscues on the typescript, following the general procedures given in Chapter 4. The typescript is now ready for miscues to be numbered and coded. Because continuous patterns are studied, once the coding begins, all subsequent miscues must be numbered and coded consecutively. The miscue numbers are written in the first column of the In-Depth Coding Form (see Betsy's In-Depth Coding Form [Figure 7.3]), and Gordon's miscues, made while reading *The Beat of my Heart*, in Appendix B). Betsy's miscues are numbered consecutively, starting from line 0112. Gordon's miscues are numbered consecutively, starting with the first line, 0101.

Miscues selected for numbering, coding, and transferring to the In-Depth Coding Form include substitutions (including reversals), omissions (including uncorrected partials), insertions, and intonation shifts (often related to punctuation) and often result in changes to syntax and or meaning of the text. These miscues are coded even if they are corrected.

Miscues *not* selected for coding and therefore not transferred to the Coding Form (unless there are research or special analysis reasons) include corrected partials, substitutions of alternative sound variations involving phonological dialect, misarticulations, split syllables, subsequent identical repeated miscues, and multiple miscues made during a correction attempt. Repetitions and pauses are not considered miscues and therefore are not coded. (However, repetitions and pauses are evidence of strategies readers use for a variety of purposes and may be the topics for special research.) Observed responses (OR) that are not coded provide important information about the reader. They are examined and then noted in the Comments section of the In-Depth Reader Profile Form (see Figure 7.7 and a blank form in Appendix C). Examples of miscues not selected for coding follow.

0302   ... all the ⓒ cells and ...

Partial attempts on words that *are corrected* are not coded. Because the linguistic intent of the reader cannot be determined, partials that *are not corrected* are coded as omissions. (See marking of omissions in Chapter 4.)

Get in the game with the kids!

Phonological dialect is not coded.

niloleum @
They slid on the linoleum floor.

Misarticulations are not coded.

What a pretty sight!

Split syllables are not coded.

0212-13   . . . the heartbeat ⓡ of a friend

Repetitions are not coded.

0512   . . . she hung / between the roof

Pauses are not coded.

Repeated Miscues

As indicated in Chapter 6, there are three types of repeated miscues. One type is the *identical* substitution or omission for the same text word. The first text word (noun, verb, adjective, adverb) is numbered and coded on the In-Depth Procedure Coding Form (Figure 7.3). We mark subsequent identical occurrences RM on the typescript but, in order not to inflate the data, we do not place them on the Coding Form. The first and subsequent identical repeated miscues are noted in the Repeated Miscues Across Text section of the In-Depth Reader Profile Form (Figure 7.7).

The second type of repeated miscue is the *varied response* for the same text word. We mark each different substitution on the typescript, code it on the In-Depth Procedure Coding Form, and record it under Repeated Miscues Across Text on the In-Depth Reader Profile Form.

The third type of repeated miscue includes substitutions and omissions of *function words*, such as determiners, verb markers, conjunctions, and prepositions. We mark all function word substitutions on the typescript, code them on the Coding Form each time they occur, and record them under Repeated Miscues Across Text on the In-Depth Reader Profile Form.

In the analysis of repeated miscues (RM), we examine what readers do when they produce an identical miscue on the same linguistic unit (usually a word or phrase), as it occurs across the text. Chapters 4 and 6 include discussions of repeated miscues that are appropriate for the In-Depth Procedure.

Multiple Miscues

Two or more attempts on the same text item at the same place in the text constitute a multiple miscue. In the In-Depth Procedure, the first complete OR (word or nonword) is coded. We select the first miscue to gain insight into the reader's initial response and subsequent choice of strategies, that is, to evaluate the reader's initial predicting and subsequent confirming strategies. When coding the other miscues in a sentence, we read the reader's final multiple attempt. See Chapter 4 for additional discussion of multiple miscues.

Complex Miscues

As stated in Chapter 4, if the miscues involve phrases, clauses, and sentences in such a way that it is not possible to determine word-for-word relationships, the entire sequence is marked and coded as one complex miscue. To determine if a miscue is complex, we compare the observed response (OR) word for word to the expected response (ER). If it is easy to compare the OR with the ER word-for-word, these are not complex miscues and each miscue is coded separately.

ANALYZING MISCUES

In the In-Depth Procedure, each miscue is analyzed separately. To appreciate the influence of the language systems and the reader's strategies on the reading process, we ask the questions concerning syntactic acceptability, semantic acceptability, meaning change, correction, graphic similarity, and sound similarity. Sociocultural influences, including pragmatics, are considered, along with the semantic system in the questions concerning semantic acceptability, correction and meaning change.

Beginners to miscue analysis find it helpful to answer question 1 for a consecutive group of five to ten miscues or all the miscues in a paragraph, then to answer question 2 for the same miscues, then question 3. However, as coders become proficient, it is preferable to code each miscue right across the coding form. In this way, coders become increasingly aware of how the various language systems and reading strategies interrelate and influence the reader. Practice and patience result in proficient coding.

We code the relations between the syntactic and semantic systems, and analyze them to determine the reader's patterns of strengths and challenges. We mark these relations on the In-Depth Procedure Coding Form (Appendix C and Figure 7.3) under Meaning Construction and Grammatical Relations.

The questions guiding the Classroom Procedure (Chapter 6) focus on the acceptability of the entire sentence. The questions of the In-Depth Procedure focus on the acceptability of the individual miscue within the sentence and the entire text. The In-Depth Procedure includes a separate question concerning miscue correction.

IN-DEPTH PROCEDURE QUESTIONS

The answers to the In-Depth Procedure questions in Figure 7.1 help evaluate a reader's reading strategies. We use Betsy's and Gordon's miscues as coding examples (Figure 7.3 and Appendix B).

SYNTACTIC AND SEMANTIC ACCEPTABILITY (QUESTIONS 1 AND 2)

As discussed in Chapter 5, language has both a syntactic organization and a semantic organization. *Syntactic acceptability* (question 1) is concerned with

Figure 7.1: In-Depth Procedure Questions

QUESTION 1: *Syntactic Acceptability*

Does the miscue occur in a structure that is syntactically acceptable in the reader's dialect?

Y (Yes)   The miscue is completely syntactically acceptable within the sentence and within the entire text.

P (Partial)   The miscue is syntactically acceptable with either the first part of the sentence or is syntactically acceptable with the last part of the sentence. Or, the miscue is syntactically acceptable within the sentence, but not within the entire text.

N (No)   The miscue results in a structure that is not syntactically acceptable.

QUESTION 2: *Semantic Acceptability*

Does the miscue occur in a structure that is semantically acceptable in the reader's dialect? Semantic acceptability cannot be coded higher than syntactic acceptability.

Y (Yes)   The miscue is completely semantically acceptable within the sentence and within the entire text.

P (Partial)   The miscue is semantically acceptable with either the first part of the sentence or is semantically acceptable with the last part of the sentence. Or, the miscue is semantically acceptable within the sentence, but not within the complete text.

N (No)   The miscue is not semantically acceptable.

QUESTION 3: *Meaning Change*

Does the miscue change the meaning of the entire text?

This question is asked only if the miscue is both syntactically and semantically acceptable (Q1 = Y and Q2 = Y).

N (No)   There is no change in meaning.

P (Partial)   There is inconsistency, loss, or meaning change of a **minor** idea, incident, character, fact, sequence, or concept.

Y (Yes)   There is inconsistency, loss, or change of a **major** idea, incident, character, fact, sequence, or concept.

QUESTION 4: *Correction*

Is the miscue corrected?

Y (Yes)   The miscue is corrected.

P (Partial)   There is either an unsuccessful attempt to correct ⓤⓒ, or the expected response is read and then abandoned ⓐⓒ.

N (No)   There is no attempt to correct.

Figure 7.1: In-Depth Procedure Questions (continued)

QUESTION 5: *Graphic Similarity*

How much does the miscue (OR) look like the text word (ER)?

H (High)   A high degree of graphic similarity exists between the miscue and the text word.

S (Some)   Some degree of graphic similarity exists between the miscue and the text word.

N (No)   No degree of graphic similarity exists between the miscue and the text word.

QUESTION 6: *Sound Similarity*

How much does the miscue (OR) sound like the expected response (ER)?

H (High)   A high degree of sound similarity exists between the miscue and the expected response.

S (Some)   Some degree of sound similarity exists between the miscue and the expected response.

N (No)   No degree of graphic similarity exists between the miscue and the expected response.

---

the degree to which the reader produces acceptable grammatical structures. *Semantic acceptability* (question 2) focuses on the success with which the reader produces meaning within an acceptable structure. The dialect of the reader is always taken into consideration when answering these questions.

How to Read for Syntactic Acceptability

■   Does the miscue occur in a structure that is syntactically acceptable in the reader's dialect?

To answer question 1, we read the entire sentence as the reader finally produced it, *except for the miscue in question.* We read the first attempt on the ER even if the miscue is corrected.

0318   "I'll light a fire in the fireplace, and the

0319   porridge will be ready in a few minutes."

To code the substitution of *the* for *a*, we read the sentence: *I'll light the fire in the fireplace and the porridge will be ready in a few minutes.* Since the miscues *I'll* and *flash* were both corrected, they are read as corrected when coding *the* for *a*.

To code the substitution of *I'll* for *the*, we read the sentence: *I'll light the fire in the fireplace, and I'll porridge will be ready in a few minutes. The* for *a* is read as the reader left it because it was not corrected. Since Betsy corrected *flash* for *few minutes*, we read *few minutes*.

To code the substitution of *flash* for *few minutes*, we read the sentence: *I'll light the fire in the fireplace, and the porridge will be ready in a flash*. The substitution of *the* for *a* is read as the reader left it, uncorrected. *I'll* is corrected to *and the*, as Betsy resolved it.

If a miscue is found to be syntactically acceptable *within the sentence*, we read the sentence to determine its acceptability within the entire story. If the miscue is acceptable within the sentence and within the entire story, the miscue is coded **Y** (yes). If the miscue is acceptable only at the sentence level, the miscue is coded **P** (partial acceptability). Syntactic acceptability at only the sentence level rarely occurs. A nonparallel structure caused by a shift in verb tense or a move from singular to plural may cause a sentence to be unacceptable within the entire text and therefore coded **P** in column 1.

If the miscue is found to be syntactically *unacceptable* within the total sentence, the next step is to determine if the miscue is partially acceptable with the beginning of the sentence up to and including the miscue, or from the point of and including the miscue to the end of the sentence. If the beginning portion of the sentence, including the miscue, is not syntactically acceptable, we judge the acceptability of the ending portion of the sentence, including the miscue. Acceptability with the ending portion of the sentence does not occur often, but when it does it suggests that the reader, knowing the sentence doesn't sound like language, accommodates to subsequent syntax. Examining acceptability of a portion of the sentence, with corrections considered, is a way to determine the reader's use of prediction strategies. If either the beginning of a sentence (including the miscue) or the end of a sentence (including the miscue) is considered syntactically acceptable, the miscue is coded **P**. If the miscue is an omission, we read one word beyond the omission or one word before the omission when judging partial acceptability within the sentence.

Miscues that occur on either the first or the last word of a sentence are coded as either acceptable in the whole sentence **P**, acceptable in the whole story **Y**, or unacceptable **N**. Miscues that occur on the first or last words of a sentence cannot be acceptable with only a portion of a sentence.

How to Read for Semantic Acceptability

■   Does the miscue occur in a structure that is semantically acceptable in the reader's dialect?

Semantic acceptability depends on syntactic acceptability. Therefore, if the miscue is syntactically unacceptable, the miscue is considered semantically unacceptable and must be coded **N** for question 2.

If the miscue is syntactically partially acceptable (**P**), the miscue may be semantically unacceptable (**N**) or partially acceptable (**P**). If the miscue is syntactically acceptable (**Y**), the miscue may be coded for semantic acceptability as **Y**, **P**, or **N**.

To determine semantic acceptability, we read the miscue exactly as it is read for syntactic acceptability; that is, we read the entire sentence, *except for the miscue in question,* as the reader finally produced it.

If the miscue is found to be semantically acceptable within the sentence, we read the sentence to determine its acceptability within the entire story or article. If the miscue is acceptable within the entire text, the miscue is coded **Y**. If the miscue is acceptable at the sentence level only, it is coded **P**.

If the miscue is found to be semantically unacceptable within the entire sentence, the next step is to determine if it is acceptable with the beginning of the sentence up to and including the miscue. If the beginning of the sentence, including the miscue, is not acceptable, we judge the semantic acceptability of the sentence portion from the point of the miscue to the end of the sentence. If only the beginning portion (including the miscue) or only the end portion of the sentence (including the miscue) is judged acceptable, the miscue is coded **P** in column 2.

If the miscue is an omission, we read one word beyond the omission or one word before the omission when judging for partial acceptability.

Sometimes miscues that might otherwise be considered acceptable are coded as unacceptable because prior or subsequent unacceptable miscues in the sentence or the sentence portion result in a structure that is syntactically or semantically unacceptable.

Examples of Responses to Questions 1 and 2 Coded YY

Y   The miscue is completely *syntactically acceptable* within the sentence and within the entire text.

Y   The miscue is completely *semantically acceptable* within the sentence and within the entire text.

0108-9   It is the/sound of your heart beating.

0328   Then listen to his heart again.

Gordon's miscues (*It's* for *It is, heartbeat* for *heart beating,* and *the* for *his* and *beat* for *heart*) result in sentences that sound like language and make sense in the total story. Each miscue is therefore considered both syntactically and semantically acceptable, **YY**.

Examples of Responses to Questions 1 and 2 Coded YP and YN

Y   The miscue is completely *semantically acceptable* within the sentence and within the entire text.

P The miscue is *semantically acceptable* with either the first or last part of the sentence only.

N The miscue is not *semantically acceptable*.

They were coming up the hill toward me, about

elves
fifteen ewes and their lambs.

The reader replaces the plural noun *ewes* with the plural noun *elves* and produces a syntactically acceptable sentence, **Y**. The miscue *elves* for *ewes* is semantically acceptable within the sentence because it may be possible, in a fantasy, for elves to own lambs, but this story is not a fantasy; therefore, *elves* is not an acceptable substitution at the story level and consequently is coded **P**.

0301-2 ⓇⒸ *feels* Ⓒc- Ⓒ *oranges*
Blood feeds all the cells and organs.

In this example, Gordon produces syntactically acceptable miscues in the entire sentence and story. He substitutes the verb *feels* for the verb *feeds* and the plural noun *oranges* for the plural noun *organs*. However, *feels* for *feeds* is semantically acceptable only with the first part of the sentence because of the miscue *oranges* for *organs*; therefore, it is coded **YP**. *Oranges* for *organs* is not semantically acceptable in the sentence; therefore the coding is **YN**.

Examples of Responses to Questions 1 and 2 Coded YN

Y The miscue is completely *syntactically acceptable* within the sentence and within the entire text.

N The miscue is not *semantically acceptable*.

building
I came down the hill like a boulder.

The substitution of *building* for *boulder* is syntactically acceptable, **Y**, since it is a noun for a noun. However, the substitution is not semantically acceptable, **N**, because a person cannot be compared to a building in relation to coming down a hill.

0116-8 *$mu-si-cle*
Your heart is a hollow muscle divided into four parts.

The substitution of the nonword *$mu-si'-cle* for *muscle* is syntactically acceptable, **Y**. Gordon's intonation of the phrase, *Your heart is a hollow $mu-si'-cle*, shows that the nonword is a noun, and therefore the phrase sounds like language. But because *$mu-si'-cle* is not an English word, the substitution does not make sense and the miscue is marked semantically unacceptable, **N**.

Examples of Responses to Questions 1 and 2 Coded PP

Miscues are *partially syntactically* and *partially semantically* acceptable in three ways:

- Partially acceptable with the first part of the sentence, including the miscue (and one word beyond if the miscue is an omission).

- Partially acceptable with the last part of the sentence, including the miscue (and one word before if the miscue is an omission).

- Acceptable within the sentence only, but not in the entire text.

P   The miscue is *syntactically acceptable* with the first part of the sentence.

P   The miscue is *semantically acceptable* with the first part of the sentence.

0502   . . . He pulled the end of the

0503   rope ⓒ up out of the fireplace . . .

This miscue is evidence of Betsy's ability to predict a possible structure. The structure is acceptable up to and including the miscue, although it is not acceptable in the entire sentence. The substitution of *up* for *out* is coded **P**, since it has the potential of resulting in a syntactically acceptable sentence, such as *He pulled the end of the rope up (the chimney)*. This miscue cannot be coded acceptable for semantic acceptability because miscues cannot be coded higher semantically than syntactically. The miscue is coded **P** for semantic acceptability because it produces a sentence beginning that makes sense up to and including the miscue and has the potential of producing an acceptable sentence.

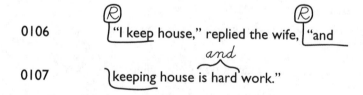

0106   Ⓡ "I keep house," replied the wife, Ⓡ "and

0107   keeping house is hard work."

Betsy's miscue, *and* substituted for *is hard*, is coded partially syntactically acceptable, **P**, because the sentence portion is acceptable up to and including the miscue. Partial acceptability is determined by attempting to add an acceptable ending after the miscue such as *"I keep house," replied the wife, "and keeping house and (looking after you) is hard work."* This miscue cannot be coded **Y** for semantic acceptability because it is not completely syntactically acceptable within the text. The miscue is coded **P** for semantic acceptability, because the beginning of the sentence makes sense up to and including the miscue, *and* for *is hard*.

P   The miscue is *syntactically acceptable* with the last part of the sentence.

P   The miscue is *semantically acceptable* with the last part of the sentence.

0112-3   *start house keeping*
                 . . . I'll stay home and keep house," said the woodman.

The substitution of *keeping* for *keep* is coded **P**; when the miscue is included with the last portion of the sentence, the resulting structure is partially syntactically acceptable. This judgment can be facilitated by adding a potential syntactically acceptable beginning, e.g., *("I like cooking) and keeping house," said the woodman.* This miscue is coded **P** for semantic acceptability because it cannot be coded higher semantically than syntactically.

Examples of Responses to Questions 1 and 2
Coded PN

P   The miscue is *syntactically acceptable* with either the first or last part of the sentence or is acceptable at the sentence level.

N   The miscue is not *semantically acceptable.*

0104-7
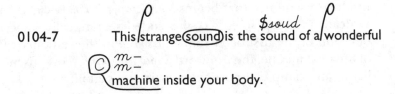

Gordon's intonation indicates that his nonword substitution of *$soud* for *sound* is a noun for a noun. However, the miscue is not acceptable in the entire sentence because of the omission of the first noun, *sound.* Because *$soud* is syntactically acceptable with the end of the sentence only, it is coded **P**. The substitution of the nonword *$soud* for *sound* does not carry semantic meaning; therefore, the miscue is not semantically acceptable and is coded **N**.

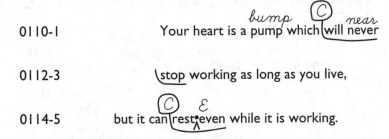

To answer questions 1 and 2 for the insertion of the period, consider Gordon's intonation as he finally read this sentence: *Your heart is a bump which will never stop working as long as you live, but it can rest. Even while it is working.* The insertion of a period is coded partially syntactically acceptable, **P,** because of the sentence fragment *Even while it is working.* The miscue is semantically unacceptable because of a previous miscue in the sentence, *bump* for *pump,* which does not make sense in this sentence and is therefore coded semantically unacceptable, **N**. In such situations, in which readers transform sentences, the unit of analysis for coding acceptability is always the sentence in the written text.

Examples of Responses to Questions 1 and 2 Coded NN

N   The miscue is not *syntactically acceptable.*

N   The miscue is not *semantically acceptable.*

Semantic acceptability cannot be coded higher than syntactic acceptability.

0104-7   This /strange (sound) is the sound of a/wonderful   *$soud*

m –
m –
© machine inside your body.

Gordon's omission of the noun *sound,* in this case the subject of the sentence, causes this miscue to be syntactically unacceptable, **N**. It is not possible to produce a sentence that begins *This strange is the.* Because this miscue is syntactically unacceptable, it is also coded semantically unacceptable, **N**. The omission of the first occurrence of *sound* in the sentence affects the coding of the next miscue, the nonword *$soud* for *sound.* This miscue is discussed earlier as an example of partial syntactic acceptability.

Here
Her name was Sandy.

The adverb *Here,* substituted for the pronoun *Her,* is syntactically unacceptable. Semantic acceptability cannot be coded higher than syntactic acceptability, **NN**.

Example of Sentences with Miscues That Are Difficult to Code

© then fingers
0503-5   Place \three fingertips of your right hand

UC worst
$wrist
w –
w –
side
on the inside of your left \wrist.

Gordon produces a sentence that is complex to code. In coding *then* for *three,* we read the sentence: *Place then fingers of your right hand on the side of your left worst.* Even though *then* for *three* is corrected, Gordon's first attempt is read when coding the miscue in question, *then* for *three.* Therefore, *then* for *three* is both syntactically and semantically unacceptable and coded **N**; it is not acceptable with either the prior or subsequent portions of the sentence. Because *worst* is the last attempt for *wrist, worst* is read as the final word of the sentence.

To code *fingers* for *fingertips,* we read the sentence: *Place three fingers of your right hand on the side of your left worst.* Because the sentence is read as the reader resolved it, *then* is read as corrected to *three. Fingers* for *fingertips* must be coded **PP**; it would have been fully acceptable both semantically and syntactically, except for the miscue of *worst* for *wrist.*

To code *side* for *inside*, we read the sentence: *Place three fingers of your right hand on the side of your left worst.* Because the sentence is read as the reader resolved it, *then* is read as corrected to *three*. Because the miscue on *wrist* results in *worst*, a word that does not fit either syntactically or semantically, *side* must be coded **PP**. These miscues (*fingers* and *side*) are acceptable only within the prior portion of the sentence (the miscue on *three* was corrected), for both semantic and syntactic acceptability.

The miscue of *$wist*, the first nonword or word substituted for *wrist*, is the miscue selected for coding and is syntactically acceptable. Gordon's intonation indicates that the nonword is the object of the preposition and therefore sounds like language. The substitution is not semantically acceptable, since there is no such word as *$wist* in English. The miscue is coded **YN** for questions 1 and 2.

Gordon's miscue numbers 44 to 47 are coded on the portion of the In-Depth Procedure Coding Form, shown in Figure 7.2. Coding for Gordon's entire reading of *The Beat of My Heart* appears in Appendix B.

Figure 7.2: Gordon's Miscues on the In-Depth Procedure Coding Form

MISCUE No./LINE No.	READER	TEXT	1 CORRECTION	2 MEANING CHANGE	3 SEMANTIC ACCEPTABILITY	4 SYNTACTIC ACCEPTABILITY
44	then	three	N	N	—	Y
45	fingers	fingertips	P	P	—	N
46	side	inside	P	P	—	N
47	$wist	wrist	Y	N	—	P

MEANING CHANGE (QUESTION 3)

■ Does the miscue change the meaning of the entire text?

The answers to question 3 help observers evaluate the degree to which readers change the author's text. See the discussion of Meaning Change in Chapter 5.

How to Read for Meaning Change

This question is asked only if the miscue is coded completely syntactically and semantically acceptable **YY**. If questions 1 and 2 result in **YP**, **YN**, **PP**, or **NN** patterns, we do not ask question 3 concerning meaning change; we place a dash on the coding sheet. The dash does not mean that there is no meaning change, but that the degree of change is indeterminate.

To analyze meaning change, read the text as written, except for the miscue in question, which is read as the reader produced it. In other words, no matter how many miscues there are in the sentence, change everything back to the ER except for the miscue under consideration. (Even if the miscue under consideration is corrected, or if there are multiple attempts on the miscue, the first attempt is read for coding.) This move causes us to focus on the potential effect of a single miscue on the entire passage. Question 3 differs from questions 1 and 2, in which the influence of all the miscues in the sentence is considered as each individual miscue is coded. Following are examples of responses to question 3. Most of the examples are from Betsy (In-Depth Procedure Coding Form, Figure 7.3) or from Gordon (Appendix B).

Examples of Miscues That Result in No Change of Meaning (N)

In the following examples there is no change of meaning. Therefore each is coded **N** for meaning change in the question 3 column.

0201   So the next mor̶n̶i̶n̶g̶ *day* the wife went off to

0202   the forest. The husband stayed home and

0203   began to do his wife's w̶o̶r̶k̶ *job*.

Betsy's substitution of *day* for *morning* and *job* for *work* involves no meaning change in this story; both are coded **N** for meaning change.

0108-9   *It's* It is the sound of your heart b̶e̶a̶t̶i̶n̶g̶ *heartbeat*

Gordon changes *It is* to the contraction *It's*. He substitutes *heartbeat* for *heart beating*. Neither miscue results in a change of meaning in this article; both are coded **N** for meaning change.

0121-2   As you grow, it (too) will grow in size.

Gordon's omission of *too* causes no change of meaning (**N**).

0328   Then listen to his heart *the beat* again.

Because the reference for *the beat* is obviously *his heart*, each substitution involves no change of meaning (**N**).

0208   *So* Soon the cream will turn into butter *buttermilk*.

To consider *So* for *Soon*, the sentence is read *So the cream will turn into butter.* Both *So* and *Soon* indicate impending action. Betsy's substitution involves no change of meaning in this story. The miscue is coded **N** in the Meaning Change column.

Examples of Miscues That Result in Inconsistency, Loss, or Change of a Minor Idea, Incident, Character, Fact, Sequence, or Concept (P)

In the following examples of inconsistency, loss, or change of a minor idea, incident, character, fact, sequence, or concept, there is a partial change of meaning. Therefore each is coded **P** in the question 3 column.

0208   *So* Soon the cream will turn into *buttermilk* butter.

To consider *buttermilk* for *butter*, the sentence is read: *Soon the cream will turn into buttermilk.* Betsy's substitution constitutes a minor change in the entire story because buttermilk is part of the process of making butter. The miscue is coded **P**.

0307   ©®*jumped RM cream* ‖It bumped into the churn, knocking it

Betsy substitutes *jumped* for *bumped*, constituting a minor meaning change. The major fact is that the churn was knocked over, not how it was knocked over. However, the substitution is coded **P** because there is a *minor* difference in meaning in this story between the pig bumping the churn and jumping into it.

0610-12   *st– st– st–* ® © ® *keep* ‖The wife‖stayed home‖to keep house and to look

uc C ①*the children* after‖their child.

The number of children in the family is a *minor* factor in this story; therefore *children* for *child* is marked **P** in the Meaning Change column. (There is no change [**N**] in the substitution of *keep after* for *look after*. And because the author has made it clear that *the child* belongs to the woodman and his wife, the substitution of *the* for *their* involves no meaning change [**N**]).

Examples of Miscues That Result in Inconsistency, Loss, or Change of a Major Idea, Incident, Character, Fact, Sequence, or Concept (Y)

Because neither Betsy nor Gordon had any major meaning changes in their miscues, the following examples of inconsistency, loss, or change of a major idea, incident, character, fact, sequence, or concept are from other readers.

But the people could (not) get the fruit from the tree.

Since getting fruit from the tree, in this story, is central to the plot, the omission of *not* is a major meaning change. The omission of *not* is coded **Y** in the Meaning Change column.

silly   *silly*

. . . so tired from his trip that he got sleepy. Very sleepy.

In this story it is important that readers know that the character is getting *sleepy*. He is not getting *silly*. This substitution constitutes a major meaning change (**Y**).

CORRECTION (QUESTION 4)

- Is the miscue corrected?

Question 4 examines successful, partially successful, and unsuccessful self-correction attempts and reflects the reader's confirmation strategies.

Examples That Show the Miscue is Corrected (Y)

Coding question 4 **Y** shows that the reader corrected miscues.

030   ⓇⒸⓇ *the*   Ⓒ   *heard*   In his hurry, the woodman had left . . .

"I know," Ben said, "We could call him up on the telephone(")"   Ⓒ

where   (")Where(?")everyone asked.

In the first example, Betsy corrects both the substitution of *the* for *his* and *heard* for *had*, resulting in no meaning change for either miscue. In the second example, the OR is *"I know," Ben said. "We could call him up on the telephone where "Where?" everyone asked.* The omission of the *period* after telephone is considered self-corrected even though the reader reread only *Where* with intonation appropriate to the ER. Since readers almost never return to a prior sentence when they correct beginning sentence intonation, the assumption is made that the correction includes the final punctuation at the end of the previous sentence. If the intonation shows that readers know how and where the corrected sentence begins, it suggests that they are aware of the termination of the previous sentence.

Examples That Show an Unsuccessful Attempt to Correct (𝒰𝒞), or Expected Response Is Read, Then Abandoned (𝒶𝒞) (P)

When a reader makes an unsuccessful attempt to correct a miscue, it is marked 𝒰𝒞. If the expected response is read and then abandoned, it is marked 𝒶𝒞. Both miscues are coded **P** in the question 4 column.

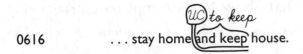

0616

Betsy reads ... *stay home to keep ... to keep ... to keep house.* The miscue is an unsuccessful attempt to correct (𝒰𝒞) and is coded **P**. The reader repeats the same miscue in an unsuccessful attempt to correct.

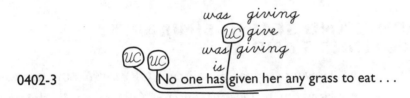

The student reads *a kind of backwa- ... backwards loop.* The unsuccessful multiple attempts to correct (𝒰𝒞) are coded **P**.

0402-3

Betsy reads *No one is ... No one was giving her any ... give ... no one was giving her any.* Betsy's unsuccessful attempts to correct (𝒰𝒞) are coded **P**.

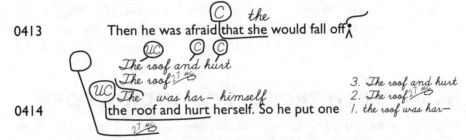

0413

0414

Betsy reads *would fall off. (period) The roof was har..........The roof ... (pause)... The ... roof and hurt himself.* The unsuccessful attempt to correct (𝒰𝒞) is coded **P**.

The student reads *He will surely ... sure know the name of the tree ... .*The reader abandons his correct response (𝒶𝒞). Therefore the miscue is coded **P**.

The student reads *His sister Suzanne was hopping around ... hoping around. Hopping* is abandoned (𝒶𝒞) for *hoping* and therefore coded **P**.

Examples That Show No Attempt to Correct (N)

When a reader miscues and makes no attempt to self correct, it is coded **N**.

0601   *cried*   *shouted*
                              baby crying, and her husband shouting for help.

Betsy read *baby cried, and her husband shouted for help.* Betsy made no attempt to correct the substituted changes in verb tense in either *cried* for *crying*, or *shouted* for *shouting*. No attempt to correct is coded **N**.

0605   *one*
                              and then count once more.

Gordon made no attempt to correct *one more* for *once more*. No attempt to correct is coded **N**.

GRAPHIC AND SOUND SIMILARITY (QUESTIONS 5 AND 6)

- How much does the miscue (OR) *look like* the text word (ER)?
- How much does the miscue (OR) *sound like* the expected response (ER)?

Follow the same evaluation guidelines for Graphic and Sound Similarity (Chapter 5) in the **Classroom Procedure** and in the **In-Depth Procedure**. Code the responses on the In-Depth Procedure Coding Form in columns 5 and 6. (See Betsy's Coding Form [Figure 7.3], Gordon's in Appendix B, and the blank form in Appendix C.)

THE IN-DEPTH PROCEDURE CODING FORM

A minimum of 25 miscues are listed on the Coding Form and analyzed for each of the six questions. For ease of reference, the six questions for the **In-Depth Procedure** are listed in Figure 7.1 and in Appendix A.

MEANING CONSTRUCTION AND GRAMMATICAL RELATIONS

Patterns

In addition to providing a place for coding questions 1–6, the In-Depth Procedure Coding Form also provides a place to check patterns of interrelations for the answers to questions 1, 2, 3, and 4. From these patterns, a percentage is computed to indicate the student's degree of proficiency in using reading process strategies. Information is subsequently entered on the In-Depth Reader Profile Form (Appendix C, Figure 7.7), which includes data from the In-Depth Procedure Coding Form.

Figure 7.3: Miscue Analysis In-Depth Procedure Coding Form

READER _Betsy_ DATE _Nov. 3_

TEACHER _Ms. Blau_ AGE/GRADE _3_

SCHOOL _York Elem._

SELECTION _The Man Who Kept House_

MISCUE No./LINE No.	READER	TEXT	1 SYNTACTIC ACCEPTABILITY	2 SEMANTIC ACCEPTABILITY	3 MEANING CHANGE	4 CORRECTION	MEANING CONSTRUCTION (See 2,3,4) No Loss	Partial Loss	Loss	GRAMMATICAL RELATIONS (See 1,2,4) Strength	Partial Strength	Overcorrection	Weakness	GRAPHIC SIMILARITY 5 H	S	N	SOUND SIMILARITY 6 H	S	N
1	so	some	P	P	—	Y	✓			✓				✓				✓	
2	start	stay	P	P	|	N		✓					✓	✓				✓	
3	house	home	P	P	|	N		✓					✓	✓			✓	✓	
4	keeping	keep	P	P	|	N		✓			✓			✓			✓		
5	well	well	Y	P	|	N		✓							✓			✓	
6	bread	butter	Y	P	|	Y		✓			✓				✓		✓		
7	all	all	Y	Y	N	Y	✓					✓		✓				✓	
8	well	we'll	Y	Y	P	N		✓		✓				✓					✓
9	you	you	Y	Y	P	N				✓									
10	day	morning	Y	Y	N	N	✓			✓					✓				✓
11	job	work	P	P	N	N	✓			✓						✓			✓
12	⊙ and	. As	Y	P	|	N		✓			✓								
13	Sshum	churn	Y	N	|	N			✓		✓			✓			✓		
14	he	. he	Y	P	|	N		✓			✓				✓				
15	the	this	Y	Y	N	Y	✓			✓				✓			✓		
16	So	Soon	Y	Y	N	N	✓			✓				✓				✓	
17	buttermilk	. butter	N	N	|	Y	✓			✓					✓				
18	couldn't	could not	Y	Y	N	Y	✓					✓							
19	There	She	N	N	N	Y	✓			✓				✓			✓		✓
20	is	was	P	P	|	Y	✓			✓						✓			
21	into	to	P	P	|	Y	✓			✓				✓			✓		✓
22	forest	far	P	P	N	N	✓					✓			✓			✓	
23	in	to	Y	Y	N	Y	✓					✓			✓			✓	✓
24	the	his	Y	Y	N	N	✓									✓			✓
25	head	had	P	P	—	Y	✓			✓				✓			✓		
			COLUMN TOTAL																
			PATTERN TOTAL																
			PERCENTAGE																

a. TOTAL MISCUES _____

b. TOTAL WORDS _____

a ÷ b × 100 = MPHW

Goodman, Watson, Burke

Figure 7.3: Miscue Analysis In-Depth Procedure Coding Form (cont.)

READER: Betsy DATE: Nov. 3

TEACHER: Ms. Blau AGE/GRADE: 3

SCHOOL: York Elem.

SELECTION: The Man Who Kept House

MISCUE No./LINE No.	READER	TEXT	1 SYNTACTIC ACCEPTABILITY	2 SEMANTIC ACCEPTABILITY	3 MEANING CHANGE	4 CORRECTION	MEANING CONSTRUCTION (No Loss)	(Partial Loss)	(Loss)	GRAMMATICAL RELATIONS (Strength)	(Partial Strength)	(Overcorrection)	(Weakness)	GRAPHIC H	GRAPHIC S	GRAPHIC N	SOUND H	SOUND S	SOUND N
26	cream	churn	Y	Y	N	N	✓			✓									✓
27	shout	shouted	P	P	—	Y	✓			✓				✓	✓		✓		
28	big	pig	P	P	—	Y	✓			✓				✓	✓		✓		
29	and	the	Y	Y	—	Y	✓			✓				✓		✓	✓		✓
30	jumped	bumped	P	P	P	Y	✓			✓		✓		✓			✓		
31	shout	splashed	P	P	—	Y	✓			✓				✓	✓			✓	
32	I'll	I've	Y	P	—	Y	✓			✓				✓	✓			✓	
33	and	in	P	P	—	P		✓						✓				✓	✓
34	home	house	P	P	—	Y	✓			✓				✓	✓			✓	
35	and	is	P	P	—	N	✓						✓			✓			
36	hard	harder	P	P	—	N		✓					✓	✓			✓		✓
37	work..."thought"	work..."thought"	P	P	—	P		✓					✓	✓		✓			
38	Then	than	Y	P	N	Y	✓			✓									✓
39	he	I	Y	Y	P	N	✓			✓						✓			
40	the	a	P	Y	N	N	✓			✓						✓			
41	basket	bucket	Y	Y	—	N		✓		✓				✓			✓		✓
42	the	a	Y	P	N	Y	✓			✓						✓	✓		
43	I'll	the	P	Y	N	Y	✓					✓							
44	flash	few minutes	Y	Y	N	P		✓				✓		✓	✓		✓	✓	
45	is	has	Y	Y	N	P	✓												
46	giving	given	P	Y	—	N			✓				✓						
47	and	.	P	P	—	Y	✓			✓									✓
48	the	he	P	P	—	Y	✓			✓				✓			✓		
49	the	she	P	P	—	Y				✓				✓					✓
50	off the	off the	P	P		P		✓					✓						
		COLUMN TOTAL																	
		PATTERN TOTAL																	
		PERCENTAGE																	

a. TOTAL MISCUES _____

b. TOTAL WORDS _____

a ÷ b × 100 = MPHW _____

Goodman, Watson, Burke

Figure 7.3: Miscue Analysis In-Depth Procedure Coding Form (cont.)

READER Betsy DATE Nov. 3

TEACHER Mr. Blau AGE/GRADE 3

SCHOOL York Elem.

SELECTION The Man Who Kept House

MISCUE No./LINE No.	READER	TEXT	1 SYNTACTIC ACCEPTABILITY	2 SEMANTIC ACCEPTABILITY	3 MEANING CHANGE	4 CORRECTION	MEANING CONSTRUCTION (See 2,3,4) No Loss	Partial Loss	Loss	GRAMMATICAL RELATIONS (See 1,2,4) Strength	Partial Strength	Overcorrection	Weakness	GRAPHIC SIMILARITY (5) H	S	N	SOUND SIMILARITY (6) H	S	N
51	was	and	P	P	—	Y	✓			✓						✓			✓
52	himself	herself	N	N	—	N			✓				✓	✓	✓		✓	✓	
53	the	a	Y	Y	N	N		✓		✓					✓				
54	to	to	P	Y	P	Y	✓			✓				✓			✓		
55	up	out	P	P	—	N	✓			✓					✓				✓
56	then	and .	Y	Y	N	Y	✓					✓			✓			✓	
57	he	and	Y	Y	N	N	✓			✓				✓			✓		
58	the	this	Y	Y	N	Y	✓			✓				✓			✓		✓
59	is	he	P	P	—	N	✓			✓				✓				✓	
60	hang	hung	P	P	—	Y		✓					✓	✓			✓		
61	never	over	P	N	—	N			✓				✓	✓			✓		
62	sprawn	ground	P	P	—	N		✓					✓	✓				✓	
63	he	she	P	P	—	N		✓		✓				✓				✓	
64	cried	crying	P	P	—	N		✓						✓			✓		
65	shouted	shouting	P	P	—	N		✓						✓			✓		
66	to	the	P	Y	—	Y	✓			✓						✓			✓
67	And	a	Y	Y	N	Y	✓					✓		✓				✓	
68	leg	legs	Y	P	N	N	✓			✓				✓			✓		
69	her	his	Y	Y	—	Y	✓			✓				✓				✓	
70	keep	look	Y	Y	N	N		✓				✓		✓				✓	
71	the	their	P	Y	—	P	✓			✓				✓	✓			✓	
72	children	child	P	P	P	Y		✓				✓		✓				✓	
73	(?)that he	"What did you	P	P	—	Y	✓			✓		✓							✓
74	the	he	P	P	—	Y	✓			✓						✓			✓
75	to keep	and keep	Y	Y	N	P		✓					✓						

	COLUMN TOTAL	PATTERN TOTAL	PERCENTAGE
MEANING CONSTRUCTION No Loss	46	75	61%
Partial Loss	25		33%
Loss	4		5%
GRAMMATICAL RELATIONS Strength	42	75	56%
Partial Strength	5		7%
Overcorrection	13		17%
Weakness	15		20%
GRAPHIC SIMILARITY H	33	60	55%
S	17		28%
N	10		17%
SOUND SIMILARITY H	26	60	43%
S	18		30%
N	16		27%

a. TOTAL MISCUES 75

b. TOTAL WORDS 711

a ÷ b × 100 = MPHW 10.55

Goodman, Watson, Burke

Meaning Construction and *Grammatical Relations* on the Coding Form provide information resulting in percentages that show interrelations of the reading strategies. It is important to be aware that the resulting percentages reflect the miscue data only and do not consider large portions of the text including words, phrases, or sentences that are read as expected, that is, read without miscues.

Patterns for Constructing Meaning

The patterns for constructing meaning indicate the influence of the miscues on the reader's concern for making sense of the text. The coding in columns 2, 3, and 4 are used to mark the patterns of No Loss, Partial Loss, or Loss of meaning.

No Loss. This pattern includes miscues that are coded as semantically acceptable with no meaning change or, if not acceptable, are corrected. No loss patterns reflect high-quality miscues and show the reader's concern for making sense of the entire text.

Partial Loss. This pattern includes miscues that are coded either fully semantically acceptable with some meaning change or partially semantically acceptable. Such miscues may have no attempt at correction, or there may be unsuccessful correction attempts. These miscues show that the reader is using some strategies appropriately.

Loss. This pattern includes miscues that are coded semantically unacceptable with no correction attempts or unsuccessful correction attempts, or the miscue is partially semantically acceptable with no attempt to correct. Loss patterns indicate that the reader is having trouble with specific portions of the text.

The Meaning Construction and Grammatical Relations sections of the In-Depth Procedure Coding Form refer to the first four columns:

1. Syntactic acceptability
2. Semantic acceptability
3. Meaning change
4. Correction

Figure 7.4 includes all the possible patterns that result in no loss, partial loss, and loss of meaning. The letters (**Y**, **N**, and **P**) in columns 2, 3, and 4 combine to establish a *meaning construction pattern*. For example, under Meaning Construction, in the No Loss column, **Y**, **N**, and **Y** under columns 2, 3, and 4 indicate a miscue that is semantically acceptable, with no meaning change, or is corrected (if there is a meaning change). The dashes in column 3 indicate that the category is not marked because the miscue is not semantically and syntactically fully acceptable and therefore meaning change is not evaluated. Only columns 2, 3, and 4 are used for determining meaning construction patterns.

Figure 7.4: Meaning Construction Patterns

No Loss			Partial Loss			Loss		
2	3	4	2	3	4	2	3	4
Y	N	Y	Y	P	N	N	—	N
Y	N	N	Y	N	P	N	—	P
Y	P	Y	Y	Y	P	P	—	N*
Y	Y	Y	Y	Y	N			
P	—	Y	Y	P	P			
N	—	Y	P	—	P			
			P	—	N*			

*This pattern is coded Loss except in a few cases. The criteria for Partial Loss and Loss need to be considered carefully.

For the most part, coding the patterns is straightforward. We note a pattern on the Coding Form (questions 2, 3, and 4), locate it on the list of Patterns for Meaning Construction and check it off in the appropriate column (No Loss, Partial Loss, Loss). However, for one pattern, **P–N** (Partial Semantic Acceptability, Meaning Change not evaluated and No Correction), it is necessary to evaluate the degree of meaning construction. In most cases, a pattern coded as **P** for question 2, left blank in question 3, and not corrected **N** is coded a loss of meaning. However, under two conditions such a pattern results in **P**, partial loss:

- If the miscue is coded acceptable, except for other miscues in the sentence, such as Betsy's insertion of *well,* and substitution of *bread* for *butter.*

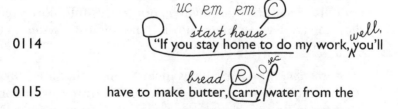

- If the miscue is acceptable except for minor syntactic shifts, such as connectives, tense, or number, as in Betsy's substitution of *and* for the *period* and *as,* line 0204, the substitution of a *period* for a *comma,* line 0205, and the substitution of *cried* and *shouted* for *crying* and *shouting,* line 0601.

0204   He began to make some butter. *and* As he put

0205   the cream into the *$shurn.* churn, he said, "This is

0206   not going to be hard work.

0407-8   some water. *and* Ⓡ "I haven't time to

A consistent rationale should be developed in making decisions about the Partial Loss Column. For example, Betsy's miscue of the substitution of *and* for the *period* and *As* (line 0204) results in an acceptable clause relationship even though the clause dependencies are changed. These two sentences are acceptable except for the nonword, *$shurn.* This miscue is therefore coded as a partial loss. The substitution of *and* for a *period* (line 0407) seems, on the surface, to be a similar miscue; however, the conjunction *and*, in this case, is used to connect a declarative sentence within the ongoing narration with a sentence representing dialogue. Therefore, this is more than a minor syntactic shift and is marked a loss.

Patterns for Grammatical Relations

The patterns of grammatical relations are found by examining syntactic acceptable (question 1), semantic acceptable (question 2), and correction (question 4). As shown in Figure 7.5, these patterns are categorized to show a reader's use of grammatical relations, that is, the ability to produce text that sounds like language.

The following four patterns are possible:

Strength. Miscue patterns include those that are syntactically and semantically acceptable and, if not, are corrected. These patterns reveal the reader's strength in integrating reading strategies.

Partial. Miscue patterns include those that are syntactically acceptable, but not fully semantically acceptable, nor successfully corrected. These patterns show the reader's strength in using the linguistic system, but not always successful in integrating meaning.

Overcorrection. Miscue patterns include those that are fully acceptable, both syntactically and semantically, and do not need correction, but the reader corrects, indicating the reader's excessive concern for exactness and focus on surface features of the text.

Weakness. Miscue patterns include those that are not fully syntactically acceptable, nor semantically acceptable, nor successfully corrected. Readers with these patterns often short-circuit their reading, attempting for accuracy on a surface level rather than using reading strategies to make their reading sound like language.

Figure 7.5: Patterns for Grammatical Relations

Strength			Partial Strength			Overcorrection			Weakness		
1	2	4	1	2	4	1	2	4	1	2	4
N	N	Y	Y	N	N	Y	Y	Y	N	N	N
P	N	Y	Y	P	N	Y	Y	P	P	N	N
Y	N	Y	Y	N	P				P	P	N
P	P	Y	Y	P	P				N	N	P
Y	P	Y							P	N	P
Y	Y	N							P	P	P

STATISTICAL ANALYSIS

After marking and coding miscues and compiling the meaning construction and grammatical relations patterns on the In-Depth Procedure Coding Form, it is time for a statistical analysis of the data. To provide statistical data to transfer to the Reader Profile Form (see Appendix C and Figure 7.7), tally both patterns (meaning construction and grammatical relations), along with graphic similarity and sound similarity, as follows:

- Count the marks for each column and place the total in the Column Total box on the Coding Form.

- Count the marks for meaning construction, grammatical relations, graphic similarity, and sound similarity and place the totals in the boxes marked Pattern Total. The totals for questions 5 and 6 may differ from the totals for the two patterns, because only word-for-word substitutions are coded for these two questions, and every selected miscue (excluding some repeated miscues) is coded for the questions that result in the two patterns. However, the totals for 5 and 6 should be the same, and the totals of the two patterns should be the same.

- Percentages are computed for each column by dividing the column total by the pattern total. The decimal answer is changed into a percentage by multiplying the quotient by 100 or by moving the decimal point two places to the right. To check for accuracy, total the column percentages for each question or pattern. Because the totals are rounded to the nearest tenth, the totals fall between 99 and 101 percent. If the observer computes statistics for both the Classroom Procedure (in which the sentences are coded from the beginning of the story or article) and the In-Depth Procedure (in which the miscues are not coded from the beginning of the story or article), there will, of course, be a discrepancy in the totals and in the percentages. (See Betsy's Classroom Procedure Coding Form [Figure 6.5] and In-Depth Procedure Coding Form [Figure 7.3] and Reader Profile Form [Figures 6.6 and 7.7].)

Figure 7.6: Retelling Guide: In Depth Procedure

Reader: _Betsy_   Date: _November 3_

The Man Who Kept House

Character Analysis:
(40 points)

Recall (20 points)
9 – Man (husband)   ✔
9 – Woman (wife)   ✔
2 – Baby   ✔
                       _20_

Development (20 points)
Husband
    2 – Woodman   ✔
    3 – Thought he worked very hard   ✔
    5 – Changed attitude over time   _1_
Housewife
    5 – Worked Hard   _4_
    5 – Accepted challenges   _1_
                                            _11_

Events:
(60 points)

- The woodman thinks he works very hard. He comes home and asks his wife what she does all day. The wife responds that she keeps house and keeping house is hard work. (10 points)   _10_

- The husband challenges the wife to change places. The wife agrees and tells husband what he has to do. The husband says they will change places the next day. (10 points)   _8_

- The wife goes off to the forest and the husband stays home. (5 points)   _5_

- The husband is involved in a number of events that cause problems: (15 points)   _13_

    Butter making.   ①

    Baby cries and woodman goes to find her. He leaves the door open.   ②

    Pig gets into the house, the woodman chases it and the pig spills the cream.   ②

    Woodman starts to clean up the mess.   ①

    The baby cries again and the woodman prepares to feed the baby.   ②

    The cow's mooing interrupts the woodman who realizes that the cow needs to be fed. He puts the cow on the roof to feed. He is afraid the cow might fall off the roof so he throws the rope from the cow's neck down the chimney. When he gets into the house he ties the rope to his own leg.   ④

    As he thinks again about the porridge, the cow falls off the roof pulling the woodman up the chimney. The cow and woodman are hanging, one in the house and one outside.   ①

Figure 7.6: Retelling Guide: In Depth Procedure (continued)

■ As the wife returns home she hears the commotion. She cuts the cow down and then finds her husband upside down with his head in the porridge pot. (10 points)   *10*

■ Every day after that the husband goes to his work and the wife to hers. The husband never again asks the wife what she does every day nor says he will do her work. (10 points)   *10*

Points – character analysis   *31*

Points – events   *56*

Total Points   *87*

Plot

The old man believes his work is harder than his wife's. When he trades places with her he discovers her work is more complicated and harder than he thought.

I'd say it was about a woodman who thought he had a harder job than his wife and he didn't so he stopped saying it.

Theme

Things aren't always as easy as they appear to be. Keeping house is demanding work. A woman's job is just as hard as a man's. The grass is always greener on the other side of the fence.

People shouldn't brag about all they have to do. Other people prove that they work just as hard as they do.

■ The In-Depth Procedure Coding Form also provides a place for the computation of miscues per 100 words. The number of words read should reflect only those words read for the miscue portion of the text. Betsy's miscue portion of *The Man Who Kept House* (McInnes 1962) starts on line 0112 and continues to the end of the story, line 0616. There are 711 words in this section. (There are 791 words in the entire story.) The total number of coded miscues is divided by the total number of words read. The quotient is multiplied by 100, which provides a miscues-per-100-words score.

■ The In-Depth Coding Form data are transferred to the In-Depth Reader Profile Form in order to have all the statistical as well as the qualitative data in one place (see Betsy's in Figure 7.7 and Gordon's in Appendix B).

RETELLING GUIDE AND SCORING

As suggested in Chapter 3, preparation for the retelling should be completed before the oral reading session. The Narrative and Expository Retelling Guides (Appendix C) are commonly used with the In-Depth Procedure.

If a retelling score is needed, it is convenient to use a Retelling Guide as a scoring form with a total of 100 points, as we have done with *The Man Who Kept House* and *The Beat of My Heart* (Retelling Guide, In-Depth Procedure, Appendix C). The point distribution chosen depends on the passage and the use made of the retelling score.

Many stories can be divided into 40 points for character analysis and 60 points for events. Character analysis is made up of (a) recall of characters and (b) information concerning each character. Events include major and minor events or idea units, with appropriate points given for each. In *The Man Who Kept House*, 40 points are assigned for character analysis (20 points for naming the three characters and 20 points for describing them). Six major events are listed with 5 to 15 points for each, depending on their importance, making a total of 60 points. For the complete story, 100 points are designated. Theme and plot may or may not be scored, depending on the use of the retelling score.

Typically, expository text is assigned 40 points for specifics, 30 points for generalizations, and 30 points for major concepts. Within each category, the point range depends on the text emphasis. In *The Beat of My Heart* (Appendixes B and C), 50 points are assigned for specific information and 25 points each for generalizations and major concepts. *The Beat of My Heart* is unusual in that, in addition to specific information, the author provides facts within the context of four experiments that the reader is to do to learn about the heart. Although these experiments lead to generalizations, their primary intent is to provide specific information.

When scoring or assigning points to the retelling, consider your own goals, the text itself, and the interests, age, and ability of the reader. For classroom or school purposes, assessment is best done by keeping students' records over time.

Betsy's scored retelling of *The Man Who Kept House* is in Figure 7.6. Gordon's scored retelling of *The Beat of My Heart* is in Appendix B.

The language of the Retelling Guide is used as a reminder of the published text. If students produce alternate language, plots, themes, generalizations, or events that are appropriate, they are considered alternatives and scored accordingly.

Teachers/researchers may prefer to use the Retelling Summary Form (Appendix C).

THE IN-DEPTH READER PROFILE

The In-Depth Procedure Reader Profile Form (Appendix C) is a form for instructional purposes and continuous recordkeeping. See Betsy's profile (Figure 7.7) below, Gordon's in Appendix B, and a blank form in Appendix

Figure 7.7: Miscue Analysis In-Depth Procedure Reader Profile

© 2005 Richard C. Owen Publishers, Inc.

READER **Betsy** DATE **November 3**

TEACHER **Mr. Blau** AGE/GRADE **3** SCHOOL **York Elem.**

SELECTION **The Man Who Kept House**

	%	%
MEANING CONSTRUCTION		PERCENT
No Loss	61	} 94
Partial Loss	33	
Loss	5	
GRAMMATICAL RELATIONS		
Strength	56	} 80
Partial Strength	7	
Overcorrection	17	
Weakness	20	
GRAPHICS/SOUND RELATIONS		
Graphic Similarity		
High	55	} 83
Some	28	
None	17	
Sound Similarity		
High	43	} 73
Some	30	
None	27	
RETELLING		
Characters	31	
Events	56	
Total	87	
Holistic Score		

MPHW **10.55** TIME **19 minutes**

REPEATED MISCUES ACROSS TEXT

LINE	READER	TEXT	COMMENTS (place in text, correction, etc.)
113-	start	stay	first occurrence of stay
114	start	stay	start home for stay home 2 times gets stayed (202); stay (513) (616)
113	house	home	no miscue on first occurrence (103)
114	house	home	no miscue on home 4 out of 6 times
			miscues home for house (312) but no miscue on house 13 times
205	tshurn	churn	never produces ER
304	cream	churn	syn. & sem. acceptable
307	cream	churn	syn. & sem. acceptable
207	the	this	In the majority of cases she gets the and this appropriately. Her substitutions of function words are either semantically and syntactically acceptable or corrected.
505	the	this	
510	hang	hung	Only two occurrences of the OR: irregular verb form.
512	hang	hung	

COMMENTS For the most part Betsy uses predicting and confirming strategies proficiently. She may be overattending to surface features of text.

Goodman, Watson, Burke

C. Biographical and procedural information are written at the top of the form; additions and changes made to accommodate the particular interests or concerns of the observer.

The percentages that show patterns for meaning construction, grammatical relations, and graphic/sound relations are taken from the In-Depth Coding Form and placed on the In-Depth Reader Profile Form. The retelling score is carried over from the Retelling Guide.

Miscues per 100 words may be entered from the In-Depth Procedure Coding Form. The length of reading time is optional information. There is a General Comments section in which relevant comments, including information from the Burke Reading Interview (Burke 1980, Squires 2001, see Chapter 9 and Appendix C), can be noted.

Repeated Miscues Across the Text on the In-Depth Procedure Reader Profile Form is the same as the Classroom Procedure Profile Form (see Chapter 6).

CHECKLIST FOR THE IN-DEPTH PROCEDURE

Figure 7.8 is a checklist for administering the **In-Depth Procedure**.

Figure 7.8: In-Depth Procedure Checklist

- ☐ Select student.
- ☐ Select material.
- ☐ Prepare typescript.
- ☐ Prepare Retelling Guide.
- ☐ Prepare tape recorder and setting.

Collect data:

- ☐ Burke Reading Interview.
- ☐ Oral reading and miscue marking.
- ☐ Retelling.
- ☐ Listen to recording and verify miscue marking.

Coding and Recording:

- ☐ Score retelling on Retelling Guide.
- ☐ Code a minimum of 25 miscues for questions 1–6.
- ☐ Code patterns of meaning construction and grammatical relations.
- ☐ Compute statistics for meaning construction and grammatical relations patterns and questions 5–6.
- ☐ Add optional data to Coding Form (MPHW, time, etc.).

Complete Reader Profile:

- ☐ Transfer statistics from Coding Form.
- ☐ Transfer retelling score.
- ☐ List repeated miscues and comments.
- ☐ Add overall comments.

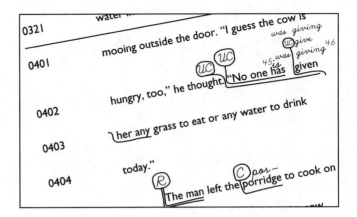

Part III
KNOWING READERS, THEIR INSTRUCTION, AND THEIR CURRICULUM

In the previous chapters of this book, we present alternative miscue analysis procedures that are used to understand the reading process and to analyze and evaluate readers' miscues as they read an entire text. Once teachers gather the miscue analysis data, they often ask, "Now that I have all this information, how do I use it to plan reading instruction for my students?" In this section we revisit the aspects of miscue analysis that support teaching and are used to plan reading instruction for individuals, small groups, and whole classes.

In Chapter 8 we bring together the reader's observed responses and the other information gathered through miscue analysis. We relate the information to different readers (Jamal, Brian, and Sara), with different reading proficiencies as they respond to specific written texts. All the combined data provide rich profiles of readers. The Burke Reading Interview is presented in Chapter 9 as a means of understanding the reader's personal model of reading. Betsy continues to inform us, and in Chapter 10 we present her case study information. In Chapter 11 we discuss reading experiences that are central to the classroom curriculum, followed by specific strategy lessons selected for Betsy and students of varied reading proficiencies.

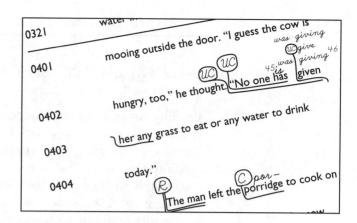

Chapter 8
Reading Miscue Analysis Information

The Reading Miscue Inventory (RMI) is an analytical assessment tool that supports the teacher's knowledge about an individual reading meaningful text. This chapter reviews the different RMI forms that the teacher uses to gather information to organize a profile or case study of a student. It is designed to help teachers look carefully at the RMI data, combined with the responses from the Burke Reading Interview (BRI) (Chapter 9), to determine the strengths and needs of readers and to learn their views of reading and reading instruction.

When a reading miscue analysis is completed, a great deal of information is available in several forms that may be used in planning students' reading instructional programs. This information is found in the reader profile forms, coding forms, typescripts (including the observer's comments in the margins), retellings, and the Burke Reading Interviews.

READER PROFILE FORM

The Reader Profile Forms (Appendix C), which summarizes much of the information from the typescript, coding forms, and retelling, is a starting point for investigating the reader's strengths and needs and for considering instructional experiences and support. Each Reader Profile Form indicates the proficiency with which readers use both their knowledge of language and reading strategies in their transaction with text. The results facilitate discussion of the reader's degree of proficiency on a *particular text*. We now consider the role of the text and provide examples of readers with different proficiency: Jamal as a proficient reader, Brian as moderately proficient, and Sara as nonproficient.

The Role of the Text

No single measure, including one RMI, can be used exclusively to evaluate readers. The text the student reads constitutes a major influence on the reading. If the text is not well-written or not selected with the interest, age, and background of the reader taken into consideration, scores are likely to be depressed.

Reading proficiency is influenced not only by how well readers control the reading process, but also by how interested they are in the material, their purpose for reading, and the background information they bring to the reading. One student may be a highly proficient reader of novels, but only moderately proficient in reading instructions. Another student may construct a great deal of meaning while reading historical fiction, but respond to a history textbook with nonproficient strategies. Reader Profiles are often maintained on students reading a variety of materials, over time, and are used for charting changes and for instructional purposes.

Every reader is unique; every text is unique. A story or article that is familiar to the teacher or to one student may use content or grammatical structures that are new to another reader. In a narrative text, the author may use long clauses and sentences that draw one reader into the story but thwart and frustrate another. In an information piece, the content may be presented in a format that is familiar to some and unfamiliar to others. And in both narrative and expository texts, unfamiliar content puts some readers into situations in which they need to pause, question, and think through new ideas. This unfamiliarity of concepts and formats helps explain why miscues at the beginning of a text reflect the reader's use of complex strategies to adapt to the author's style, unfamiliar formats, and new concepts. All readers face unfamiliar styles and text features. As proficient readers meet such features, they solve problems about unfamiliar concepts, meanings, grammatical structures, and wordings.

We now consider three broad categories of readers by looking more closely at Jamal's, Brian's, and Sara's strengths and at the support they need for reading instruction. We must remember that these readers are identified as proficient, moderately proficient, and nonproficient only as they transact with a particular text.

Proficient Readers

Proficient readers are comfortable meeting new challenges in written texts. They enjoy the undertaking and know they are becoming better readers when they tackle a new and interesting text. Proficient readers know tacitly that sampling from print, predicting, inferring, and confirming or disconfirming their predictions through correction procedures, along with integrating new information with prior knowledge, are necessary for building meaning. Proficient readers constantly ask and answer questions such as, "Does this make sense?" "Does this sound like language?" "What will happen next?" "Does this remind me of anything I know?" "Do I agree with this?" "I don't understand this, so I need to shift my strategies." Proficient readers know that reading new material is exploratory and requires using their knowledge, language, and reading strategies to meet the author's challenges. These readers come to understand that miscues at the beginning of a piece often require them to use complex strategies as they adapt to the genre, format, and author's style. In this way, proficient readers are confident and patient with themselves and know that the results of reading new content and varied structures expand their reading ability.

K. Goodman (1996a) describes proficient readers as those who make both effective and efficient use of the language cuing systems and reading strategies. Such readers produce syntactically and semantically acceptable structures most of the time, either by predicting appropriate structures or by correcting unacceptable ones. They use graphophonic information selectively. Proficient readers' graphic and sound similarity scores may be in a moderate range or lower than those of less proficient readers who depend heavily on graphophonic information. Figure 8.1 is from an In-Depth Procedure Reader Profile of a proficient reader, Jamal. We have chosen the In-Depth Procedure to help us discuss these three readers because it provides the most complete data about the reader.

Figure 8.1: The Pattern Section from Jamal's In-Depth Procedure Reader Profile Form.

PATTERNS	%	%
MEANING CONSTRUCTION	PERCENT	
No Loss	70	}89
Partial Loss	19	
Loss	11	
GRAMMATICAL RELATIONS		
Strength	61	}90
Partial Strength	20	
Overcorrection	9	
Weakness	10	
WORD SUBSTITUTION IN CONTEXT		
Graphic Similarity		
High	62	}79
Some	17	
None	21	
Sound Similarity		
High	62	}78
Some	16	
None	22	
RETELLING		
Characteristics	9.0	
Events	55	
Total	95	
Holistic Score		
MPHW 1.9 TIME ___		
COMMENTS		
See Teacher's Notes		

Goodman, Watson, Burke

While reading *Time Pieces* by Virginia Hamilton (2002), Jamal uses the cues of language selectively and flexibly to produce syntactically and semantically acceptable miscues (shown by 89 percent Meaning Construction and 90 percent Grammatical Relations). He selects graphophonic cues but does not overuse them, since 21 percent and 22 percent of his graphic and sound similarity scores include miscues with no similarity at all. These miscues are all high-level substitutions that do not change the meaning of the passage. Figure 8.2 shows Jamal's teacher's notes that she wrote to help her plan for Jamal's reading development.

Figure 8.2: Teacher's Notes: *Jamal*

Name: *Jamal*   Date: *Jan. 23*   Grade: *7*

Text: *Time Pieces by V. Hamilton*   Genre: *Realistic Fiction*

From Reader Profile Form	Reader's Needs	Support
Meaning Construction 89% (Combined No Loss & Partial Loss)	Needs more time to read and think.	Extend silent reading time. Rethinking and Rereading
Grammatical Relations 90% (Combined Strength, Partial Strength, & Over Correction)	Select from a broader range of genres.	Introduce variety of genres Interests: animals, outdoors, conservation. Begin with science fiction e.g., *Green Boy* by Susan Cooper; *The Exchange Student* by Kate Gilmore.
Graphic & Sound 79% 78% (Combined High & Some)		Brief conference about Jamal's high level miscues. Commend proficient reading.
Retelling, BRI, Conferences, Observations, etc.	Build confidence. Deepen exploration of characterization. Extend writing experiences. Jamal handles most fiction texts proficiently.	Discuss high level miscues. Retrospective Miscue Analysis[1, 2] Characterization Strategy[2] Encourage Critical Conversations[1] in Literature Discussion Group about books, e.g., *The Patchwork People* by Louise Lawrence, that also lead to critical writing.

[1]See Chapter 11.
[2]See *Reading Strategies: Focus on Comprehension* (Y. Goodman, Watson, and Burke 1996).

Moderately Proficient Readers

Moderately proficient readers often see unfamiliar texts as proof they can't read well. Their responses to the BRI (Chapter 9) indicate that, once you become a reader, you should be able to read and understand all texts. It is important for these students to know that at some time all readers struggle with text and the struggles can result in becoming a better reader. Through such understandings, readers come to revalue not only themselves as readers but also the reading process.

Most moderately proficient readers (see Brian's Reader Profile Form, Figure 8.3) make effective use of reading strategies but they are not always efficient. They are often good readers who lack confidence in themselves. These readers produce syntactically and semantically acceptable structures most of the time, but also rely a great deal on graphophonic information. They have a tendency to overcorrect semantically and syntactically acceptable miscues. Their reading is sometimes slow and they often repeat themselves. When this is the case, they are constructing meaning, but they are not efficient in their selection of cues. Although some moderately proficient readers read quickly with appropriate intonation, they may be unable to organize their retellings and usually retell facts or events rather than discuss relations between characters and among concepts. Moderately proficient readers may be able to retell a great deal of what they have read, although they may not, for example, understand subtlety or follow the development of characters.

Moderately proficient readers are proficient with predictable and familiar texts; however, when they read unfamiliar texts with complex sentence structures or with multiple concepts, especially the sort found in content area materials, they may produce a fairly high percentage of syntactically and semantically acceptable sentences while not constructing a great deal of meaning of the text as a whole.

In reading the folktale *The Old Man, the Son and the Donkey* (Y. Goodman and Burke, 1972), Brian's major strength is in constructing meaning 80 percent of the time. However, 30 percent of his miscues are syntactically unacceptable. On these occasions he seems unaware that his reading does not sound like language and disrupts any attempt to create meaning. When he pays close attention to graphophonic cues, he tends to ignore the meaning-making process. Brian pauses often; he may be silently correcting disruptive constructions. His retelling of events and names of characters is good, but he does not comment on theme or plot. In the Burke Reading Interview (Chapter 9), Brian offers positive comments about the reading process and reading instruction. Figure 8.4 contains Brian's teacher's notes in discussion with the researcher, which help her plan Brian's reading development.

Figure 8.3: The Pattern Section from Brian's In-Depth Procedure Reader Profile Form

PATTERNS	%	%
MEANING CONSTRUCTION		PERCENT
No Loss	56	}80
Partial Loss	24	
Loss	20	
GRAMMATICAL RELATIONS		
Strength	45	}70
Partial Strength	16	
Overcorrection	9	
Weakness	30	
WORD SUBSTITUTION IN CONTEXT		
Graphic Similarity		
High	75	}90
Some	15	
None	10	
Sound Similarity		
High	70	}84
Some	14	
None	16	
RETELLING		
Characteristics	35	
Events	45	
Total	80	
Holistic Score		

MPHW _5.07_   TIME ___

COMMENTS

See Teacher's Notes

Nonproficient Readers

Nonproficient readers use procedures that interrupt the reading process, such as overuse of small units of language like letters, sounds, syllables, and words, and they do not develop facility and flexibility with the integration of the reading strategies. In general, they produce unacceptable and uncorrected structures. In addition to overreliance on graphophonic information, they fail to relate the text to their lives and their background knowledge. They are often easily distracted and resist reading.

Nonproficient readers are discouraged, think they will always be behind other students, and are sure they are not winning their struggle with reading. They believe proficient readers never have reading problems. They do not find the reading of new ideas, new formats, and new authors motivating or interesting, and they have not learned to take risks with unfamiliar

Figure 8.4: Teacher's Notes: *Brian*

Name: *Brian*   Date: *Sept. 13*   Grade: *4*

Text: *The Old Man, the Son and the Donkey*   Genre: *Folktale*

From Reader Profile Form	Reader's Needs	Support
Meaning Construction 80% (Combined No Loss & Partial Loss)	Needs to build on his ability to make the text make sense to him.	Determine interests. Ask librarian to help locate appropriate material. Help Brian select books of his interest to read to younger kids. Language Experience[1, 2] Predicting Strategies[1] Preview, Overview, Review[1] Retelling Strategy[1]
Grammatical Relations 70% (Combined Strength, Partial Strength, & Over Correction)	Doesn't always use syntactic structure to help predict.	Introduce variety of genres based on Brian's interests. Schema Stories[1,2] Selected Deletions—syntax[1] Varieties of Grammatical Function[2] Hard to Predict Structures[2] Format Variations[2]
Graphic & Sound 90% 84% (Combined High & Some)	Often gives up making sense for sounding out.	Conference about Brian's high level miscues. Making Meaning Without Graphophonic Cues[2]
Retelling, BRI, Conferences, Observations, etc.	Help in selecting books. Brian has not yet indicated his interest in any particular genre. Needs to understand that he knows a lot about what to do when reading.	Mine, Yours, Ours Strategy[1] Review with Brian his answers on the BRI (especially his positive comments). Retrospective Miscue Analysis[1,2] Retelling Strategy[1]

[1]See Chapter 11.
[2]See *Reading Strategies: Focus on Comprehension* (Y. Goodman, Watson, and Burke 1996).

material. Nonproficient readers are unaware of their own strengths and therefore do not have a good strategy base. For example, they aren't aware that sometimes they read ahead to gain meaning or that they substitute something that makes sense but the substitution is not a graphophonic match. In fact, they may believe that these strategies are wrong and that they

Figure 8.5: The Pattern Section from Sara's In-Depth Procedure Reader Profile Form

PATTERNS	%	%
MEANING CONSTRUCTION		PERCENT
No Loss	35	⎫
Partial Loss	20	⎬ 55
Loss	45	⎭
GRAMMATICAL RELATIONS		
Strength	48	⎫
Partial Strength	5	⎬ 59
Overcorrection	6	⎭
Weakness	40	
WORD SUBSTITUTION IN CONTEXT		
Graphic Similarity		
High	68	⎫
Some	25	⎬ 93
None	7	⎭
Sound Similarity		
High	62	⎫
Some	30	⎬ 92
None	8	⎭
RETELLING		
Characteristics	25	
Events	45	
Total	70	
Holistic Score		
MPHW _12_ TIME ___		
COMMENTS		
See Teacher's Notes		

should be stopped. Nonproficient readers often fail to correct when they predict grammatical or semantic information that is not confirmed by subsequent text information or by their own knowledge. The nonproficient reader may believe it is more critical to sound out names accurately, for example, than it is to construct a thorough understanding of a character's motivation or personality traits. Figure 8.5 is from an In-Depth Procedure Reader Profile of a nonproficient reader, Sara.

Sara's primary reading strategy is sounding out letters, syllables, and words, resulting in high percentages for graphic and sound similarity. Less than half of Sara's miscues result in sentences that are semantically and syntactically acceptable or corrected with little or no meaning change, as shown by the 45 percent loss of meaning construction and 40 percent loss of grammatical relations. Sara's retelling lacks detail, but she knows the two main characters and that "something happened to a cow." Figure 8.6 contains Sara's teacher's notes, that help her plan Sara's reading development.

Figure 8.6: Teacher's Notes: *Sara*

Name: _Sara_   Date: _March 10_   Grade: _4_

Text: _The Man Who Kept House_   Genre: _Folktale_

From Reader Profile Form	Reader's Needs	Support
Meaning Construction 59% (Combined No Loss & Partial Loss)	Appears to have little interest in making sense of the story.	Assisted Reading with Teacher and/or Parent[1] Language Experience Writing[2] Conference re. bringing own experiences to story to make sense.
Grammatical Relations 59% (Combined Strength, Partial Strength, & Over Correction)	Needs to fully use syntactic structure to help predict.	Predicting Strategies[1] Selected Deletions—syntax[1] Listen to Books on Audiotapes while reading along. Keep a Listening Journal.
Graphic & Sound 93% 92% (Combined High & Some)	Believes first and major strategy is to sound out.	Conference about Sara's high level miscues in which she makes sense rather than sounding out. Making Meaning Without Graphophonic Cues[2]
Retelling, BRI, Conferences, Observations, etc.	Strengths: Listens to stories. Shows interest in reading with a partner. Loves the Franklin books. Likes drama.	Continue Partner Reading. Get new Franklin books. Get books on drama, e.g., *The Jumbo Book of Drama*, by Deborah Dunleavy. Ask librarian.

[1]See Chapter 11.
[2]See *Reading Strategies: Focus on Comprehension* (Y. Goodman, Watson, and Burke 1996).

CODING FORM

Although the Reader Profile Form summarizes the data provided by the Coding Form (Appendix C), it does not reflect it all. For this reason, teachers review the Coding Form to consider information that does not appear on the Reader Profile Form. For example, additional information found on the In-Depth Procedure Coding Form has to do with the kinds of miscues the reader makes. By scanning the Coding Form, the observed response (OR) listed under Reader can be quickly compared with the expected response (ER) listed under Text. Knowledge concerning the kinds of miscues a reader makes helps teachers select appropriate strategy lessons and instructional procedures. For example, omissions of nouns and verbs sometimes suggest that a reader is not willing to make predictions or infer.

Acceptable insertions and substitutions indicate a reader is using cues selectively and constructing meaning confidently. In the first case, the teacher plans lessons to encourage risk taking; in the second, the teacher talks with the reader about how acceptable miscues support meaning making.

The In-Depth Procedure Coding Form reports syntactic acceptability, semantic acceptability, meaning change, and correction separately. Examination of each of these columns is informative. For example, a reader's partially acceptable (**P**) miscues, under the syntactic and semantic acceptability headings in relation to correction, provide insight into the reader's predicting, inferring, and confirming strategies. Examination of partially acceptable miscues that are corrected reveals the degree to which a reader understands, for example, certain themes, concepts, or plot development.

The second column of the first section, Language Sense, on the Classroom Procedure Coding Form (Appendix C) shows the number of miscues in each sentence. For Betsy, sentences 34 and 49 (see the Classroom Procedure typescript, Figure 6.1) reflect large numbers of miscues that may be investigated to determine whether the syntactic structure of the text and/or concept load contribute to producing the miscues. The second section, Word Substitution in Context, provides a comparative look at the OR (listed under Reader), and the ER (listed under Text), of all word-level substitution miscues.

Miscues that are influenced by the reader's dialect are indicated on the Coding Form with a d inside a circle *ⓓ* beside the OR under the Reader column. (Dialect is discussed in Chapters 4 and 5.)

TYPESCRIPT

Teachers often consult the typescript for confirmation and clarification of the Coding Forms and Reader Profile, as well as for data that do not appear on other forms.

Repeated Identical Miscues (*RM*) on a Single Item Across Text

Studying a reader's response to the same linguistic unit throughout the entire text helps identify the many strategies a student uses. For example, if a student reads a text in which the word *canary* occurs eight times, substitutes *cannery* for *canary* three times, then substitutes *carry*, then *cardinal*, then again *cannery*, and finally reads the last two occurrences correctly as *canary*, the teacher examines the text for factors influencing the OR changes. Because repeated miscues provide a powerful way to view students' changing strategies across a text, a place is provided to summarize repeated miscue information on the In-Depth and Classroom Procedures Reader Profile Forms (see Chapter 4, 6, and 7 for marking and coding repeated miscues).

Using other assessment procedures, evaluators sometimes make recommendations based on a single miscue occurrence. For example, if the reader reads *saw* for *was* or *left* for *felt* on a list of words, the reader is sometimes diagnosed as having a significant reading disability. However, careful examination of these same words in a complete story provides evidence that readers are responding to grammatical and meaning cues, and in many instances in the text the miscues do not occur.

Multiple Miscues on a Single Text Item

If a reader substitutes two or more words for a single text item, the first complete word or nonword is coded on the In-Depth Procedure Coding Form. The additional attempts on the same item provide information about the reader's strategy use. In the following example, the reader activates more and more linguistic information, first graphophonic and then syntactic, on each attempt to produce the final OR. The reader's first strategy makes the most use of graphophonic cues. By the time the reader substitutes *songs* for *signs*, he is using both syntactic and graphophonic cues with little focus on the story's meaning.

Mr. Pine put up all the signs in Little Town.

Partials

Investigating partial attempts on words helps confirm what the Reader Profile and Coding Form indicate in terms of the reader's sampling and predicting strategies. Frequency of partials gives information about reading efficiency. Proficient readers tend to produce more partials than less proficient readers, but proficient readers' partials are almost always immediately corrected. Partials provide information about the reader's use of initial consonant and vowel cues.

0213   baby at the far end of the garden and

Betsy's miscue in line 0213 indicates that she uses graphophonic, grammatical, and semantic information to produce *f-, forest* before she self-corrects to the ER, *far end.*

Repetitions

The position, extent, and frequency of repetitions reflect the reader's problem-solving efforts. Sometimes the repetitions reflect text complexity, while other times they reflect a reader's lack of efficiency and confidence. Examining points in the text where the reader's repetitions diminish or increase indicates the predictability or complexity of the text features. After Betsy turns the second page of the story, she meets an unusual use of an idiom (line 0301). The common idiom *in a hurry* is written as *in his hurry.* Betsy possibly predicts that the author is providing information about what is *in the house,* but *hurry* doesn't fit. Her grammatical and semantic knowledge causes her to self-correct, but she has to assure herself by repeating several more times. Is it possible that the author originally wrote *in his haste,* and an editor, thinking this was too complicated for a young reader and attempting to make the text easier, inadvertently produced a more complex structure by substituting a higher-frequency word? Many readers of this story make miscues similar to Betsy's in this sentence.

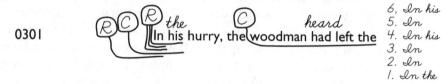

0301

6. *In his*
5. *In*
4. *In his*
3. *In*
2. *In*
1. *In the*

Peripheral Field

The possibility and extent to which something in the ER periphery can influence readers, possibly causing them to miscue, can be investigated only by looking at the typescript. Checking the peripheral field helps us see that the reader is examining written information beyond the specific word.

0211   pointing to your heart.

                                  your
0212   Listen to the heartbeat

Although there are syntactic and semantic considerations in Gordon's reading, his substitution of *your* for *the* may have been influenced by *your* appearing in the preceding line. (See Appendix B for Gordon's complete marked typescript.)

Corrections

Both unsuccessful attempts to correct *UC* and instances in which a correct reading is abandoned *AC* are marked **P** on the In-Depth Procedure Coding Form. The markings on the typescript clarify this coding. Betsy's miscue on line 0312 reflects her reading of *keeping house,* then substituting *keeping home.* Here she abandons the correct form *AC* rather than trying the more usual unsuccessful attempt at correction *UC.*

Pauses

Pauses made during reading sometimes indicate that the reader is sorting out information, hesitating before taking a risk, anticipating syntactic or semantic problems, working with unpredictable text, thinking about possibilities, and problem solving. Betsy's three pauses in line 0512 indicate that she is possibly reflecting on the improbability of a cow hanging anywhere, especially between the roof of a house and the ground.

Additional Miscues

Miscues other than those in the coded portion of the text, as well as dialect and misarticulations, are noted on the transcript. Although we usually choose not to begin coding until the second or third paragraph, the miscues made in the earlier text often shed light on reading proficiency, especially on how a reader approaches unfamiliar genre, concepts, and formats.

Types of Miscues

The kinds and complexity of miscues are identified and evaluated in the context of the total text. A reader who constantly omits words is less of a risk taker than one who is willing to predict and produce a substitution miscue on the basis of syntactic or semantic cues. Insertions suggest the reader is confident in editing the text and they provide evidence of proficient reading. Information about types of miscues helps the teacher select and develop appropriate strategy lessons.

Miscue Clusters

Examination of text units (phrases, clauses, sentences) containing large numbers of miscues help identify points in the text that are complex and affect the reader's performance. Analysis of the text at these points sometimes reveals unpredictable beginnings, extraneous or irrelevant information, or abrupt shifts in the expected linguistic or conceptual sequence. Betsy's miscues 50 and 51 (lines 0413–0414) illustrate how a text may not be supportive of a reader's expectations.

Location of Miscues

Examination of the typescript sheds light on where certain readers are likely to miscue. For example, more miscues may occur during the beginning sections of text, at the beginning or ending of a sentence, or in titles, headings, and subheadings. Such miscues suggest the reader might benefit from reading more materials with similar occurrences and discussing the function such features serve in text.

Comments Written in the Margin of the Typescript

The reader's extraneous responses ("That's a hard word, I'm going to skip that" or deep sighing), as well as the teacher's comments about the reader's behavior during the session (working hard with text, pointing, laughing out loud, looking at illustrations, yawning), provide information about the reader's response to the text.

Teachers/researchers may want to build on the available research by collecting additional examples of interesting and informative text features as data for their own study. Some features from the typescript are researched in depth (Brown, Goodman and Marek 1996; Gollasch 1980; Xu 1998).

RETELLING

Observers are often surprised when students considered to be poor readers give extensive and in-depth retellings. They also are sometimes bewildered when students who read well orally do not give substantial retellings. Miscue analysis always includes a retelling. Information about retellings is found in Chapter 3 (Readers' Retellings and Presentations), Chapter 6 (Betsy's Retelling Summary), Chapter 7 (In-Depth Procedure Retelling Guide), and Chapter 10 (Betsy's Retelling).

TRANSITION TO THE BURKE READING INTERVIEW

The Burke Reading Interview (BRI), discussed in depth in Chapter 9, is an instrument used to explore the views and attitudes students have about reading and reading instruction, as well as how their perceptions influence the ways they think of themselves as readers. These insights, combined with RMI data found in this chapter, build a rich case study of a reader. Such information can lead to successful instructional practices. In the following chapter, we add to our information about Betsy by investigating her responses to the Burke Reading Interview questions.

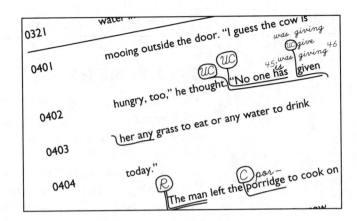

Chapter 9
Perceptions of the Reading Process: Models of Reading and the Burke Reading Interview

What students (as well as teachers) believe about reading powerfully affects learning and the teaching of reading. To help us gain insight into a reader's perception of the reading process, and to understand the complex relations between how people read and what they believe about their own reading, Carolyn Burke developed the Burke Reading Interview (BRI) (Burke 1980). The interview is usually given before starting the miscue analysis and often it is used periodically, depending on the purpose of the teacher/researcher. In this way, we find out if the reader's views of the reading process has changed and we are able to explore why with the reader.

By examining readers' responses to the BRI, we categorize their views of reading according to three different models of reading instruction. Miscue analysis has been instrumental in the development of a holistic view of reading. However, alternative theories of reading are held by other scholars in the field and the general public, and they are reflected in commercial reading programs. Everyone in a literate society develops beliefs and attitudes about reading and reading instruction. The BRI helps us to examine these views and to understand why readers use certain reading strategies. Such information is useful when planning students' reading instruction.

MODELS OF READING

We categorize the most commonly held beliefs about reading into three major models of reading instruction: a subskills or word recognition view, a skills or eclectic view, and a holistic or whole language view.

Subskills Model

The *subskills,* or *word recognition,* model of reading instruction is based on behaviorist or connectionist learning theory. The underlying assumption of these theories is that reading is word recognition. In this view reading is learned from parts to wholes through a sequential hierarchy of skills, and each skill is taught, reinforced, mastered, and tested before the next skill in the hierarchy is presented. The simplest units of language are assumed to be letters and sounds. Recently "phonemic awareness," including where phonemes appear in oral words have become a basic component of the subskills model. Teaching the smallest units of language, one at a time, precedes the teaching of word recognition, and the mastery of these subskills precedes a focus on the meaning of what is being read. Generally, consonants are introduced first, followed by long vowels and short vowels. Larger units of language are taught after tests show that beginning subskills are mastered.

In this model, reading is taught explicitly with practice and drill on small units of language, all leading to mastery of the skills. Because it is assumed that errors will become learned responses, they are not acceptable and must be eradicated. To discourage error, reading instruction is tightly organized and focuses on exactness and fluency. The teacher monitors the reader's progress and uses a test-teach-test curriculum model. This model can be envisioned as a triangle with a strong base of letter-sound relations, which supports the next level, word recognition, which eventually supports the top tier, word meanings or vocabulary.

Skills Model

The skills or eclectic model of reading instruction has been the most generally accepted view promoted in schools, and it is reflected in the curricula of most commercially produced reading instruction programs. The proponents of this view often claim that they are eclectic, using what they believe represents the best insights from all views of reading. Beginning reading instruction, based on this theory, includes phonemic awareness, phonics, and the teaching of relations between letters and sounds. In many programs, irregular words are taught as whole units through the use of flash cards or games that focus on words in isolation. In addition to phonemic awareness, phonics, word recognition, and vocabulary, reading instruction may include the reading of children's literature and the integration of the other language arts (writing, speaking, and listening). Three language cuing systems (graphophonics, syntax, and semantics) are taught, although each is usually presented in separate lessons using prescriptive language rules.

Many commercial reading instruction materials are written to control letter-sound relations, word frequency, spelling patterns, and grammatical structures in a sequential order. In recent years, they include a range of genres and excerpts from professionally authored literature. Meaning, particularly of words, is important in this model but takes its place in a hierarchical set of comprehension skills. Instruction is driven by the belief that the teaching of language must be simplified for children to learn to read. This model can be envisioned as a circle with equal divisions provided for comprehension, phonics, and vocabulary skills.

Holistic Model

The holistic or whole language model of reading instruction reflects a transactional, psycholinguistic, and sociolinguistic view of the reading process that is discussed in depth throughout this book. This view can be envisioned as a multilayered circle or sphere that represents the systems of language used to construct meaning. At the heart of the circle is the semantic system. Surrounding and supporting the semantic system is the syntactic system, and on the surface is the graphophonic system of language. All the systems are used simultaneously within a sociocultural, pragmatic context. To construct meaning, the reader integrates his or her reading strategies with the language systems within a social-cultural context (see Chapter 2). See Chapter 11 for instructional experiences and strategy lessons that are based on the holistic model of reading instruction.

Based on our experience, we support the holistic view of reading instruction as it is based on research in miscue analysis, research that reveals how readers integrate the language cuing systems and reading strategies.

UNDERSTANDING THE BURKE READING INTERVIEW (BRI)

To plan students' reading instruction, we need to be aware of their beliefs about reading, and consider how their reading proficiency is influenced by past and current reading instruction. What students believe about reading and reading instruction affect the decisions they make about their reading strategies. The BRI provides information about the reader's metalinguistic knowledge, that is, the language people use to think and talk about reading as an object of study. Readers' responses (Burke 1980; Harste and Burke 1977; Squires 2001) often correspond to the models of reading instruction just described. Similar research has been used in the examination of teachers' views about reading and reading instruction (DeFord 1981; Squires 2001).

Although readers' combined responses usually correspond to a particular model of reading instruction, no single interview question provides a definitive profile of a student's view of reading. In fact, what some readers believe and say about the reading process does not always reflect how they read. Some proficient readers suggest, through their responses, a skills view of the reading process, while some nonproficient readers, despite their reading, report that reading is making sense of the text. Additionally, responses sometimes reflect what the reader believes the interviewer wants to hear. Nevertheless, because the BRI asks several questions that focus on the same information, it is not difficult to spot rote responses. It is also interesting that some readers respond differently to the questions in diverse settings or with dissimilar materials (Coles 1981). However, because (we hope) students spend a good deal of time reading in school, it makes sense to examine how they respond in school settings. Given the nature of the reader and the purpose for conducting the interview, it is often helpful to conduct more than one interview in different sociocultural contexts and over time.

Teachers/researchers find it informative and sometimes surprising to consider their own responses to the BRI and then to compare their responses with students' responses, as well as to compare and discuss the responses with other adult readers. Teachers can help parents understand the reading process and miscue analysis by asking parents to respond to the interview and then compare their responses with their children's.

Following are the BRI questions with discussions of their significance. The responses of three readers, whom we introduced in Chapter 8, are then presented. The blank forms, including the BRI found in Appendix C, may be copied for teacher/researcher use.

- **Question 1:** *When you are reading and come to something you don't know, what do you do?*

  One issue addressed by this question is what the student believes the word *something* refers to, that is, with which linguistic unit (letter, word, phrase, sentence, or section of text) the reader is primarily concerned. The word *something* is purposefully used to avoid unintentionally focusing the reader on the *word* or the *sentence*. The response to this question also concerns strategies readers believe they use when they come to a unit of language they don't know. Their answers indicate whether they believe it is best to sound out, skip, substitute, or keep reading, as well as who or what the reader depends on for help while reading.

  The follow-up question: *Do you ever do anything else?*

  This question is asked to gain additional information about the characteristics of what *something* refers to. Additionally, answers to this question provide insight into whether readers have a single strategy in mind or believe they need to change strategies depending, for example, on purpose or setting.

- **Question 2:** *Who is a good reader you know?*

  The answer to this question helps us understand what readers believe are the characteristics of good readers. This information is useful for comparison with answers to subsequent questions. When students indicate they do not know any good readers or nominate themselves as good readers, the following questions (especially question 3) often reveal a student's understanding of what makes someone a good reader.

- **Question 3:** *What makes _____ a good reader?*

  (The blank is filled with the name or pronoun for the person mentioned in the answer to question 2.) The answer to this question adds to the reader's list of characteristics of a good reader.

- **Question 4:** *Do you think _____ ever comes to something he/she doesn't know?*

  This question relates to question 1. If students, in response to question 4, say that good readers never come to *something* they don't know, this suggests that they equate good reading with errorless performances by readers who know everything. Such students may believe they are not smart enough to learn to read or to read well. Different questions are asked next depending on whether the response to this question is yes or no.

- **Question 5:**

  If the answer to question 4 is yes: *When _____ does come to something he/she doesn't know, what do you think he/she does?*

  If the answer to question 4 is no: *Suppose _____ comes to something he/she doesn't know. What would he/she do?*

  This question encourages the reader to take a stand on which aspect of language is most important in reading and which strategy is most productive.

- **Question 6:** *How would you help someone having trouble reading?*

  In addition to indicating possible strategies the reader might use, the response to this question reveals whether the reader believes troubled readers are different or should be treated differently from other readers.

- **Question 7:** *What would a/your teacher do to help that person?*

  This question is similar to questions 5 and 6, in that readers are asked again to focus on what is important in teaching, especially for teaching the less able reader. Questions 6 and 7 together suggest how instruction might influence readers' beliefs.

- **Question 8:** *How did you learn to read?*

  People who have pleasant memories about reading often think they learned to read before they started to school, or they don't remember learning to read. Such readers may credit family members—parents, grandparents, or siblings—with teaching them to read, or they remember being told they were self-taught readers who read before school. Readers who believe they are problem readers often remember negative experiences while learning to read in school.

- **Question 9:** *What would you like to do better as a reader?*

  Answers to this question provide additional information concerning readers' beliefs about the reading process. Even good readers think they would like to be able to read faster or to remember everything they read. This question presents an opening to discuss reading in terms of the reading process and the need for prior knowledge. (For very young children, this question may need to be rephrased: *Would you like to read better? How would you do that?*)

- **Question 10:** *Do you think you are a good reader? Why?*

  By the time this question is asked, teachers/researchers can often predict the reader's answer. The response frequently reflects what readers believe other people think of them as readers and as students. When using the BRI with bilingual or multilingual people, it is interesting to ask the readers to reflect on how they would answer the questions if they were thinking about reading in their second or third language.

An adaptation of the BRI for older readers, the Burke Interview Modified for Older Readers (BIMOR) is available in Appendix C. (Watson and Chippendale 1979, Y. Goodman and Marek 1996.) When ESL readers respond to the BRI, teachers usually ask about their reading in English. It is useful to ask these students if they would respond differently if they were reading in their native language.

BRI Interviews of Three Readers

The following responses to the interview questions are from the three readers we introduced in Chapter 8 who represent different reading proficiencies and different views of reading. Sara's and Jamal's interviews were conducted by their teachers (T), and Brian's interview was conducted by a reasearcher (R).

Name	Age	Education Level	Sex
Sara (S)	9	3	F
Brian (B)	8	3	M
Jamal (J)	13	7	M

Sara	Brian	Jamal
Question 1: *When you are reading and come to something you don't know what do you do?*		
I ask you.	Figure it out—like break it into two parts.	J: Do you mean when I don't understand something? T: Yes, anytime you come to something ... J: I usually can work it out. I keep reading.
Do you ever do anything else?		
S: I look close at the word. I sound it out and I try to figure it out. T: What do you mean? How do you figure it out? S: I sound it out. Sometimes I try to see if I know the beginning and the end.	My mom helps me. She gives me a sentence with the word left out to see if I can fill in the blank. Like the word is *not* and she will say: "You were *blank* there." And that will help me.	Well, if I'm really interested, when I'm finished I might look back at it and work it out.
Question 2: *Who is a good reader you know?*		
You're a really good reader [*talking to teacher*].	My mom.	My dad is a good reader.
Question 3: *What makes [me, your mom, your dad] a good reader?*		
You know all the words. When you read to us, it's really good.	She just reads a lot.	He reads a lot and he knows a lot.

Sara	Brian	Jamal
Question 4: *Do you think [I, your mom, your dad] ever comes to something I/she/he don't/ doesn't know when reading?*		
No!	Yes.	Well, maybe.
Question 5: If Yes: *When [your mom, your dad] does come to something she/he doesn't know, what do you think she/he does?*		
	B: She says a wrong word, and then she'll try to say it again. **R:** How does she figure it out? **B:** There's a hard word or something ... a wrong word. She'll say it a couple more times and it comes out all right. **R:** What is she doing when she says it a couple more times so that it comes out right? **B:** Thinking about it.	He thinks about it, I guess. Sometimes he talks about what he is reading to us ... to Mom and me.
Question 6: If No: *Suppose [I] came to something [I] didn't know. What do you think [I'd] do?*		
S: You always know it. **T:** Just suppose—pretend. **S:** You would ask your husband. **T:** Who else is a good reader? **S:** Janis. [a classmate] **T:** Why? **S:** Because she can pronounce all the words. **T:** What does Janis do when she doesn't know? **S:** Asks the teacher. **T:** Anything else? **S:** She sounds it out.		
Question 6: *How would you help someone having trouble reading?*		
S: Tell them to ask the teacher. **T:** Anything else? **S:** Give them a worksheet.	**B:** I don't know ... do shared reading. **R:** What's shared reading? **B:** I read a page and then the other one does. Or you read three and they read three. **R:** How does that help? **B:** I don't know. You just get to read and like if they make mistakes it doesn't matter. Or something like that.	**J:** I'd take them to the library. **T:** What would you do there? **J:** They'd [librarians] help him find a book he likes real well. I could help them do that, too.
Question 7: *What would a/your teacher do to help that person?*		
Tell them to sit down and work on the word 'til they get it.	**B:** Have them read and then stop them. **R:** What would they do after they stopped them? **B:** I don't know. **R:** That's okay. I'll give you a couple of minutes to think. **B:** Read with them and written conversation and read stories like picture books and stuff.	She'd give them some good stories to read and try to get them to understand it.

Sara	Brian	Jamal
Question 8: *How did you learn to read?*		
I don't know. I learned at school. My teacher helped me. I learned from her. I needed help.	**B:** By my mom helping me and teachers helping me. **R:** What kinds of help did your mom and teachers give? **B:** Encouraged me and stuff. **R:** Anything else? **B:** Don't give up, keep trying. **R:** Can you remember when you were in first grade? **B:** Yeah. I was in the low reading group. **R:** What did you do there? **B:** We read easy books. Some of the higher kids made fun of us because we weren't that good of readers ... My mom said ignore it. In second grade my teacher tutored me. **R:** What did you do? **B:** Read books. I read books to her and that helped me. **R:** When you came to something you didn't know, what did your teacher do? **B:** She told me to sound it out. **R:** Anything else? **B:** No.	My dad. He taught me to read and then I read and then my teacher taught me, too. But I'm still not a great reader.
Question 9: *What would you like to do better as a reader?*		
S: I'd like to know all the words. **T:** What does it mean to know all the words? **S:** I'd know how to pronounce them.	**B:** Just read quicker. **R:** How can you read quicker? **B:** Practice a lot. **R:** Practice what? **B:** Books, just reading books and stuff. And words, just like saying them. **R:** What do you think will help you say the words better? **B:** Saying them over and over.	Understand everything in the book.
Question 10: *Do you think you are a good reader?*		
No. Maybe, sometimes ... a little bit.	So-so.	I could be better.

Discussion of Students' Interviews:

> *Sara's* responses indicate a focus on atomistic language units. She "looks close at the word," sounds out words, checks the beginnings and ends of words, and believes that good readers know everything and never have problems with reading. Sara, representing a nonproficient reader, believes that, when readers have problems, they usually rely on other people for help, especially a teacher, and that she herself is "maybe, sometimes ... a little bit" a good reader. She admires her teacher's oral reading. Her teacher "knows all the words." Sara's answers reflect a subskills view of reading. For supportive instructional experiences, see the Teacher's Notes in Chapter 8 and the curriculum suggestions for a nonproficient reader in Chapter 11.

Brian, a moderately proficient reader, is more eclectic in his views. He thinks reading is focusing on words: "like break it into two parts" or "saying them [words] over and over." But he also thinks that "reading books and stuff" is part of reading practice. Brian views himself as a "so-so" reader. Brian's answers reflect a skills view of reading. For supportive instructional experiences, see the Teacher's Notes in Chapter 8 and the curriculum suggestions for a moderately proficient reader in Chapter 11.

Jamal, a proficient reader, takes on the responsibility of understanding the text as he focuses on reading for meaning: "I usually can work it out. I keep reading. If I'm really interested ... I might look back at it and work on it." Jamal's answers reflect the importance he places on understanding what he is reading, on his interests, and on the need for stories and books. Jamal thinks that others, such as his dad, his teacher, and librarians are helpful to readers. Jamal's realistic grasp on reading is evident when he says it may be possible that his dad, a good reader, would come to something while reading that he doesn't know. He believes there is a connection between his Dad's reading well and knowledge. Despite his proficiency, Jamal thinks he could be a better reader. His answers reflect a holistic view of reading. For supportive instructional experiences, see the Teacher's Notes in Chapter 8 and the curriculum suggestions for a proficient reader in Chapter 11.

When collected over time, the knowledge we gather from the BRI reflects ongoing changes in students' attitudes about reading, and helps teachers adjust their reading programs to make the most of readers' strengths and to address their needs. A summary of the information gained from the BRI is often placed in the Comments Section on the Classroom Procedure or the In-Depth Procedure Reader Profile Forms.

Once we have gathered the wealth of information about the reader from various appropriate sources that we discussed in Chapter 8 and the BRI, we are ready to build a profile of a student in relation to the reading of a particular text. In the next chapter we demonstrate how to integrate the data we have gathered about Betsy in order to construct a profile based on her reading of *The Man Who Kept House.*

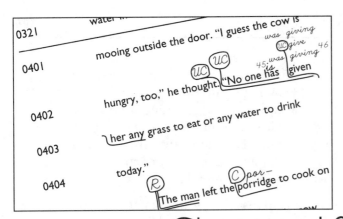

Chapter 10
Betsy as a Reader: Case Study

We now use information about Betsy gathered from various sources (the Reader Profile Form, Coding Form, typescript, retelling, and Burke Reading Interview) to provide a case study or profile of her as a reader of *The Man Who Kept House*. We present the statistical information from each of the miscue analysis procedures and then discuss Betsy's strengths and needs as a reader. One way of considering the information summarized on the Reader Profile Form is to focus on categories and patterns that deal specifically with the reading strategies: initiating and sampling, predicting, inferring, correcting, confirming, and integrating (see Chapter 2). Betsy's scores, taken from the Reader Profile Forms of the Classroom and the In-Depth Procedures, are presented below as a means of examining and discussing how the scores reflect her use of the reading strategies. Scores from the different procedures vary because miscues and sentences are coded differently for each procedure, and the questions in each procedure focus on different linguistic units and patterns. This information, along with the other miscue analysis data discussed earlier, is the basis for planning Betsy's reading instruction (Chapter 11). Although researchers/teachers select, depending on their interest, the Classroom or the In-Depth Procedure, we discuss both. Teachers often use the Informal Procedure throughout the year to have current information.

BETSY'S READER PROFILE FROM THE IN-DEPTH PROCEDURE

Figure 10.1 is from the In-Depth Procedure Reader Profile Form of a moderately proficient reader, Betsy. Betsy's In-Depth Reader Profile Form indicates that her use of graphic similarity is 55 percent High, 28 percent Some, and 17 percent None, and her use of sound similarity is 43 percent High, 30 percent Some, and 27 percent None. When the combined scores of High and

Figure 10.1: The Pattern Section from Betsy's In-Depth Procedure Reader Profile Form

PATTERNS	%	%
MEANING CONSTRUCTION		PERCENT
No Loss	63	} 96
Partial Loss	33	
Loss	4	
GRAMMATICAL RELATIONS		
Strength	56	} 80
Partial Strength	7	
Overcorrection	17	
Weakness	20	
WORD SUBSTITUTION IN CONTEXT		
Graphic Similarity		
High	55	} 83
Some	28	
None	17	
Sound Similarity		
High	43	} 73
Some	30	
None	27	
RETELLING		
Characteristics	31	
Events	56	
Total	87	
Holistic Score		

MPW _10.55_   TIME _19 min._

COMMENTS

For the most part Betsy uses predicting & confirming strategies cmfortably. She may be overattending to surface features of the text.

Some are considered, we see that in 83 percent of her miscues Betsy's responses involve her use of graphic cues, and that in 73 percent she uses sound cues. Such high scores indicate a heavy reliance on the surface features of the text. On the other hand, Betsy proficiently integrates graphic and sound information when the meaning is clear to her. This is evident from the In-Depth Procedure (see Chapter 7) and Classroom Procedure Coding Forms (see Chapter 6). In every instance of either no graphic or no sound similarity, Meaning Construction is marked No Loss, and Grammatical Relations is marked Strength.

A look at such substitutions in context illustrates this pattern.

0201	_nn,_ _day_
So the next morning the wife went off to

0214	_nn_ _in_
brought her back to the house.

Betsy's numerous repetitions on a single text item also indicate that she is overly concerned with surface-level (graphophonic) accuracy; when she tunnels into small units of language, the difficulty becomes greater. Betsy sometimes attends so closely to the letters and words (*has given* in line 0402) that she does not sample larger units of text; she continues to work without information more text could provide.

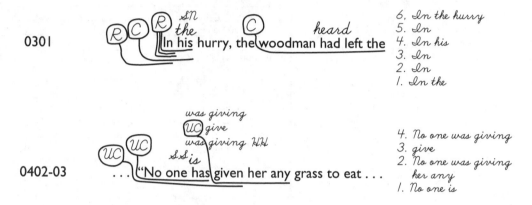

PATTERNS FROM BETSY'S CLASSROOM PROCEDURE READER PROFILE

Betsy's Language Sense and Word Substitution in Context (Figure 10.2) are taken from her Classroom Procedure Coding Form (Figure 6.5) or from the last page of the Classroom Procedure typescript (Figure 6.1) and placed on her Classroom Procedure Reader Profile (Figure 6.6).

The scores shown in Figure 10.3 are taken from the bottom of the last page of Betsy's typescript.

Figure 10.2: From Betsy's Classroom Procedure Reader Profile Form

PATTERNS	%	%
LANGUAGE		
SENSE		PERCENT
Strength	78	} 84
Partial Strength	6	
Weakness	16	
WORD SUBSTITUTION		
IN CONTEXT		
Graphic Similarity		
High	55	} 84
Some	29	
None	15	
Sound Similarity		
High	43	} 75
Some	32	
None	25	

Figure 10.3: From Betsy's Classroom Procedure Reader Typescript

Reader Transcript

Syntactic Acceptability	Semantic Acceptability	Meaning Change	Graphic Similarity	
Yes 88%	Yes 84%	Yes 0%	High 55%	} 84%
No 12%	No 17%	Partial 7%	Some 29%	
		No 93%	None 15%	

SCORING BETSY'S READING WITH THE INFORMAL PROCEDURE

There is no profile form for the Informal Procedure, but the teacher can place scores and comments on the Conference Form (Appendix C) for references to the reader's use of strategies. The Informal Procedure often reveals a reader's strengths or needs that are addressed immediately in a conference setting.

BETSY'S USE OF LANGUAGE SYSTEMS

Betsy's ability to make predictions using all the language systems, especially through the use of her knowledge of English grammar, is evident (grammatical relations in the In-Depth Procedure and language sense in the Classroom Procedure indicate this strength). Betsy's grammatical knowledge supports her ability to make predictions, thus allowing her to move along in the text, and to disconfirm and then self-correct responses that do not sound right to her. Betsy usually makes her reading syntactically acceptable; that is, she is concerned that her reading sounds like language.

To get a better understanding of Betsy's ability to use the grammatical system of language, we consult the Coding Forms, the typescript, and the Reader Profile Form. Only twice in the coded section of *The Man Who Kept House* did Betsy produce a totally syntactically unacceptable sentence. In the first case (line 0211), she corrected the miscues, and the second time (line 0414) she did not.

In line 0211, Betsy had not yet established the gender of the baby, and therefore she may have predicted a more generalized structure, such as *there is [no one to help the woodman in the house]*. Since *there is not in the house* does not sound like English to Betsy, the unacceptable structure supports her correcting strategy.

However, in line 0413, once Betsy predicts *fall off* is the end of a sentence, she predicts the next line is the beginning of a sentence. These miscues are obvious by her intonation patterns. Betsy attempts to correct, not realizing that the problem is with an earlier segment of the sentence rather than at the beginning of the line (0414). Betsy eventually continues reading, leaving a syntactically unacceptable segment of the original sentence.

When readers such as Betsy make a number of miscues in a short amount of text (as with lines 0413 to 0414), they are often overwhelmed with the complexity of the situation and consequently leave the unacceptable segment without attempting to correct. When this happens, the retelling indicates whether the reader corrects silently as she or he continues reading and subsequently understands all or part of the complex section of the text. (Betsy's early reading experiences consist of predominantly simplistically written texts, thus depriving her of opportunities to read more complex English structures.)

When Betsy's miscues are syntactically acceptable, they almost always are semantically acceptable, or she corrects them to achieve total acceptability. When the miscues are partially syntactically acceptable, they are also partially semantically acceptable, or Betsy corrects them to acceptability. Such strategies indicate effective use of her semantic and syntactic knowledge for purposes of meaning construction.

Betsy's *overcorrection* (17 percent) does not interfere with her story comprehension because all her miscues in this category are both syntactically and semantically acceptable with no meaning change. In the total context of the story, correction is unnecessary. Betsy's *overcorrection* confirms what is indicated by her intonation when reading and by her numerous repetitions and corrections; she focuses on graphophonic features and is therefore hesitant to continue reading even though her miscues are acceptable. The following examples illustrate that this overuse does not diminish Betsy's effectiveness as a reader, but does diminish her efficiency.

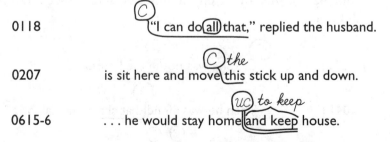

Betsy's use of grammatical relationships provides a base for her reading strategies. Almost all miscues that result in a *weakness* of grammatical relations are a result of partial syntactic acceptability and partial semantic acceptability; that is, Betsy is able to use the beginning of the sentence, in addition to her comprehension of the text, to help her make reasonable predictions, but unfortunately she does not always confirm her predictions.

For the most part, Betsy produces language structures in acceptable English. However, in the following instances, apparently there is not enough semantic disruption to cause a reconsideration of her reading, and the language sounds acceptable; Betsy does not attempt to correct.

0516   (R) ...she could hear the cow mooing, the

0517-18   *cried*   *shouted*
                baby crying, and her husband shouting for help.

In the preceding instances (lines 0517–0518) no meaning is lost; Betsy transforms the second and third clauses to simple past tense, separating them syntactically from the first clause.

When her miscues result in partial semantic acceptability, Betsy corrects them well over half the time. These miscues show that she predicts potentially meaningful sentences. Following are typical corrections.

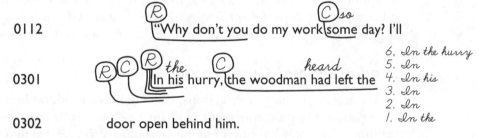

0112   (R)   (C) *so*
                "Why don't you do my work some day? I'll

0301   (R)(C)(R) *the* (C)   *heard*   6. *In the hurry*
                In his hurry, the woodman had left the   5. *In*
                                                          4. *In his*
                                                          3. *In*
                                                          2. *In*
                                                          1. *In the*

0302   door open behind him.

For the most part, Betsy does not bother to correct miscues that are semantically acceptable and cause no change in meaning:

0111   *I'll*
                "I'd be glad to," said the wife.

0201   *day*
                So the next morning the wife went off to

0202   the forest. The husband stayed home and

0203   *job*
                began to do his wife's work.

When Betsy produces a semantically acceptable miscue that causes a minor meaning change, the Partial Loss column shows that she usually does not correct.

0208   *So*   *buttermilk*
              Soon the cream will turn into butter."

0415-6   ⓡ ...⌐He dropped the other end down⌐to⌐the chimney.

BETSY'S USE OF READING STRATEGIES

At this point we move from Betsy's use of language cuing systems to her use of reading strategies. We need to remember that Betsy does not miscue in large portions of the text. These nonmiscued portions add to the evidence of Betsy's proficient use of language cuing systems and reading strategies.

Initiating and Sampling

Betsy's initiating and sampling strategies are reflected in her use of graphic and sound information. The combined totals of High and Some graphic and sound similarity (83 percent and 73 percent on the In-Depth Reader Profile) suggest that her efficiency is diminished by overuse of graphic and sound information. Her slow oral reading, numerous repetitions, and grammatical relations overcorrection score of 17 percent add evidence that she pays a great deal of attention to every word, thus becoming inefficient in her sampling and selecting strategies. Betsy's instructional materials may have influenced her expectation that sentences begin and end on a single line, resulting in her use of correction strategies that are not always successful.

Predicting and Confirming

As mentioned, to make predictions, Betsy makes considerable use of syntactic and graphophonic information. In the case of the following pronoun substitution, Betsy may have predicted a masculine pronoun related to the male woodman rather than a feminine pronoun related to the cow. (Nine-year-old Betsy might not attribute a gender to cows, or she might think that all cows are males just because they are large animals.) Also, Betsy might have thought it incomprehensible for a cow to be on a roof and therefore cannot confirm the meaning. After considering more text in which she gains additional syntactic information, Betsy corrects her miscue in line 0413.

0413   © *the*
              Then he was afraid⌐that she⌐would fall off⌐

0414   ⓤⓒ *The* ⓤⓒ *was har-* © *himself* ©
              ⌐the roof and hurt herself."

Betsy's use of predicting and confirming strategies, as well as silent correction (next section) is evident when we consider her reading of *house* and *home*. *House* occurs 14 times (in lines 106, 107, 113, 116, 211, 214, 303, 312, 412, 502, 516, 606, 611, and 616), *home* occurs six times (in lines 103, 113, 114, 202, 611, and 616). It is important to determine not only when Betsy miscues on these two words, but also when she predicts *house* and *home* appropriately.

Betsy reads *home* as expected once, before she miscues on it; she reads *house* seven times before she miscues on it. She miscues on *home* twice out of the six text possibilities, and on *house* once out of the 14 possibilities. If we simply count miscues, it is easy to conclude that Betsy confuses the two words. However, it is clear as we examine her reading of *house* and *home*, that there is more going on than not understanding the meaning of two words. The following patterns emerge. Betsy:

- Miscues on *home* only when *stay* precedes it.
- Miscues on *house* only when *keeping* precedes it.
- Regresses before *keep* and *keeping house* in lines 0106 and 0107.
- Never uses the term *keeping house* in the retelling.
- Eventually, by transacting with the story, solves the problem of *staying home* and *keeping house*.

Betsy ultimately resolves the problem with the concept of *keeping house* as she continues reading. Her retelling reveals that she understands the concept when she tells about the chores the woodman faces as he attempts to keep house. Additionally, her reading of *stay home* on lines 0611 and 0616, as well as *to keep* in line 0616, show that she learns to handle the syntax and semantics of these words and phrases as she reads the story.

Betsy's substitutions of *$shurn* (0205) and *cream* (0304 and 0307) for *churn* also show her concern for making sense. She first substitutes a nonword (*$shurn*), then predicts a meaningful real word (*cream*) the next two times the word *churn* occurs. By doing this, she produces syntactically and semantically acceptable sentences.

Correction

When we consider Betsy's correction strategies, the role of meaning construction is especially significant. As always, we begin with what the reader does well, that is, what Betsy does that results in no loss of meaning. Betsy uses the correction strategy proficiently; she corrects when the miscues are not completely semantically acceptable, but she often continues reading when the miscue is acceptable and does not cause a significant change in the meaning of the total text. However, to understand Betsy's use of correction strategies more fully, we look at the patterns that emerge in the Loss column of the In-Depth Procedure. On only three occasions does Betsy allow a completely semantically unacceptable miscue go without correction.

Twice she substitutes a nonword for a text item (0205, *$shurn* for *churn*, and 0513, *$gorun* for *ground*), and once she substitutes a masculine pronoun for a feminine pronoun (0414, *himself* for *herself*). The long thoughtful pause before *$shurn* and the regressions before *$gorun* suggest that Betsy is reflecting on her reading.

The following represent partially semantically acceptable, but uncorrected miscues. Betsy often repeats and makes unsuccessful attempts to correct, suggesting she is problem solving, but is not proficient at correcting these miscues to acceptability.

0112-13   . . . I'll stay home and keep house," said the woodman.

0204   He began to make some butter. As he put

0312   room. Perhaps keeping house is harder work.

0313   than I thought.

0406   . . . He gave the cow some water.

Betsy's Integrating

Betsy's integrating of the author's text with her own existing knowledge is evident in at least two connected ways. Linguistic integration involves using the reading strategies, along with the systems of language, in the attempt to construct meaning. Her observed responses, especially repeated miscues, involving the use of reading strategies are clues to linguistic integration that cannot be separated from conceptual integration. Conceptual integration, in the attempt to construct meaning, involves the relation of Betsy's ideas, theories, and themes with the perceptions of the author's ideas, theories, themes, and it shows she is comprehending, that is, focusing on making sense of the text. In addition to the miscue analysis, retellings provide information about Betsy's integration of the author's and her own thinking and reasoning.

BETSY'S RETELLING

Betsy's retelling of *The Man Who Kept House* (Chapter 1) indicates that she understands the story, despite what some might consider as halting and slow reading; Betsy's oral reading took 19 minutes, during which time she produces an average of 11 miscues per 100 words. She shows a grasp of setting, characterization, and inferential information, such as theme and plot. Both Betsy's miscues and her retelling indicate that she has a sense of the author's grammar; her retelling includes phrases and clauses that closely follow the author's sentence construction. Betsy has a sense of story grammar in that she uses her knowledge of the structure of stories to provide an orderly retelling with little change from the author's presentation of the story. Betsy's grasp of sentence and story grammar are strengths that should become part of the foundation of her reading program.

As Betsy retells the story, there is no indication that she sees any humor in it or that she relates it in any way to her own life or to literature she previously may have heard or read. In contrast, when another student read *The Man Who Kept House,* he gave this personal response:

> I was thinking about when we first moved into our new house. There was a garage outside that was full of junk and stuff people left. We had to do so much. It seemed like every time we got one thing done there was lots more things to do. It took us forever to get everything right. The harder the woodman worked, the bigger mess he made. That was kind of like us.

Nor does Betsy indicate any critical thinking in terms of the male/female roles. She does not comment on the woodman's attitude about his importance. In contrast, another female reader turned a critical eye on the woodman:

> That old man! He thought he was the best. Better than his wife. Better than all the women, probably. And when she showed him up, he didn't even apologize. Just shut him up good!

SUMMARY OF BETSY'S STRENGTHS AND NEEDS

It is helpful to summarize Betsy's strengths, because her reading program will be built on them.

- Betsy uses all the reading strategies to comprehend and move forward in the text. She activates *initiating* and *sampling strategies* by readily reading the title and beginning the story in the conventional upper left-hand corner. Despite the fact that Betsy occasionally labors over discrete surface-text features to the point of disrupting her reading, most of her miscues indicate that she samples on the basis of all available language cues. Betsy's *predicting strategies* are evidenced by use of all the systems of language to take linguistic risks, especially with the grammatical system. Her *confirming strategies* are revealed in her concern with constructing meaning by making her reading sound like language and making sense; she often corrects her miscues to achieve this.

- Betsy *learns from text*, that is, she learns to read by reading, as evident in the integration of linguistic and conceptual knowledge. Her repeated miscues indicate that she uses text to develop familiar concepts and language structures. Betsy's repeated miscues indicate that a well-written story provides opportunities to learn more about reading across the text as concepts about the content are building. Substitutions for *home* and *churn* are examples of Betsy's learning as she moves through the text.

- Betsy uses her *knowledge of story grammar*. Her miscues, especially those made during the last two-thirds of the text, along with her retelling, indicate her knowledge of how a story is organized. Such knowledge helps her move through the text and supports her retelling of the story.

- Betsy has insights into *characterization*, even when characters are not explicitly described in the text. These insights are revealed in her retelling.

- Betsy activates *inferring strategies* by using her *background experiences and information*. She brings to the reading of *The Man Who Kept House* knowledge about folktales and the chores males and females are usually assigned in such stories. She has concepts about the meaning of porridge and fireplaces.

- Betsy *has control of language*. Her retelling indicates that she can take turns during a conversation. She is able to articulate her ideas, thus communicating through language.

Areas of concern become evident through the analysis of Betsy's miscues, retelling, and BRI (see Chapter 1).

- Betsy needs to broaden her linguistic experiences related to certain idioms and structures (i.e., *in his hurry, staying home, keeping house* and the past perfect tense, *has given*).

- Despite her understanding of the plot, Betsy is unaware of mood (humor) in the story.

- Occasionally Betsy overuses the surface-level cuing systems involving graphics and sounds.

- Betsy sometimes repeats a phrase over and over rather than continuing to read to experience more structures and meanings provided in the text.

- To fully grasp meanings in *The Man Who Kept House*, Betsy needs to develop concepts relating to sod houses, to cows eating on roofs of houses, and to making butter in churns.

- Betsy lacks confidence in herself, evident through her hesitancy in selecting her own reading material as well as her lack of understanding that past experiences are of value and should be brought to her reading.

- Betsy needs to revalue herself as a reader to gain confidence that will support more risk-taking abilities.

Once we have gathered the wealth of information about the reader from various appropriate sources and developed a rich profile or case study, we are prepared to plan a reading program. In the next chapter we focus again on Betsy to create an instructional program for her and to make suggestions for her classmates.

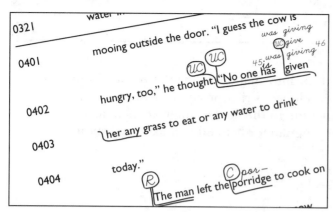

Chapter 11
Reading Curriculum and Strategy Lessons

As teachers develop "miscue ears" and focus on how students construct meaning through reading, they realize that all readers, in regular or special classes, improve their reading when they are in settings with a teacher who:

- Places students' interests and needs at the center of the program.
- Observes students on a regular basis through miscue analysis and kid watching (Owocki and Y. Goodman 2002).
- Plans instruction with a focus on students' strengths.
- Selects materials and instructional procedures that include a wide range of rich and supportive reading materials (Mooney 2001; 2004).
- Engages students in reading and writing across the curriculum.

In this chapter we consider the classroom curriculum and specific reading strategy lessons. Although Betsy is our focus in developing a rich literacy curriculum and instructional program, we also consider the other students in her classroom. We present specific strategy lessons for moderately proficient readers like Betsy and follow these with strategy lessons for proficient and non-proficient readers. We recommend a range of learning experiences, many reading and writing opportunities, and strategy lessons that are modifiable to engage members of Betsy's learning community.

Research in miscue analysis shows that the more personally involved students are in their reading the more proficiently they read and the more eagerly they expand their reading opportunities. Although whole language programs mean different things to different people, one essential attribute provides the foundation for all such programs: Personal involvement develops in a curriculum that *keeps the systems of language unified in a mutually supportive way.* By *whole* we mean the language utilized in the program is real reading and writing (Edelsky and Smith 1984). Students are invited to participate in a meaningful program, in which they are learning their language by *using it* and *talking about it.*

THE ONGOING READING CURRICULUM

Experiences essential to a holistic curriculum include listening to literature, reading, writing, integrating past experiences with new information, searching for knowledge, asking and answering questions, and becoming consciously aware of and discussing reading and the reading process. The following literacy experiences and opportunities are essential in a rich literacy curriculum.

Listening to a Variety of Texts

Reading to students on a daily basis from a variety of texts is integral to a holistic curriculum. Students quickly become aware of the parallel between listening and reading. When teachers encourage listeners to predict what will happen next in a story or to guess how a character might solve a problem, they are inviting them to take cognitive and linguistic risks—a way of becoming actively involved in assimilating information and constructing meaning. By listening and responding to teachers reading aloud (*Read Alouds*), Betsy and her classmates use the strategies of sampling, predicting, inferring, confirming, and integrating new information in a stress-free setting. The teacher enlists the librarian's help in selecting a variety of genres that broaden and deepen the students' knowledge of literature. The various kinds of literature relate to their inquiry projects in a range of subject areas. Their interests are stimulated by listening to audiotapes and CDs. Following listening experiences, time is set aside for writing and sketching in a listening log.

Newspapers, magazines, and nonfiction are all sources for listening experiences. When readings relate to current events and controversies, or when they are a part of ongoing inquiry projects, listeners and readers develop understandings of previously unfamiliar concepts and vocabulary. By listening to their teachers and their peers read, students become familiar with the structures of news features, scientific reports, political essays, and other literary forms while they share their concerns about the significant events of the day. In addition to sharing professionally authored texts, students' compositions read aloud provide evidence that the class values and celebrates their authorship. The content and form of a variety of stories and articles that students listen to, while expanding their linguistic experiences, also provide a model for writing.

Listening to Stories and More

Students value reading when they hear good stories told or read well. Such experiences are invitational demonstrations of the power of story, and, as a result, students often want to read to themselves and to others. Stories, poems, and songs that students hear again and again become "family stories" and classroom traditions that help create a bond among all the members of the classroom community. Literature heard often motivates students to extend the literature by adding another chapter, verse, or incident, or to write stories using the same characters that were central to their listening experience. In response to hearing stories, students dramatize or illustrate favorite ones.

Literature shared is culture shared, or at least it is a beginning of understanding. Experiencing the culture of other groups and societies through literature, perhaps as part of social studies, is another important reason for listening to stories on a regular basis.

Throughout the reading and retelling of *The Man Who Kept House*, Betsy showed little sign of enjoying or being amused by the story. Betsy and her peers need to experience stories that make them laugh and cry. The teacher selects stories to read aloud that move both children and teacher to laughter or tears. The 2003 Newbery Award winner, *The Tale of Despereaux* by Kate Di Camillo might appeal to Ms. Blau's students. Betsy might be moved by *A Taste of Blackberries* by Doris Buchanan Smith (1973) and amused by *Poems for the Very Young* by Michael Rosen, a British poet (1994), *Petrifying Poems* by Australian Jane Covernton and Craig Smith (1988), or *The Elevator Family* by Douglas Evans (2000). Laura Ingalls Wilder's Little House series still reaches out to children emotionally and provides background knowledge (for example, information about sod houses) for readers of stories such as *The Man Who Kept House.*

Silent Reading

Students need time for their own reading. Betsy's reading strategies become stronger with the opportunity to practice reading undisturbed during reasonable amounts of time on a daily basis. We suggest that the majority of students' reading be done silently. At least 75 percent of their reading time should be devoted to real reading and writing for real purposes across the curriculum, and no more than 25 percent spent on instructional lessons. School personnel and parents also need to understand that silent reading for authentic purposes is integral to developing reading proficiency.

Students are encouraged to self-select their reading fare, while teachers invite readers to try materials with a variety of content and diverse literary forms. To bring students and good reading material together, teachers become familiar not only with their students' interests and abilities, but also with accessible and suitable literature. There are excellent annotated resources for keeping informed about books, magazines, and other reading materials for children and youth on web sites and in professional journals.

Selecting Material

An important step in becoming an independent reader is learning to self-select material. Betsy must take the initiative in finding her own material or at least in making selections from a collection of materials that reflect her background and interests. Betsy may initially need help choosing reading material, but, as she discovers she can read what interests her, she will be motivated to make more challenging selections.

By self-selecting stories, poems, and books from a variety of genres (folk stories, nonfiction, fantasy, realism, history, science), Betsy will expand and deepen her reading proficiency. With the teacher's encouragement, students might have at least three pieces of reading material in their desk at all times. Many teachers invite students to have a book of their own choosing (*mine*), a book suggested by the teacher or librarian (*yours*), and a book chosen with the teacher, a friend, or a parent (*ours*). Teachers discuss reasons for their choices, and students tell what criteria they use for making their selections. By having a combination of materials always available, whether a magazine, a novel, or a poetry book, Betsy and her classmates make choices—developing a sense of control and accomplishment.

Reading Aloud

Students' oral reading is, for the most part, a somewhat formal presentation that includes making audio- or videotapes or reading stories to younger children, conducting radio broadcasts, reading one's own writings to classmates, making reports, reading recipes and directions to others, dramatizing plays, and participating in reader' theater or choral reading. Such presentations require time for practice. As Betsy develops a read-aloud voice for real audiences, her repetitions and multiple attempts on single words will diminish. To gain confidence as a reader, Betsy must be involved in reading experiences that are productive, that help her construct meaning, and that bring to her awareness strategies that support proficiency.

Content Area Reading and Conceptually Related Materials

When students have opportunities to experience and read in social studies, science, math, art, and other content areas, they expand their knowledge base as they build a range of concepts. In addition to conceptually related experiences, such as visiting a farm, discussing shelters (including sod houses), and actually seeing an old-fashioned churn at a local history museum, gathering information from various reference and nonfiction materials helps students such as Betsy build background knowledge that clarifies, expands, and extends unfamiliar concepts in stories like *The Man Who Kept House.*

When content area textbooks are unsuitable for Betsy because of overly complex syntax, format, or vocabulary, a group of conceptually related materials provides support. Pairing nonfiction materials with fiction on related topics provides a way of discussing and comparing similar concepts written in different genres. One group of students may select a nonfiction account of an event, while another group reads a fictionalized version. *The Thought of High Windows* by Lynn Kositsky (2004), *The Diary of Anne Frank* (1991), and *The Cage* by Ruth Minsky Sender (1988) are accounts, fiction and nonfiction, of female adolescents coping with Nazi domination of their countries during World War II. Paired materials or text sets include professionally authored single-concept texts, reference materials, student- and teacher-authored pieces, short chapters or articles from books, magazines, and newspapers that add appropriate and related background information.

Literature Study Groups

Literature groups provide Betsy and her peers opportunities to discuss numerous topics relating to the book they are reading, but none is more important than talking about the relationship between their lives and the literature (Short and Pierce 1998). In literature study, the teacher selects, with the students' interests and abilities in mind, four to six books depending on the size of the class. The students are invited to indicate their first and second preferences. On the basis of their book selections, the teacher organizes readers into groups of five or six. The most proficient and least proficient reader may be in the same group. Each group member has a copy of the book. The group decides on a number of pages to read in the time available between meetings. Those who want to read beyond that number do so if the members agree, but the advance information is not discussed so as not to spoil the discovery for others. If the group decides it is better that individuals not read ahead, those students are encouraged to read conceptually related materials or books by the same author while waiting for other group members to complete the mutually assigned pages. Students who need help keeping up with the group may take the book home so that parents become involved in enjoying a book with their child, listen to an audiotaped section of the text, or read with a partner or tutor. Less proficient readers must feel that they are keeping up with their group and contributing to it.

Because students are provided adequate reading time in class, it usually takes no more than one or two weeks to read and discuss a book. The amount of time allotted depends on the length and complexity of the text. The students often keep a log in which they note their reactions, responses to the literature, and any questions they have. Sticky notes are sometimes used to mark important places and questions for the group. Twice each week, the children and teacher meet to discuss the book and their reactions and to share the impact the literature has on them. For their own reasons (it grabbed me, I didn't understand this, this is a good description, this part reminds me of *The Wanderer*, I wish I could write like this), they read short sections aloud to each other.

Students benefit from the continuity of group meetings. However, if it is not possible to meet regularly, there are other ways to organize literature study groups. Students organize for group meetings by writing their names and the titles of the books they have finished reading on the board. When enough class members have read the same book, they come together to share their responses. Initially the teacher meets with groups to discuss and to demonstrate ways of sharing literature. Eventually, most students are able to handle literature-sharing groups on their own. Some groups have "a student researcher" sit outside the circle taking notes on the members' contributions and interactions. The researcher reports briefly to the group following the session, and all the students then evaluate the strengths as well as the needs of their group. Plans are made for improvement of their discussion techniques.

Readers compare the themes and plots of stories, talk about similarities and differences in characters and their relations, and talk about how they use their reading to learn. They realize that readers do not always respond in the same way and that it is possible to learn different things from the same material. Students begin to use and value their own background of experience and come to appreciate that what they already know helps them understand what the author is expressing. The teacher, as a member of the group, also reads, writes, and responds with the students.

Writing for Personal and Social Reasons

Betsy needs not only to talk and read about experiences that connect with her life and interests, but also to write about them. Through discussions about the function and forms of the literacy that surrounds them, Betsy and her classmates come to realize that reading and writing take place in everything they do. They are readers when they get information from a carton on the grocery shelf or follow traffic signs, and they are writers when they take phone messages, write a note, or make a shopping list. Students of all proficiencies and ages, including those in kindergarten, are expected to write daily: send pen-pal letters; keep records; make lists, labels, captions, and learning plans; order materials and supplies; author stories, poems, plays, and research reports; publish magazines and books; and engage in a range of literacy experiences available on the computer. Their writings are read aloud to different audiences for enjoyment and supportive responses.

With constant invitations and effective demonstrations, Betsy generates her own topics for writing stories, poems, songs, plays, and reports. The teacher organizes opportunities for students to write in journals and to return to those logs for writing inspiration, for example, "I feel just like Slow Loris" after reading Alexis Deacon's *Slow Loris* (2002), "I want to be just like Jackie Robinson" after reading Sharon Robinson's *Promises to Keep* (2004), or "*The Summer of the Swans* (Byars 1970) made me think about people with handicaps."

When reading and writing are a continuous part of the curriculum, students "learn to read like writers" (F. Smith 2004). They begin to ask, "Why and how did the author do that?" and over time, as they consider how professional authors write, they use the information, including conventions of spelling and writing, in revising and editing their own compositions and those of their friends.

Our focus now turns to the organization of strategy lessons for Betsy and other students, based on careful analysis of their reading.

READING STRATEGY LESSONS

Reading strategy lessons encourage readers to:

- Become consciously aware of the ways they sample, predict, infer, confirm, and integrate.
- Use their prior experiences and knowledge.
- Attend to the context of circumstances and situation.
- Use what they know about language (pragmatics, semantics, syntax, graphics, sound, phonics) to read for the purpose of making sense.

Reading strategy lessons are authentic literacy events (Edelsky and Smith 1984), in which the reader's strengths are emphasized to minimize weaknesses. As we have said, strategy lessons are a small part of reading instruction embedded in a rich literacy curriculum to solve problems, to respond to students' inquiries, and to increase the joy of reading (Y. Goodman, Watson and Burke 1996). Strategy lessons are conducted with individuals, small groups, or the entire class. The lessons are for readers who demonstrate a need for support in a particular area, and they are used when students benefit most from them. The instructional time is typically ten to twenty minutes. If a group is formed, the members change regularly, depending on need and interest.

The teacher, taking the role of facilitator, involves students as active participants in the experience. Students learn to evaluate their own abilities, select their own materials, and help plan their own learning experiences. Later, students may take on the roles of teacher and resource person. At the heart of strategy lessons are actively involved students in nonthreatening and nonjudgmental settings, in which learners have continuous opportunities to transact with each other and the teacher as well as with the author through the text. Students and teachers are engrossed in exploratory talk about content, language, and the reading process. Whether the discussion is about how reading works, about the subject matter and concepts of a text, or about responses to a specific passage, students examine, question, and listen thoughtfully to each other's ideas and opinions.

Strategy lessons tie reading to other aspects of the curriculum. Students *apply* the developing concepts about both language and the reading process to new reading events; they *expand* and integrate the concepts when appropriate with other sign systems, genres, and knowledge domains or disciplines.

The strategy lessons presented here build on Betsy's strengths in using all the systems of language and help her gain greater proficiency in her use of the reading strategies of sampling, predicting, inferring, and confirming. The lessons are suitable not only for Betsy and other moderately proficient readers, but they can be modified for readers of all proficiencies. At the end of this chapter, we also suggest strategy lessons for proficient and nonproficient readers.

Strategy Lesson: Conscious Awareness of Reading: Retrospective Miscue Analysis

Retrospective Miscue Analysis (RMA) is a strategy lesson that engages readers in an experience that values them as intelligent learners. Research in Retrospective Miscue Analysis clearly shows that readers become more proficient as they participate in RMA, inquiring into the reading process and becoming consciously aware of their own capabilities as a reader (Y. Goodman and Marek 1996; Y. Goodman 2000; Moore and Gilles 2005). All students, regardless of proficiency, are capable of thinking and talking about their reading. These metalinguistic and metacognitive discussions help students notice that miscues are related to "editing" the author's text and to translating the author's language into the reader's understandings.

To engage Betsy in talking and thinking about her reading, she is encouraged to listen to her own reading on audiotape and ask, "Am I making sense? Does my reading sound like language?" As she answers these questions, Betsy discusses with her teacher, and possibly other students, various appropriate strategies that help her focus on constructing meaning. Betsy comes to understand that proficient reading is not free of miscues. A retrospective discussion of her overcorrections and examples of her own syntactically and semantically acceptable miscues, as well as the miscues of other readers and teachers, highlights the positive influence of high-quality miscues on reading comprehension. It is important for students such as Betsy to understand that the goal of reading is not to struggle for accuracy, but to read for meaning. The students discover that high-quality miscues provide evidence that the reader is predicting and making sense. Nonproficient and moderately proficient readers gain insights into their own reading when they hear proficient readers explore their reasons for making miscues. Students who *appear* to comprehend, and who try to convince others and themselves that they have actually understood what they read, benefit from audiotaping and then critiquing their own reading and retelling.

Some moderately proficient readers reflect a subskills model of reading (mastering fragments of language in a hierarchy), in response to the Burke Reading Interview. The gap between what students think they should do as readers and what they actually do often causes them to lack confidence in their ability, especially when they come to difficult or unpredictable texts. Discussions about how they read allows them, often for the first time, to realize that what they thought was wrong—sometimes readers say they were "cheating"—is exactly what they *should* do to construct meaning. Betsy needs to understand that it is permissible to substitute or even skip some words, to continue reading even if she is uncertain about some concepts and vocabulary, and always to relate what she is reading to her past experiences and knowledge. Through these understandings, Betsy learns that she is capable of applying her successful reading strategies to predictable texts as well as to more complex and diverse texts. Debra Goodman (1999) helps readers see themselves as reading detectives, searching for clues to meaning and discarding those that don't make sense. The following strategy lessons fit well with the RMA experience.

Strategy Lesson: What Smart Readers Do

Discussions during small-group or one-on-one conferences are excellent venues for helping students understand that they have accomplishments and that they are not alone in their needs. To help Betsy think of herself as a more proficient reader, she must gain confidence in herself as a thinker and a learner and build on her strengths. Ms. Blau points out Betsy's high-quality miscues, that is, miscues that show she is constructing meaning, and how she almost always tries to make the text sound like language and to make sense of what she is reading. Some teachers, working with an entire class or a small group of students, put examples on an overhead or the board from readers who have proficiently handled text and discuss why these are high-quality miscues. Calling this strategy lesson *What Smart Readers Do* helps Betsy and other insecure readers think more positively about their abilities.

Strategy Lesson: How to Reach Your Goal

Many students, in response to the BRI question, *What would you like to do better as a reader?* say they want to read more, to comprehend better, or to read faster. Through RMA with students who have such goals, the teacher discusses what it means to be an efficient and flexible reader, to be able to read with greater understanding, and to read faster. When Betsy listens to an audiotape of her own reading, noting her overcorrections and repetitions, she and Ms. Blau discuss what she does when she reads proficiently, such as producing high-quality predictions and making sense. After such talk it is appropriate to discuss how overcorrections keep Betsy from reaching her goal, to read with greater understanding. Discussing what efficient readers do gives moderately proficient readers such as Betsy strategies to reach their goals.

Brian's teacher asked him if his prediction strategies helped him reach the goal he mentioned in the BRI, to read faster. He was sure they did. His teacher decided to discuss reading rate with Brian to help him and other students understand when it is appropriate to read fast but also to appreciate that there are times to slow down to savor the reading experience and think more deeply about the content and meaning of a text. Teachers help students understand that the more they know about a topic and the more interest they have in it, the faster and easier it is to read and understand, thereby reaching their goal.

Strategy Lesson: Functions of Reading and Writing

Another way for Betsy to see herself as a more proficient reader and to bolster her self-confidence, is to focus on developing conscious awareness of the role literacy plays in her life. To achieve this, Betsy and her classmates may participate in a series of strategy lessons. The first lesson begins by listing everything they read in school that day and on the previous day. For the next few days, the students keep lists of as many uses of reading and writing that they and their family members participate in at home and on their way to school or work. During subsequent strategy lessons, the students add to their lists of literacy engagements, who benefits from them, and what functions and purposes they serve.

Young children may go on an Environmental Print Walk with their teacher, sometimes taking photos but always jotting down all the written language they are able to read in their school and around their neighborhood. Returning to their classroom, students talk about the places print was found, as well as for whom it is written and the purpose it serves. Sometimes students recreate signs and post them around the room and make individual or class *I Can Read* books, writing about the photographs or drawings of the signs selected for their books. These books are added to the classroom library.

Strategy Lesson: Brainstorming (Preview, Overview, Review)

Brainstorming draws on what students know about a particular subject before they begin their reading. If they are to read a chapter, for example, in their science book, a number of strategy lessons are planned to prepare them for their reading. First, if students indicate they do not know enough about the subject to ask good questions or to volunteer information, the teacher sets up a browsing table with a variety of materials conceptually related to the topic. The students examine the artifacts, read books and articles, check the internet, and talk among themselves about the information. This preview gives students information, language, and confidence to enter into a preliminary discussion. When the students believe they are ready to plunge in, the teacher asks them to mention everything they know about the subject. They talk together in groups of two or three for a few minutes, listing everything they know. They then come together in a larger group to read their lists to the class. The teacher guides the students in organizing the information and then writes their contributions on the board or overhead transparency.

Graphic organizers provide a way of categorizing information. For example, if the topic of study is pollution, the students are encouraged either to list items under headings such as air pollution, noise pollution, and so on, or to place the word *pollution* in the center of the board and draw lines out in spokes to related subheadings. Some of the lines may connect (for example, industrial pollution has to do with more than one kind of pollution), thus forming a web or *idea frame*. After this preview, students *overview* the materials to be studied through their inquiry and reading, adding to the graphic display. If necessary, the teacher contributes to the overview. The appropriate language of the subject matter is used. As students continue their reading, they add to and amend the web. Sometimes, they keep their own copy of the graphic in their notebooks to update it as they read.

After reading the text, students *review* and discuss their lists or webs to relate what they have learned to previously known information. Brainstorming helps students understand how they use their own knowledge and information provided by classmates as a resource to support reading, as well as how new information relates to and builds on old information. These lessons often become the basis for writing research reports.

Strategy Lesson: Schema Story

Betsy has a strong sense of grammar at both the sentence and the story level (see her Grammatical Relations and Retelling). This language knowledge helps her predict and construct semantically cohesive sentences even though she does not completely understand a number of the concepts. On the other hand, another moderately proficient reader, Brian, the student mentioned in Chapter 8, needs to focus on the structures of sentences and stories, integrating all the systems of language.

In the schema story strategy lesson, the teacher divides or cuts up a structurally and conceptually well-written story or article into several sections. A high-quality short story or article is suitable as long as it has a definitive beginning, middle, and end. Good pieces to use are found in newspapers written for students or carefully selected chapters or sections from science and social studies texts. The divisions are made at points that are highly predictable both syntactically and semantically. Each section is pasted on a separate piece of construction paper, and one section is given to each member of a small group. The students read their sections silently. The readers are encouraged to think about what happened in the text before their section and to predict what will occur in the following section. The teacher asks the readers if they have the beginning of the story; if so, ask the student to read it and explain why it is the beginning. The students listen for clues and volunteer to read their passages when they think it is their turn. After the entire text is read, the students discuss how they made decisions about the position of their section in the total passage. The teacher shares the original with the class to verify their problem solving.

If this strategy is used individually, the student receives the scrambled sections of the text, reads them, and then arranges the sections in an order that makes sense syntactically and semantically. This strategy and the discussion of what happens as students participate in it help readers such as Brian understand that they make decisions based on their knowledge of the text's organizing structure and semantic intent.

Strategy Lesson: Selected Deletions or the Cloze Procedure

One means of encouraging Betsy to take risks by predicting and confirming involves the careful deletion of words within a syntactically and conceptually well-constructed story or article. Ms. Blau selects a story suitable to Betsy's interests. After the first paragraph or two, which does not include any deletions, a few highly semantically and syntactically predictable words or phrases are deleted, for example, one noun significant to the story and repeated three or more times, such as *house* or *husband* in *The Man Who Kept House*. Only words or phrases that Betsy is certain to supply are deleted. The text word or a synonym is acceptable. For more confident readers, less predictable words may be deleted; for example, typically every seventh word is removed in the cloze procedure.

A single miscue does not provide enough information on which to make decisions about strategy lessons, but, if in subsequent readings Ms. Blau finds instances involving a past perfect verb tense such as *has given* (line 0402), a strategy lesson can be conducted in which such verbs are deleted.

Success with this strategy lesson may indicate that miscues involving the past perfect tense have more to do with overattention to graphic information than with syntax. In Betsy's case, it appears that *has given* is an unfamiliar syntactic structure. The selected deletion strategy lesson allows her to become more familiar with the past perfect structure. Look through the typescript to determine whether a reader has miscued on any similar form or unit of language. (*The Man Who Kept House* has no other instances of the past perfect verb tense.)

The class and teacher hold a discussion concerning the strategy lesson procedure and how decisions are made about which word or phrase is acceptable. This helps students become confident that they can substitute meaningfully when they meet unfamiliar words or phrases. Students begin to realize they can fill the slots or offer a substitution because of the knowledge they bring to their reading.

Strategy Lesson: Meaningful Substitutions

As we've mentioned, the strategies Betsy uses to construct meaning should be discussed with her as strengths; she must understand that they are aids to her comprehension. Betsy often produces high-quality miscues efficiently, such as the substitution of *day* for *morning* and *job* for *work*, but on occasion she accepts nonsense (the substitution of the nonword *$gorun* for the text item *ground*). Because of Betsy's strong focus on meaning, her teacher may decide to encourage Betsy to produce meaningful substitutions rather than sounding out. Ms. Blau points out Betsy's high-quality miscues and discusses with her how she uses predicting and confirming strategies based on constructing meaning. Betsy needs assurance that it is more important to make sense of text than to sound out letters, syllables, and words. Given this kind of permission, Betsy develops confidence that she and the author, as a team, are constructing meaning.

A strategy that is similar to the previous lesson involves using a selection that has an unfamiliar term in it. The term may be unfamiliar in three ways:

- The concept is unknown.
- The pronunciation is unknown.
- Both are unknown.

The students read the text individually, with a partner, or in a small group. When they come to the word they don't know, they write all the possible substitutions on paper or on the board. As the author provides more information and as the readers progress through the text, they list additional possible substitutions, deleting previous ones that they now reject. Students discover that the more information they gather from the author, the more the meaning of the word or phrase is narrowed and evident. By the end of the text, the students select their best substitution and explain the clues used to predict and ultimately confirm their decision. The students conclude that, when they keep reading, they are often able to figure out what they were unsure of earlier.

Betsy should be reminded that using letters and sounds is a way of confirming good guesses, but it is not to be used as the only cuing source. Students come to understand that all concepts and words are not equally important and that proficient readers select the most important, helpful, and interesting ones. It is not necessary to pronounce every unfamiliar term or to learn every concept in depth; rather, each reader is selective about what is most important and meaningful in each text. Continuing to read in related materials adds to their knowledge. Discussion concerning the use of resources is helpful at this time, for example, when it is appropriate and efficient to use the dictionary, other reference books, or the internet, and when it is helpful to ask someone for information.

The selected deletions and the meaningful substitutions lessons encourage readers of all proficiencies to keep reading the text, to continue bringing their past experiences to their reading, and to construct a meaningful text that makes sense and sounds like language. Readers less proficient than Betsy may be advised to omit unknown words, to say *blank* and go on reading, or to produce a nonword placeholder, as Betsy does with *$gorun* for *ground*. Except in rare occurrences, Betsy needs to move from placeholders to substituting high-quality synonyms. The rationale for using placeholders is to allow readers to focus on meaning, to keep them from stalling on a word. This doesn't mean that we withhold the conventional pronunciation of words from readers. Students learn vocabulary and pronunciation through hearing and using the language in discussions and other meaningful situations. Students who have an interest in the meaning of a particular word quickly learn its pronunciation

Strategy Lesson: Name and Keep Going

Another strategy lesson that involves helping readers produce meaningful substitutions by gaining cues from the entire text to make sense of unknown names is Name and Keep Going. This strategy encourages readers to make acceptable substitutions for difficult-to-pronounce names of people, places, and things. The students gather information about the character such as *Kokovinis* in *The Great Brain*, or the place, *Appalachian Mountains*, mentioned in their social studies text, rather than laboriously sounding out each name. To keep reading, the students decide that substitutions (*Koko* for *Kokovinis* and *the mountains* for *Appalachian*) are acceptable. These suggestions are not meant to show disregard for conventional pronunciations; rather, the intent is to show moderately proficient readers that the major emphasis in reading is to make sense and discover the author's intent, not simply to sound out a label. Pronunciation can be determined later by consulting a resource or through class discussions.

Strategy Lesson: You Become the Author

To help Betsy become more of a risk taker, to strengthen her proficiency in predicting, and to encourage her ability to confirm, she is invited to choose, on the basis of the title only, one book from five or six with interestingly illustrated covers. The illustrations and print, with the exception of the title, are initially covered. On the basis of the title only, Betsy predicts what the book will be about. She presents her predictions, by writing or drawing them. After discussing her writing or illustrations, Betsy adds further predictions. She is invited to become an author by writing a story based on her predictions or illustrations that she compares later with the professionally authored text. This experience can involve small groups of students.

A similar lesson helps readers become interested in writing other kinds of texts. Students make predictions using headlines of news articles, titles of chapters, captions for graphs or illustrations, and then write their own article, chapter, or caption. After reading the original, classmates compare their predictions and writings. During a subsequent strategy lesson, Betsy and the members of her small group might discuss the information provided by the author and the information they added, and as well as whether the reading is easier because they first made predictions.

Strategy Lesson: After Retelling

Following a retelling, teachers often engage in one-on-one strategy lessons that focus on the material read. When the aided retelling is completed, Ms. Blau might ask questions specific to Betsy's retelling. She wants to learn why Betsy uses a particular reading strategy and to know more about how Betsy's background knowledge influences her comprehension. This strategy, similar to the RMA, provides an opportunity to ask students why they did what they did as they read. If, for example, a reader persistently substitutes one word for another and then at a certain point in the text self-corrects, the teacher reviews the various substitutions with the reader and asks the reader what prompted the correction. The following questions expand on retellings (Chapter 3) and help the teacher and reader gain insights into the reader's strategies.

- Did any (concept, idea, sentence, word) in the story give you trouble? (Offer the book to the reader to find the trouble spot.)
- Why did you leave out this word?
- You said (reader's word, nonword, or phrase here). What do you think that means?
- Have you ever heard this word or phrase before? What does it mean?
- Did you know what this was before you began the story, or did you learn it as you read?
- What clues before or after this helped you understand the text?
- What was the easiest part of this story for you? Explain.
- What was the hardest part of this story for you? Explain.
- Did you understand the story (text) from the very beginning? What helped you understand it?
- Were there times when you didn't understand the story (text)? Tell about those times. Where are those parts?
- Did the illustrations (or graphs or maps) help you or not? Explain.

Ms. Blau discussed the following with Betsy after the aided retelling of *The Man Who Kept House*:

T: Betsy, would you read this part again? [*Turns to the second page of the story.*]

B: "He began to make some butter. And he put the cream into the churn, he said ..."

T: How did the woodman make butter?

B: He put the cream in a ... sh ... churn?

T: What is a churn?

B: You can make butter in it I suppose. I never saw one. We made butter last year, but in a jar.

T: Well, you've got the right idea. You put the milk in a jar. A churn is a special kind of container for making butter. If you are interested let's look in some of our reference books or look up churn on the computer. Betsy, when the cow fell off the roof, you said she had the rope tied to her leg. Then what happened?

B: She was hanging on the roof.

T: [*Sketches a house with a flat roof.*] Betsy, will you draw where the cow was hanging?

B: [*Draws the cow hanging between the roof and the ground.*]

T: Now, will you tell me where the cow was hanging?

B: The cow fell off the roof and the rope caught her and she was hanging between the roof and the ground.

T: [*Points to the text.*] Betsy, will you read this again?

B: "As for, as for the cow, she hang between the roof and the ground, and there she had to stay."

T: You didn't read ground before and now you know it.

B: I had a picture in my mind.

T: Betsy, would you like to read another story similar to the one you just read?

B: Yes, I liked it pretty good.

T: Well, Wanda Gág wrote a story called *Gone Is Gone* (2003). Remember that she wrote *Millions of Cats* (1956)?

B: I know that book. I read it. I liked it.

T: *Gone Is Gone* is in the library. Ms. Bender (librarian) will help you find it and some other books Wanda Gag wrote.

Ms. Blau suggests that Betsy look at other authors' versions of the folktale about a bragging husband who changes places with his wife for a day. David McKee's adaptation is *The Man Who Was Going to Mind the House* (1973); William Wiesner's is *Turnabout* (1972). Ms. Blau used *Happily Ever After: Sharing Folk Literature with Elementary and Middle School Students* (2004) edited by Terrell Young as a resource about folk literature. This book offers suggestions for using folktales across the curriculum and presents ideas for helping students write their own.

Cambourne and Brown (1990) suggest a retelling strategy lesson, somewhat similar to the predicting strategies, that calls on students of varied proficiencies to write their predictions. The authors suggest that the teacher ask students in a small group to predict a story plot on the basis of a title only and to write their predictions quickly (in no more than two minutes). The students predict words or phrases that a reader would expect to encounter in the text. Students read and compare with others their plot and word predictions. Each student makes one comment about other group member's predictions; everyone listens. The students then read the text silently. The teacher directs the students to read either as if they were going to tell the story to their best friend when finished or as if they were going to take a test on the material. After reading, students write out the story as if they were writing it for someone who has not read it. In pairs, the students compare their retellings. They ask each other:

- What did I include/omit that you did not?
- Why did you include/omit this?
- Do you think I changed anything that alters the meaning?
- Did I use any words/phrases that are not in the story, but are good substitutions?
- If you could take a bit of my retelling and include it in yours, which part would you take? Why?

READING STRATEGY LESSONS FOR PROFICIENT READERS

We have made suggestions for moderately proficient readers such as Betsy and now turn to strategy lessons for proficient and non-proficient readers. We often say that the best way to help proficient readers is to *stay out of their way unless we are needed*. Certainly we must not impede readers by requiring them to participate in instructional experiences that are uninteresting and demeaning. RMA research shows that proficient readers benefit from strategy lessons when they are involved in talking and thinking about their own reading and writing processes (Goodman and Marek 1996). What is important is for the teacher to establish a supportive environment in which students discover their power with language. By providing more support and using appropriate materials, the following lessons are also adaptable to less proficient readers.

Strategy Lesson: Understanding Story Conventions

Through individual conferences, literature studies and book discussion groups, teachers help students become acquainted with authors' styles and their ways of developing themes, plots, and settings. They help readers understand *characterization* by asking questions that lead students to investigate how authors reveal their characters: How do we come to know, love, or hate a character through conversations, actions, reactions, and the character's thoughts? Questions concerning the *plot* include the following: What language does the author use to show action or what happens to make a story drag? Is the story believable and is it original, or is it unbelievable and old hat? How do you know? Is the reader prepared for events, and is there a logical sequence of cause-and-effect happenings? Is there a climax, and, if so, do the events credibly lead to the climax? Students are encouraged to think about *themes* that emerge easily from the text and engage them, as well as those that overwhelm them. Students chart or make webs to show the similar and different ways that their favorite authors use story conventions. By discussing authors' uses of conventions, readers build understandings about the writing process and are motivated to use these features to add richness to their own compositions.

Strategy Lesson: Exploring Literature

Students are encouraged to take responsibility for literature discussions and to respond to the literature with critical comments and real questions. Readers examine human relationships such as those between children and parents or among their own friends. For example, they compare such relationships in *Love, Ruby Lavender* (2001) by Deborah Wiles and in *Homecoming* (1981) by Cynthia Voight. Readers contrast books on the same subject, or books written by the same author. They may collect folktales of one country and then present orally or in writing what they learned about that country, including information about its geography, climate, people, beliefs, customs, and products. Students may compare what they learned in folktales with what they read in historical material.

Students often enjoy studying the *characteristics, language,* and *style* of one poet or illustrator. One student might present a poem using an audio- or videotape-recorder with background music and sounds; or create a PowerPoint presentation or a poster with text and photographs. Others might collect and write informational books and materials on a topic of interest such as the solar system, transformers, computers, cooking, or ecology, and then share these with others, including younger students.

Strategy Lesson: Critical Conversations

Gee (2001) says, "The forms of literacy learned in school usually do not lead to the urge or ability to think 'critically' in the sense of understanding how systems and institutions interrelate to help or harm people." Harste, Vasquez, Lewison, Breau, Leland, and Ociepka (2000) argue that readers need to go beyond discussions concerning what they have read or what has been read to them. Rather, teachers should involve students in age-appropriate materials and topics that kindle critical conversations. For example, students of various ages are capable of considering the topic of stereotyping and are encouraged to look for instances in their reading. When reading stories such as *The Man Who Kept House*, Betsy and her friends might ponder gender roles in workplaces and in homes. Younger students can deepen their thoughts by reading *Goin' Someplace Special* (2001) by Patricia McKissack while older students discuss the many social issues evident in *Hush* (2002) by Jacqueline Woodson, and Lois Lowry's *The Giver* (1993), *Gathering Blue* (2000), and *Number the Stars* (1989). Readers develop a deeper understanding of stories as they explore their own beliefs and expose the values of the characters with critical questions such as: Whose story is this? Who benefits? and What voices are not being heard? (Comber and Simpson 2001).

Strategy Lesson: Notice Something New

Many stories, such as *The Quiltmaker's Gift* (2001) by Jeff Brumbeau, are invitations for critical conversations as well as for a strategy lesson that a group of children named Notice Something New. Critical conversations arise in *The Quiltmaker's Gift* when readers are introduced to a generous quiltmaker who makes the most beautiful quilts in the world and then gives them away to the poor and needy. Readers meet a greedy king who hoards treasures but continues to yearn for more. He is sure one of the quilts will make him happy. The quiltmaker says she will make a quilt for him only if he gives away everything he owns. The questions that arise are critically social in nature as children ponder the king's dilemma and wonder if they are willing to part with their treasures and, if so, to whom. To encourage critical conversations, try reading a story a second or third time. In the Notice Something New strategy, one reader at a time closes his/her eyes and points to something in one of the lovely and detailed illustrations. The student then explains whether he/she *noticed* this item when the story was first read and who might benefit from the treasure. What is critical, as well as surprising, is the number of times the students say, "I didn't see that before." In one second-third grade group, the children mentioned that the items could be given away to the Salvation Army, a homeless shelter, their Sunday school class, and a local nursing home. Students often add that they would like the item for themselves or for their classroom

READING STRATEGY LESSONS FOR NONPROFICIENT READERS

Strategy lessons help nonproficient readers keep their focus on making sense. At the same time, they provide students with language to talk about reading, strategies, and language cuing systems. Some nonproficient readers respond to their reading with such negative emotions that they develop strategies to avoid reading as much as possible (Coles 1999). Nonproficient readers need teachers to help them revalue themselves as readers (Rhodes and Dudley-Marling 1996). The following lessons are adaptable for moderately proficient and proficient readers by using more sophisticated concepts and language materials.

Strategy Lesson: Reading Along with Me

Three different strategy lessons help readers examine the print in their world and to focus on authentic reading and writing. The lessons provide nonproficient readers with demonstrations of the flow of their reading, along with the appropriate intonation that allows them to focus on meaning. These lessons promote satisfying and meaningful reading experiences. Sharing these lessons with parents help them engage their children in comfortable *read-alongs* at home (Trelease 2001).

- Books on tapes and CDs allow students to listen and follow along at a listening center. Initially, the teacher sits with reluctant readers to show them how to follow along with the print while they listen to the recordings. Eventually, readers comfortably and independently participate in these lessons.

- Reading along as a teacher reads is similar to the taped-reading strategy lesson but provides teachers with opportunities to observe readers' reactions more directly. As the reader follows along, the teacher occasionally asks, "Where am I reading?" This invites readers into the process, letting them know the importance of attending to the print while constructing meaning. As readers become more comfortable with the lessons, the teacher suggests that they read aloud together. As they become more proficient, the teacher moves in and out of the supportive reading role depending on the confidence of the reader. When the reader is reading comfortably, the teacher becomes more silent; when the reader hesitates or slows down, the teacher reads louder to keep the reading flow going and to support the reader. Some reading professionals call this Assisted Reading (Hoskisson 1975).

- Buddy reading involves two readers, usually with similar reading proficiencies, reading together. The readers, often with the help of the teacher, select a predictable and accessible text that they will enjoy. The teacher involves the entire class in understanding the role of miscues, so that students know that, whenever they listen to their peers read, their roles are to support each other in making sense and not to correct miscues. Readers of all proficiency levels find discussion about miscues useful. It is easy to engage readers in learning to wait while the person reading orally solves his or her own problem. Readers soon discover that there are high-quality miscues that do not need to be corrected. Buddy readers often have wonderful discussions about language as they discuss appropriate reading strategies.

Strategy Lesson: Big Books

Holdaway (1979) helped popularize the "big book" concept, in which favorite picture books are enlarged so that a group of students can see, read, and discuss the text. Such discussions engage readers in exploring text features, the relations between text and illustrations, how language works, and the use of appropriate reading strategies. After reading with the teacher, children enjoy revisiting the big book as well as reading the standard-size book on their own. Big books need to be selected carefully. The language should be predictable, with repetitious or cumulative words and phrases, as well as familiar concepts. With enlarged features, big books facilitate class discussions about letter-sound patterns, rhyming, spelling patterns, punctuation, and other writing conventions. Big books are available from many publishing companies, or teachers and students make them. Many older students like to write and illustrate big books for younger children.

Strategy Lesson: Estimate, Read, Respond, Question

In this strategy lesson, students quickly look over the text (often content-area material) and estimate how far they can read with comprehension. They then make a check mark with a pencil in the margin at that spot. Each student begins reading. In most cases the reading is silent, but for some it may be oral. The teacher might use Assisted Reading (see Reading Along with Me Strategy Lesson above). When the readers reach the check mark, they briefly respond to the text in any way they choose (retelling, telling what it reminds them of, offering a critique or opinion). The reader then asks the teacher a question about the text. The teacher keeps notes about the kinds of questions asked; they may be "real" ones, in which the student seeks information and uses the teacher as a resource person, or they may be inconsequential questions that require only surface-level information to answer. (In a later session, the class discusses which types of questions promote more meaningful and relevant conversations.) Depending on the student's responses, the teacher asks a question. The procedure moves quickly so that readers do not get bogged down with asking or answering questions. The estimating procedure should not be omitted because it gives the reader control of the experience. Discussion that closes the session has to do with which factors cause readers to make the estimations they make, how readers in their responses relate the text to their lives, and what happens when readers ask rather than answer questions (Watson and Gilles 1987).

Strategy Lesson: Language Experience

Involving students in writing their own stories, articles, directions, songs, school chants and cheers, jokes, finger plays, advertisements, and commercials, whether in small groups or with the teacher, provides opportunities for students to express themselves creatively and meaningfully. The teacher serves as a scribe, taking dictation while the student-composers watch carefully, making sure the teacher gets the language down appropriately. Based on important events or significant personal experiences (the necessary *experience* part of *the language experience*) (Allen 1982; Sampson, Allen, and Sampson 1990), the teacher invites the student authors to compose the event for a book, article, or newsletter that eventually is prominently displayed in the classroom or school library. The teacher/scribe makes it obvious that the student is in control of the language event. On a regular basis, but especially when the student shows interest in the writing process, the teacher invites him or her to take the pencil and continue writing. The teacher uses professional judgment in selecting the appropriate time to be a scribe, when to turn the writing over to the student, and when to take the pen back because the student needs support or is tired. The stories become reading material for the entire class. Students respond with great interest to student-authored writing. They can usually read their own writing proficiently.

Classroom-publishing of student-authored books, magazines, and newspapers build on students' familiar language, which is highly predictable and easily read by nonproficient readers. When older students share the language unique to teenagers and write *A Dictionary of Adolescent Language Use* or a list of their instant messaging abbreviations, they learn about variations of language, as well as how and why it changes. Students use computers to publish posters, signs, leaflets, maps, CD and video jackets, baseball cards, bumper stickers, and T-shirts. Students make books of family sayings and stories (See the Foxfire Series, Collins 1999), nursery rhymes, song lyrics, favorite recipes—all of which bring their world and their language into the classroom and demonstrates their capability and ownership of their reading and writing. When first-graders talk about and then teach a jump rope rhyme to their teacher, who writes it on the board while they write it on paper for themselves, the children are using their own resources and familiar language. When they write (whether it is mock letters, "pretend," or conventional print), or when they dictate to their teacher, they use their memory of past experiences as well as familiar language to help them write and then read what they have written.

AN INVITATION

The reading curriculum and strategy lessons in this chapter are based on the theory, research, and view of reading explored in this book and do not, by any means, exhaust the possibilities of rich and supportive experiences that help students become enthusiastic and proficient readers. We hope that the lessons here serve as prototypes to be modified by teachers for their students. We invite our readers to use their professional knowledge of language about reading, writing, listening, human development, curriculum, learning, and teaching to organize a literate community of students by creating positive reading experiences for all.

water in...

0321

mooing outside the door. "I guess the cow is

was giving

0401

UC *UC* *is give* 46

45. *was giving*

hungry, too," he thought. "No one has given

0402

her any grass to eat or any water to drink

0403

today."

0404

R The man left the *C* *por-* porridge to cook on

cow

APPENDICES

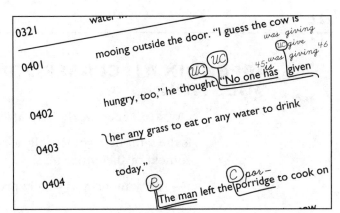

Appendix A

Summary of Procedures

APPENDIX A1: CLASSROOM PROCEDURE QUESTIONS

QUESTION 1: *Syntactic Acceptability*

Is the sentence syntactically acceptable in the reader's dialect and within the context of the entire text?

Y—The sentence, as finally produced by the reader, is syntactically acceptable.

N—The sentence, as finally produced by the reader, is not syntactically acceptable. (Partial acceptability is not considered in this procedure.)

QUESTION 2: *Semantic Acceptability*

Is the sentence semantically acceptable in the reader's dialect and within the context of the entire text? (Question 2 is coded N if Question 1 is coded N.)

Y—The sentence, as finally produced by the reader, is semantically acceptable.

N—The sentence, as finally produced by the reader, is not semantically acceptable. (Partial acceptability is not considered in this procedure.)

QUESTION 3: *Meaning Change*

Does the sentence, as finally produced by the reader, change the meaning of the entire text? (Question 3 is coded only if Questions 1 and 2 are coded Y.)

N—There is no change in the meaning.

P—There is inconsistency, loss, or change of a *minor* idea, incident, character, fact, sequence, or concept.

Y—There is inconsistency, loss, or change of a *major* idea, incident, character, fact, sequence, or concept.

QUESTION 4—*Graphic Similarity*

How much does the miscue (OR) *look like* the text word (ER)?

H—A high degree of graphic similarity exists between the miscue (OR) and the text word (ER).

S—Some degree of graphic similarity exists between the miscue (OR) and the text word (ER).

N—No degree of graphic similarity exists between the miscue (OR) and the text word (ER).

QUESTION 5: *Sound Similarity* (Optional)*

How much does the miscue (OR) sound like the expected response (ER)?

H—A high degree of sound similarity exists between the miscue (OR) and the expected response (ER).

*Miscue analysis research shows that sound similarity is similar (lower in High and Some) to graphic similarity, therefore, sound similarity is optional in this procedure.

S—Some degree of sound similarity exists between the miscue (OR) and the expected response (ER).

N—No degree of sound similarity exists between the miscue (OR) and the expected response (ER).

APPENDIX A2: IN-DEPTH PROCEDURE QUESTIONS

QUESTION 1: *Syntactic acceptability*

Does the miscue occur in a structure that is syntactically acceptable *in the reader's dialect?*

Y (Yes)—The miscue is completely syntactically acceptable within the sentence and within the entire text.

P (Partial)—The miscue is syntactically acceptable with the first part of the sentence or is syntactically acceptable with the last part of the sentence. Or, the miscue is syntactically acceptable within the sentence, but not within the entire text.

N (No)—The miscue is not syntactically acceptable.

QUESTION 2: *Semantic acceptability*

Does the miscue occur in a structure that is semantically acceptable *in the reader's dialect?* Semantic acceptability cannot be coded higher than syntactic acceptability.

Y (Yes)—The miscue is completely semantically acceptable within the sentence and within the entire text.

P (Partial)—The miscue is semantically acceptable with either the first part of the sentence or is semantically acceptable with the last part of the sentence. Or, the miscue is semantically acceptable within the sentence, but not within the entire text.

N (No)—The miscue is not semantically acceptable.

QUESTION 3: *Meaning change*

Does the miscue change the meaning of the entire text? This question is asked only if the miscues are both syntactically and semantically acceptable (Q1 = Y and Q2 = Y).

N (No)—There is no change in meaning.

P (Partial)—There is inconsistency, loss, or change of a minor idea, incident, character, fact, sequence, or concept.

Y (Yes)—There is inconsistency, loss, or change of a major idea, incident, character, fact, sequence, or concept (see note below).

QUESTION 4—*Correction*

Is the miscue corrected?

Y (Yes)—The miscue is corrected.

P (Partial)—There is either an unsuccessful attempt to correct, or the expected response is read and then abandoned.

N (No)—There is no attempt to correct.

QUESTION 5: *Graphic similarity*

How much does the miscue (OR) look like the text word (ER)?

H (High)—A high degree of graphic similarity exists between the miscue and the text word.

S (Some)—Some degree of graphic similarity exists between the miscue and the text word.

N (None)—No degree of graphic similarity exists between the miscue and the text word.

QUESTION 6: *Sound similarity*

How much does the miscue (OR) sound like the expected response (ER)?

H (High)—A high degree of sound similarity exists between the miscue and the expected response.

S (Some)—Some degree of sound similarity exists between the miscue and the expected response.

N (None)—No degree of sound similarity exists between the miscue and the expected response.

Note: Many have raised questions about the use of Y to equal loss in Question 3, while Y is equal to acceptability in Questions 1 and 2. This is a purposeful shift in order to cause coders to consider the quality of the miscue in relation to all the cuing systems and strategies, rather than automatically code Y for no meaning change.

APPENDIX A3: IN-DEPTH PROCEDURE PATTERNS

Meaning Construction Patterns

No loss				Partial Loss				Loss	
2 3 4	2 3 4			2 3 4	2 3 4			2 3 4	
Y N Y	Y Y Y			Y P N	Y Y N			N — N	
Y N N	P — Y			Y N P	Y P P			N — P	
Y P Y	N — Y			Y Y P	P — P			P — N*	
					P — N*				

*This pattern will be Loss except in a few cases. The criteria for Partial Loss needs to be considered carefully (see discussion).

Patterns for Grammatical Relations

Strength			Partial Strength			Overcorrection			Weakness		
1	2	4	1	2	4	1	2	4	1	2	4
N	N	Y	Y	N	N	Y	Y	Y	N	N	N
P	N	Y	Y	P	N	Y	Y	P	P	N	N
Y	N	Y	Y	N	P				P	P	N
P	P	Y	Y	P	P				N	N	P
Y	P	Y							P	N	P
Y	Y	N							P	P	P

APPENDIX A4: GENERAL PROCEDURE FOR MARKING MISCUES

Substitutions
Write the miscue above the appropriate text:

> *There*
> Where is Sven?
>
> *this is a*
> "No," said the voice.
>
> ⟨Was⟩something⟨wrong⟩ with Papa?

Omissions
Circle the omitted text item:

> We thought ⟨up⟩ different ways to jump.

Insertions
Write the OR above the carat ∧ used to mark the insertion:

> 0321   First listen. ∧
>
> 0718   The other way
>
> 0719   *is*
>   ∧to take care of your heart

Repetitions
Draw a line under the repeated text portion and up in front of the first word repeated, ending in a circle. The letter in the circle shows the reason for regressing.

1. Anticipating and Reflecting

    (R)
    The village where I grew up . . .

2. Repeating and Correcting

    0301   © feels
                Blood feeds

    0302   ©c– ©oranges
                all the cells and organs

3. Repeating and Abandoning a Correct Form

                (ac) complaining
    She was always comparing.

4. Repeating and Unsuccessfully Attempting to Correct

    (UC)   Clarida
                Clarence
    Her name was Clarible.

5. Repeating That Affects More Than One Miscue:

    0408-9   © sense   (UC)
                . . . the heart is a sensitive machine

Additional Markings

1. Partial Attempts:

    0405   © por–
                The man left the porridge . . .

2. Nonword Substitutions:

    $distroubles
    If it bothers you to think of it as baby sitting . . .

3. Dialect and Other Language Variations:

                like (d)
    . . . about everybody likes babies.

4. Misarticulations:

ⓐ$pecific
He had a specific place in mind.

$hangabers ⓐ
They make hamburgers over the fire.

5. Intonation Shifts:

récord
He will record her voice.

6. Split Syllables:

The lit/tle girl yelled her head off.

7. Pauses:

0105   *23 sec Ⓟ*
              do all day/while I am away cutting wood?"

8. Complex Miscues:

0104   *Ⓒ I want you*
              from work, he said to his wife, "What do you

9. Repeated Miscues:

0304   *cream*
              nose in the churn. "Get out! Get out!"

0307   *cream RM*
              room. It bumped into the churn, knocking it

10. Multiple Miscues:

0308   *Ⓒ shadow / shout*
              over. The cream splashed all over the room.

0321 water in

mooing outside the door. "I guess the cow is

0401 hungry, too," he thought. "No one has given

0402 her any grass to eat or any water to drink

0403 today."

0404 The man left the porridge to cook on

Appendix B
Gordon's Miscue Analysis:
The Beat of My Heart

APPENDIX B1: MARKED TYPESCRIPT

Name *Gordon*   Date *May 23*

Grade/Age *9 years*   Teacher *Mr. Murphy*

Reference *The Beat of My Heart*

THE BEAT OF MY HEART

0101   *Lu-bump* / Lub-dup . . . *(Lu sounds like initial sounds in love.)* / *RM*

0102   *Lu-bumps* / Lub-dup . . . / *RM*

0103   *Lu-bump* / Lub-dup . . .

0104   This strange (sound) [2]

0105   *$soud* [3] / is the sound

0106   of a wonderful (machine) *m—* / *m—* ©

0107   inside your body.

0108   © *It's* [4] It is the sound [6]

0109   *heartbeat* [5] / of your heart beat(ing.)

0110   Your heart is a pump *bump* [6]

0111   © which (will never *near* [7]

0112   stop working

0113   as long as you live,

0114   but it can (rest) © [8]

0115   *E* even while it is working.

0116   Your heart

0117   is a hollow muscle   *$mu-si-cle* [9]

0118   divided into four parts.   C *in—*

0119   It is about the size

0120   of your fist.   R   C *first* [10]

0121   As you grow,

0122   it too will grow in size.   *//* [11]

0201   To find out

0202   where your heart is,   C *the* [12]

0203   put your right hand

0204   in the middle   R

0205   of the left side of your chest.   C *chests* [13] *ch—*

0206   Now move your fingers around

0207   until you find

0208   the spot where

0209   the heartbeat is strongest.   *strong* [14] *st—*

0210   Your hand is now

0211   pointing to your heart.

0212   Listen to the heartbeat   *your* [15]

0213   Ⓡ ⌐of a friend

0214   by putting your ear

0215   to his chest.   *on* [16]

0216   To hear the sound ˄even better,   [17]

0217   hold an empty mailing tube   *a* [18]

0218   or a ⌐rolled-up piece   Ⓒ *roll–*

0219   of heavy paper

0220   to your ⌐friend⌐s heart.   Ⓒ [19]

0221   When the heart goes lub,   *lump* [20]

0222   it is ⌐drawing in blood.   Ⓒ *d–*

0223   When it goes dup,   *bump* [21]

0224   it is pushing blood out

0225   to all parts of the body.   *RM your* [RM]

0226   Your heart has

0227   this most important job⌐to do —   Ⓡ

0228   ⌐pumping blood   Ⓒ *pum–*

0229   to all parts of your body.

0301   ⌐Blood⌐feeds   Ⓡ Ⓒ *feels* [22]

0302   Cc – C oranges [23]
all the cells and organs

0303   of your body

0304   so that they can do

0305   C sp – sp –
their own special work

0306   5 O 24 fat [25]
to keep you physically fit.

0307   Your heart pumps blood

0308   from your head

0309   to your toes,

0310   C$ liver [26] (Rhymes with diver)
to your liver

0311   and your lungs.

0312   C if [27]
Just as a wheel

0313   can turn slowly or fast,

0314   R
your heart can work

0315   the [28] C race [29]
at a slow or a fast pace.

0316   If you want to see

0317   C chances [30] [31] d
how your heart changes quickly

0318   C place [32]
from working at a slow pace

0319   6 O
to working at a faster pace,

0320   try this.

0321   ⓒ First listen [33]

0322   *To* to a friend's heartbeat

0323   and count the number of beats

0324   *few* in a minute [34]

0325   Now ask your friend

0326   to run fast

0327   for about a minute.

0328   *the beat* [35] [36] Then listen to his heart again.

0329   ⓒ *Now* [37] How many times a minute

0330   *yet* [38] is his heart beating now?

0401   Count his heartbeats again

0402   ⓒ *finished* [39] after he has rested

0403   for a minute.

0404   [40] *$coopering* ⓡ By comparing the number

0405   of heartbeats

0406   ⓒ *dif*– ⓒ *con*– under these different conditions,

0407   you will discover that

0408   the heart is

0409   [41] ⓒ [42] *sense* ⓤⓒ a sensitive machine

0410   *RM*
            (C) *your*
            working inside the body.
- -

0501   (C) *face* [43]
            You can test this fact again

0502   by checking your own heartbeat.

0503   (C) *then* [44] *fingers* [45]
            Place three fingertips

0504   of your right hand   (UC) *worst* [47]
                                         $wrist
                                         w —
                                         w —   *"No"*

0505   *side* [46]
            on the inside of your left wrist.

0506   *find* (C) *b—* [48]
            You will feel the beat

0507   of your heart.

0508   (UC) *That* [49]
            Then   20 *sl* / *O*
            This is called your pulse.   *"Oh, pulse. And that's
                                          wrist" (pointing to wrist
                                          on line 0505)."*

0509   Count the number of times

0510   (C) *you* [50]
            your heart beats in a minute.
_____

0601   Now, run for a minute

0602   and count the heartbeats

0603   in your pulse again.

0604   Lie down and rest for a minute

0605   *one* [51]
            and then count once more.

0606   (R)   (C) *ex—*
            See how exercise makes

0607   your heart work

0608   harder and faster?

0609   (C) *Ex-*
        Exercise helps your heart

0610   *52*
        (to) become stronger

0611   and be able

0612   to do its work better.

0613   Your heart beats

0614   (C) *a* [53]
        as long as you live.

0615   *one-six* [54] *minute* [55]
        It rests for 1/6 of a second

0616   between every beat.

0617   (C) *on* [56]   [57]
        When you are asleep (or resting,)

0618   your heart beats

0619   (C) *that* [58]
        at a slower rate.

0620   This rest gives your heart

0621   (C) *chan-*
        a chance to keep

0622   [59] *a* (C)   [60] (C) *con-*
        in (good working) (condition

0623   [61] *you*
        as well as to grow

0624   [62]   [63]
        (bigger) and (stronger.)

- -

0701   (C) *S-*
        Since you are becoming

0702   taller and heavier

0703   (R)   [64]
        every (school) year,

0704 *C you* RM   *C large* 65
        your heart must grow larger, too.

0705 RM
        Your bigger body needs

0706   a bigger motor to keep it

0707   in good working order.

0708 *C Then* 66
        There are many ways

0709   to take care of your heart,

0710 67   68 *ways*
        but the two best ones are

0711   the easiest to do.

0712 *a lot* 69
        One is to get lots of exercise

0713 70
        by playing vigorous games

0714   out of doors.

0715   Play games that have lots

0716   of running and jumping,

0717   or hitting and kicking balls.

0718 *R*
        The other way

0719 *is* 71
        to take care of your heart

0720   is to be sure you get

0721   at least ten hours of sleep

0722   every night

0723   and do restful things

0724   ⓒ for 72
                └from time to time

0725   throughout the day.   10 sec

0726   On and on your heart beats—

0727   ⓒ   73
                └year ⓘn and year out.

0728   *Lu-bump* RM
                Lub-dup . . .

0729   *Lu-bump* RM
                Lub-dup . . .

0730   *Lu-bump* RM
                Lub-dup . . .

Note: Gordon's miscues are numbered for coding on the In-Depth Procedure Coding Form.

APPENDIX B2: GORDON'S EXPOSITORY RETELLING

Gordon's Combined Aided and Unaided Retelling

T: Thank you, Gordon. Now, if you'll close the book I'd like to ask you some questions. First, would you tell me what you remember about this selection?

G: Well, it was telling you about ... about your body and how ... how it works and ... um ... it tells you where ... from what place ... to what place your blood goes and ... um ... as you get bigger everything has to get bigger with it or else it stops. Ah, it was telling you how you can listen to your heart beat ... um ... and it tells you what to eat and ... um ... how to test out ... *(20 seconds)*

T: Anything else?

G: Well, no.

T: You said it told how you can listen to your heartbeat. How did it say to do that?

G: It said that ... ask your friend to run and then listen to his heartbeat. To count how many heartbeats and then you can lie down and then count again and ... um ... um ... it said that you could listen to a friend's heartbeat and ... um ... you could do it by yourself. I can't think of anything else.

Vannier, Maryhelen. 1967. In *Sounds of Mystery.* Edited by Bill Martin, Jr. New York: Holt, Rinehart and Winston.

T: So, you said a couple of things. You said that it said this is how it works. Do you remember how it said it works?

G: Oh, not really.

T: Do you remember anything else about how it works?

G: Well *(15 seconds)*, you remember where the blood went?

T: Okay, tell me about it.

G: First it goes to your ... goes to your ... I forget where. I think it was your heart and then it goes to your toes and then it goes to your liver ... ah ... then it ... it, I think it goes up again and it keeps on doing that and you can also put your finger on your heart to see how ... to see where you heart beats the most ... beats the heaviest.

T: Tell me about that beating the heaviest.

G: You put your fingertips on where your heart is and you try to find where it is the heaviest just with your fingers and then you count how many thumps you hear.

T: Have you ever done anything like that?

G: No.

T: So you said that you counted the thumps. Did it tell about what the heart sounded like at all?

G: Yeah, it said it was something like the bump.

T: Why do you think this selection was in a book? What do you think they wanted you to remember from reading?

G: Well, because in school you have to read things like that. You have to know all those things about your body. They told you a little bit about it so you could answer questions.

T: What was the main thing that this was about.

G: Your heartbeat.

T: Um hum, so from reading this, what did you figure out was the most important thing?

G: That it beats.

T: And why is that important?

G: So you can stay alive.

T: So what does the blood do to help you stay alive?

G: It goes?

T: (10 seconds) Yes?

G: It goes from the heart. It goes down to your toes, it goes to your liver and it goes back down again ... in a pattern.

T: You told me what you learned from reading this. Did you know anything about the heart before you began reading this?

G: Well, I knew blood went through your body, but I didn't know where it was going ... what parts it was going to.

T: Okay, so the new information you got from this was what? Can you just sum that up?

G: That where the blood goes from place to place and um ... ah ... let's see ... There were so many things, but I can't remember them all. I can't remember.

T: You said something about ... that you could ... um ... test out? What was that part about?

G: I learned that you can ... well ... I knew that you could test some parts of your body. You could count how many heartbeats you had after you did certain things.

T: Like what?

G: Like running.

T: What happens when you run?

G: You get out of breath ... uh ... and your heart beats faster?

T: Is that ... tell me about the heart beating faster.

G: It just does.

T: Did this selection tell you anything about what you should do for your heart?

G: Not really.

T: Do you know how you can take care of your heart?

G: You can take vitamin pills. You can drink milk and eat things that are good for you.

T: Gordon, the author told us something about the size of the heart. Can you remember what that was?

G: I think it gets bigger as you get bigger.

T: Do you remember the size of the heart?

G: It's one-six or something like that.

T: In this chapter the author tells us about certain ... uh ... experiments you can do to find out about the heart. You've mentioned asking your friend to run and then listening to his heartbeat. Can you tell me more about how you would do that?

G: You just listen.

T: How?

G: I don't know.

T: You also said you could put your finger on your heart to see where your heart beats the heaviest. Where exactly would you put your fingers?

G: On your chest.

T: Anywhere else?

G: Uh-uh *(no)*

T: Did the author compare the heart to anything?

G: Not that I can remember.

T: Gordon, would you draw a picture of the heart?

G: *(Draws a heart shape. Does not indicate the four parts as mentioned in the passage.)* Well, that's sorta like it, but not too much like the picture in the book.

T: I understand that.

Gordon's Retelling Specifically Related to the Reading Process

T: Gordon, did you think that story was easy or hard to read?

G: Kinda hard.

T: Why?

G: I didn't know a lot of the stuff.

T: *(hands the book back to Gordon)* Would you show me some part that you thought was hard?

G: *(spends 45 seconds looking at the story)* I think it was all hard.

T: Was any part easy?

G: It wasn't too bad, but not too easy.

T: What does this mean? *(points to "Lub-dup, Lub-dup ...")*

G: That's the heartbeat.

T: Did you know that at the beginning of the story?

G: No. I found out and kinda guessed.

T: Gordon, can you remember what you were thinking as you read this? *(points to lines 0116–18)* Will you read it?

G: "Your heart is a hollow ..." I don't know that word (muscle) ..." divided into four parts."

T: What are you thinking about.

G: I could divide my heart in four parts. *(divides his picture of a heart into four parts)*

T: You did divide it into four parts. Another question ... how did you get this? (points to wrist on line 0505)

G: "... left wrist." I knew it wasn't right, but I got it when ... *(reads silently ahead to line 0508)* ... I read this about your pulse.

T: Is there anything else you want to tell me about how you felt when you read that passage?

G: Um ... no ... it was kinda long.

T: Anything else?

G: Uh uh (no)

T: Gordon, thanks for reading. I enjoyed talking with you.

APPENDIX B3: GORDON'S SCORED EXPOSITORY RETELLING GUIDE: *THE BEAT OF MY HEART*

Reader _Gordon_

Date _May 23_

**Specific Information
(50 points)** _25_

The Heart *(10)* _4_

Is a pump (Analogy)
Rests even while working   *"tells how your body works"*
Is a hollow muscle
Divided into four parts   *(Gets this on rereading)*
About the size of your fist
Grows as you grow *"as you get bigger everything has to get bigger"*

Blood *(8)* _6_

With one beat blood is drawn in; with the next beat blood is pushed out
Blood feeds cells and organs which is needed for the body to be physically fit
*<u>Blood pumps to liver to lungs</u> *"goes in a pattern to toes"*

Heartbeat *(8)* _2_

The heart can beat slow or fast
Heartbeat felt in your wrist is your pulse
Rests 1/6 second between beats
Beats at a slower rate when asleep or resting

Conditions *(8)* _5_

Exercise helps heart become stronger and do work better.
Two best ways of taking care of heart: vigorous games and at least 10 hours of
    sleep every night.

Experiments Making Use of Specific Information

<u>Find your heart by moving fingers</u> around on the left side of your chest. Find
where the <u>beat is strongest.</u> *(3)* *"beats the heaviest"*   _2_

Listen to the heartbeat of a friend by putting your ear to his chest. Listen by
using a mailing tube or paper roll. *(3)* *"you can listen to his
heart"*   _1_

Learn how heart changes quickly from slow to fast pace by listening to a friend's
heart. Count beats in a minute. <u>Ask friend to run</u> fast for a minute. <u>Count beats</u>
in a minute. Count beats again after friend has <u>rested</u> for a minute. Compare
number of beats. *(6)*   *"then count again"*   _3_

Check own heartbeat by taking your pulse rate for a minute. *Run* for a minute
and count again. Lie down for a minute and count again. *(4)*   _2_
        "you could do it to yourself."

*Underlining indicates Gordon's responses.

**Generalizations
(25 points)**   _6_

        Heart is a machine inside the body
        Heart has an important job to do
        Exercise makes heart work harder and faster   *(partial)*   _3_
        Rest gives heart a chance to go slower   *(partial)*   _3_

**Major Concepts
(25 points)**   _3_

        Is a most important organ for life
        There are ways we can find out about our hearts   _3_

Retelling

Specific Information	25
Generalizations	6
Major Concepts	3
Total Points	34

Inferences *Did not appear to infer from text. After talking with the teacher about the heart (after retelling), drawing a picture of the heart, and rereading, Gordon divided his picture of the heart into four parts.*

Comments *Gordon shows very little interest in this article. He apparently did not bring much background information— "I didn't know a lot of that stuff." Learned a few things as he read: Lub-dup is a heartbeat. Has bits of information but can't tie the pieces together.*

APPENDIX B4: MISCUE ANALYSIS IN-DEPTH PROCEDURE CODING FORM

READER: Gordon DATE: May 23
TEACHER: Mr. Murphy AGE/GRADE: 9 yrs.
SCHOOL: M.L. King
SELECTION: The Beat of My Heart

MISCUE No./LINE No.	READER	TEXT	1 SYNTACTIC ACCEPTABILITY	2 SEMANTIC ACCEPTABILITY	3 MEANING CHANGE	4 CORRECTION	MEANING CONSTRUCTION (See 2,3,4) No Loss	Partial Loss	Loss	GRAMMATICAL RELATIONS (See 1,2,4) Strength	Partial Strength	Overcorrection	Weakness	GRAPHIC SIMILARITY 5 — H	S	N	SOUND SIMILARITY 6 — H	S	N
1	Lub-bump	Lub-dup	Y	Y	N	N	✓			✓				✓			✓		
2	—	sound	N	N	|	N			✓				✓	✓					
3	Sound	sound	P	N	|	Y			✓				✓	✓			✓		
4	It's	It is	Y	Y	N	Y	✓					✓		✓			✓		
5	heartbeat	heart beating	Y	Y	|	N	✓			✓				✓			✓		
6	bump	pump	Y	N	|	Y			✓		✓			✓				✓	
7	near	never	N	N	|	Y	✓			✓				✓					
8	rest: Even	rest even	P	N	|	N	✓			✓				✓					✓
9	Smu-si-cle	muscle	Y	N	|	N		✓			✓			✓				✓	
10	first	fist	Y	P	|	Y	✓			✓				✓			✓		
11	too	too	Y	Y	|	Y	✓			✓									
12	the	your	Y	Y	N	Y	✓					✓		✓					✓
13	chests	chest	Y	N	N	Y	✓			✓				✓			✓		
14	strong	strongest	P	Y	N	Y	✓							✓		✓			✓
15	your	the	P	P	|	N		✓					✓			✓			✓
16	on	to	P	P	|	N	✓			✓				✓					✓
17	sounds	sound	Y	Y	N	N	✓			✓				✓			✓		
18	a Ⓐ	an	P	N	N	Y	✓			✓				✓					
19	friend	friend's	Y	Y	|	N	✓			✓				✓			✓		
20	bump	lub	Y	Y	N	N	✓			✓				✓			✓		
21	bump	dup	Y	Y	N	Y	✓			✓				✓			✓		
22	feels	feeds	Y	P	|	Y	✓			✓				✓			✓		
23	oranges	organs	Y	N	|	N		✓		✓				✓			✓		
24	physically	physically	Y	P	—	N	✓				✓								
25	fit	fat	Y		—	N			✓		✓			✓			✓		

COLUMN TOTAL
PATTERN TOTAL
PERCENTAGE

a. TOTAL MISCUES _____
b. TOTAL WORDS _____
a ÷ b × 100 = MPHW _____

Goodman, Watson, Burke

APPENDIX B4: MISCUE ANALYSIS IN-DEPTH PROCEDURE CODING FORM (CONT.)

READER: Gordon DATE: May 23
TEACHER: Mr. Murphy AGE/GRADE: 9 yrs.
SCHOOL: M.L. King
SELECTION: The Beat of My Heart

No.	READER	TEXT	1 SYNTACTIC ACCEPTABILITY	2 SEMANTIC ACCEPTABILITY	3 MEANING CHANGE	4 CORRECTION	No Loss	Partial Loss	Loss	Strength	Partial Strength	Overcorrection	Weakness	Graphic H	Graphic S	Graphic N	Sound H	Sound S	Sound N
26	sliver (sounds like diver)	liver	Y	N	—	Y	✓			✓				✓			✓		
27	if	a	P	P	—	Y	✓			✓				✓					✓
28	the	a (a)	P	P	—	N		✓					✓			✓		✓	
29	rate	pace	N	N	—	Y	✓			✓									
30	chances	changes	Y	P	N	Y	✓			✓				✓			✓		
31	quick (l)	quickly	Y	Y	—	Y	✓			✓				✓			✓		
32	place	pace	Y	P	—	Y	✓					✓		✓				✓	
33	listen : To	listen to	P	P	P	Y		✓		✓							✓		
34	a few minutes.	a minute.	Y	Y	N	N	✓			✓				✓					✓
35	the	his	Y	Y	N	N	✓			✓							✓		
36	beat	heart	Y	Y	—	N	✓			✓				✓			✓		
37	Now	how	N	N	P	Y		✓		✓				✓	✓			✓	
38	yet	now	Y	Y	P	N	✓			✓		✓				✓			✓
39	finished	has rested	Y	Y	—	Y			✓	✓				✓			✓		✓
40	scoopering	comparing	Y	N	—	N			✓		✓								
41	___	a	N	N	—	Y	✓			✓				✓		✓	✓		
42	sense	sensitive	Y	Y	—	N	✓				✓			✓					
43	face	fact	Y	P	—	P	✓			✓				✓			✓	✓	✓
44	then	three	N	N	—	Y			✓	✓				✓					
45	fingers	fingertips	P	P	—	N		✓			✓			✓			✓		
46	side	inside	P	P	—	N		✓			✓			✓			✓		✓
47	wrist	wrist	Y	N	N	P			✓	✓							✓		
48	feel	feel	Y	Y	—	N	✓						✓	✓			✓	✓	
49	find Then	This	N	N	N	N	✓			✓				✓	✓		✓	✓	✓
50	you	your	P	P	—	Y	✓			✓									
		COLUMN TOTAL																	
		PATTERN TOTAL																	
		PERCENTAGE																	

Column header groupings:
- MEANING CONSTRUCTION (See 2, 3, 4): No Loss / Partial Loss / Loss
- GRAMMATICAL RELATIONS (See 1, 2, 4): Strength / Partial Strength / Overcorrection / Weakness
- 5 GRAPHIC SIMILARITY: H / S / N
- 6 SOUND SIMILARITY: H / S / N

a. TOTAL MISCUES _____
b. TOTAL WORDS _____
a ÷ b × 100 = MPHW _____

Goodman, Watson, Burke

APPENDIX B4: MISCUE ANALYSIS IN-DEPTH PROCEDURE CODING FORM (CONT.)

READER _Gordon_ DATE _May 23_
TEACHER _Mr. Murphy_ AGE/GRADE _9 yrs._
SCHOOL _M. L. King_
SELECTION _The Beat of My Heart_

Miscue No./Line No.	READER	TEXT	1 SYNTACTIC ACCEPTABILITY	2 SEMANTIC ACCEPTABILITY	3 MEANING CHANGE	4 CORRECTION	MEANING CONSTRUCTION (See 2,3,4) No Loss	Partial Loss	Loss	GRAMMATICAL RELATIONS (See 1,2,4) Strength	Partial Strength	Overcorrection	Weakness	GRAPHIC SIMILARITY (5) H	S	N	SOUND SIMILARITY (6) H	S	N
51	one	once	Y	P	—	N			✓		✓			✓			✓		
52	—	to	Y	Y	N	N	✓			✓									✓
53	a	as	P	P	—	Y	✓			✓				✓					✓
54	1–6 (one-six)	1/6	N	N	—	N			✓				✓	✓			✓		
55	minute	second	P	P	—	N			✓				✓			✓			✓
56	on	or	P	P	—	Y	✓			✓				✓			✓		
57	rest	resting	P	P	—	Y	✓			✓				✓			✓		
58	that	at	P	P	—	N	✓			✓				✓			✓		
59	a	in	P	P	—	Y			✓				✓			✓			✓
60	work	working	P	P	—	N	✓			✓				✓			✓		
61	you	to	P	P	—	N			✓				✓				✓		
62	big	bigger	N	N	N	N		✓					✓	✓	✓		✓		
63	strong	stronger	Y	Y	N	Y	✓			✓				✓			✓		
64	school	school	Y	Y	N	Y	✓			✓									
65	large	larger	N	Y	N	Y	✓			✓				✓			✓		
66	Then	There	Y	Y	N	N	✓			✓				✓				✓	
67	best two	two best	N	Y	—	Y	✓			✓									
68	ways	ones	Y	Y	N	N	✓			✓						✓			✓
69	a lot	lots	Y	Y	N	N		✓					✓						
70	vigorous	vigorous	Y	Y	P	N	✓			✓									
71	—	is	P	P	—	N	✓			✓									
72	for	from	N	N	—	Y			✓	✓				✓				✓	
73	—	in	Y	N	—	Y	✓						✓						

COLUMN TOTAL / PATTERN TOTAL / PERCENTAGE

	No Loss	Partial Loss	Loss	Strength	Partial Strength	Overcorrection	Weakness	Graphic H	Graphic S	Graphic N	Sound H	Sound S	Sound N
COLUMN TOTAL	47	9	17	45	10	5	13	45	5	7	35	9	13
PATTERN TOTAL	73			73				57			57		
PERCENTAGE	64%	12%	23%	62%	14%	7%	18%	79%	9%	12%	61%	16%	23%

a. TOTAL MISCUES _73_
b. TOTAL WORDS _635_
a ÷ b × 100 = MPHW _11.5_

Goodman, Watson, Burke

APPENDIX B5: MISCUE ANALYSIS IN-DEPTH PROCEDURE
READER PROFILE FORM

READER _Gordon_

TEACHER _Mr. Murphy_   AGE/GRADE _9_   DATE _May 23_

SELECTION _The Beat of My Heart_   SCHOOL _Dewey_

	%	%	PERCENT
MEANING CONSTRUCTION			
No Loss	64	⎫ 76	
Partial Loss	12	⎬	
Loss	23		
GRAMMATICAL RELATIONS			
Strength	62	⎫	
Partial Strength	14	⎬ 83	
Overcorrection	7		
Weakness	18		
WORD SUBSTITUTION IN CONTEXT			
Graphic Similarity			
High	79	⎫ 88	
Some	9	⎬	
None	12		
Sound Similarity			
High	61	⎫ 77	
Some	16	⎬	
None	23		
RETELLING			
Generalizations & Major Concepts	9		
Specific Information	25		
Total	34		
Holistic Score	2		

MPHW _11.5_   TIME ____

REPEATED MISCUES ACROSS TEXT

LINE	READER	TEXT	COMMENTS (place in text, correction, etc.)
101–03	Lu-bump	Lub-dup	Fits syntactically and semantically
728–30	Lu-bump	Lub-dup	Intonation and retelling show that he understands these are the heart beats.
104	_____	sound	Miscue on 3rd occurrence of sound is syn. & sem. acceptable.
105	$sound	sound	Gordon learns from the text.
216	sounds	sound	
202	the	your	These miscues relate to the 2nd person voice in this article. They
212	your	the	show Gordon's syntactic knowledge.
225	your	the	All miscues are syntactically and
410	your	the	semantically acceptable except 510
510	you	your	and 704 and they are self corrected.
623	you	to	Your occurs 24 times: you occurs 3 times and to occurs 23 times.
704	you	your	Your and to are almost always read as expected.

COMMENTS _Strong awareness of syntactic structures as shown by repeated miscues and grammatical relations. Many high quality miscues and appropriate correction strategies. He is monitoring his meaning constructing during his reading (see lines 503–508) but he's not interested enough to look for main concepts and generalizations. Background experience and lack of interest limits his meaning search. Develop greater interest in non-fiction in Gordon's interest areas._

Goodman, Watson, Burke

Appendix C
Blank Forms

APPENDIX C1: MISCUE ANALYSIS CLASSROOM PROCEDURE CODING FORM

READER _____ DATE _____

TEACHER _____ AGE/GRADE _____ SCHOOL _____

SELECTION _____

WORD SUBSTITUTION IN CONTEXT

READER		TEXT	GRAPHIC (4)			SOUND (5)		
Dialect ⓓ			H	S	N	H	S	N
LINE NO.								
SENTENCE NO.								

a. TOTAL MISCUES _____
b. TOTAL WORDS _____
a ÷ b × 100 = MPHW _____

COLUMN TOTAL / TOTAL MISCUES / PERCENTAGE

LANGUAGE SENSE

PATTERN (See 1, 2, 3)		3 MEANING CHANGE	2 SEMANTIC ACCEPTABILITY	1 SYNTACTIC ACCEPTABILITY	NO. MISCUES IN SENTENCE	LINE NO./SENTENCE NO.
Weakness	NN- YN-					
Partial Strength	YYY YYP					
Strength	YYN					

COLUMN TOTAL / PATTERN TOTAL / PERCENTAGE

Goodman, Watson, Burke

APPENDIX C2: MISCUE ANALYSIS CLASSROOM PROCEDURE READER PROFILE FORM

READER _____ DATE _____

TEACHER _____ AGE/GRADE _____ SCHOOL _____

SELECTION _____

PATTERNS	%	%
LANGUAGE SENSE		PERCENT
Strength		
Partial Strength		
Weakness		
WORD SUBSTITUTION IN CONTEXT		
Graphic Similarity		
High		
Some		
None		
Sound Similarity		
High		
Some		
None		
RETELLING		
Holistic Score		
Comments		

REPEATED MISCUES ACROSS TEXT

LINE	READER	TEXT	COMMENTS (place in text, correction, etc.)

MPHW _____ TIME _____

COMMENTS

Goodman, Watson, Burke

APPENDIX C3: MISCUE ANALYSIS RETELLING SUMMARY

READER _____

DATE _____

SELECTION _____

Holistic Retelling Score (optional): _____

Plot Statements

Theme Statements

Inferences

Misconceptions

Comments

Goodman, Watson, Burke

APPENDIX C4: MISCUE ANALYSIS INFORMAL PROCEDURE CONFERENCE FORM

READER _____ DATE _____

TEACHER _____ AGE/GRADE _____

SELECTION _____

Does the sentence, as the reader resolved it, make sense within the context of the entire text?

Yes _____ Total _____

No _____ Total _____

Number of Sentences Read _____ Comprehending Score _____

Divide total Yes by Total number of sentences for Comprehending Score

Retelling Information

Comments

Goodman, Watson, Burke

APPENDIX C5: MISCUE ANALYSIS IN-DEPTH PROCEDURE CODING FORM

READER

TEACHER

DATE

SCHOOL

AGE/GRADE

SELECTION

MISCUE No./LINE No.

TEXT

READER

	1 SYNTACTIC ACCEPTIBILITY	2 SEMANTIC ACCEPTIBILITY	3 MEANING CHANGE	4 CORRECTION	See 2, 3, 4 MEANING CONSTRUCTION			See 1, 2, 4 GRAMMATICAL RELATIONS				5 GRAPHIC SIMILARITY			6 SOUND SIMILARITY		
					No Loss	Partial Loss	Loss	Strength	Partial Strength	Overcorrection	Weakness	H	S	N	H	S	N

COLUMN TOTAL

PATTERN TOTAL

PERCENTAGE

a. TOTAL MISCUES _____
b. TOTAL WORDS _____
a ÷ b × 100 = MPHW _____

Goodman, Watson, Burke

APPENDIX C6: MISCUE ANALYSIS IN-DEPTH PROCEDURE
READER PROFILE FORM

READER _____ DATE _____

TEACHER _____ AGE/GRADE _____ SCHOOL _____

SELECTION _____

REPEATED MISCUES ACROSS TEXT

LINE	READER	TEXT	COMMENTS (place in text, correction, etc.)

PATTERNS	%	%
MEANING		
CONSTRUCTION		PERCENT
No Loss		
Partial Loss		
Loss		
GRAMMATICAL		
RELATIONS		
Strength		
Partial Strength		
Overcorrection		
Weakness		
WORD SUBSTITUTION		
IN CONTEXT		
Graphic Similarity		
High		
Some		
None		
Sound Similarity		
High		
Some		
None		
RETELLING		
Characteristics		
Events		
Total		
Holistic Score		

MPHW _____ TIME _____

COMMENTS

Goodman, Watson, Burke

253

APPENDIX C7: *THE MAN WHO KEPT HOUSE* TYPESCRIPT

Name _____

Date _____ Grade/Age _____

Teacher _____

Reference _____

THE MAN WHO KEPT HOUSE

0101   Once upon a time there was a woodman

0102   who thought that no one worked as hard as

0103   he did. One evening when he came home

0104   from work, he said to his wife, "What do you

0105   do all day while I am away cutting wood?"

0106   "I keep house," replied the wife, "and

0107   keeping house is hard work."

0108   "Hard work!" said the husband. "You don't

0109   know what hard work is! You should try

0110   cutting wood!"

0111   "I'd be glad to," said the wife.

0112   "Why don't you do my work some day? I'll

0113   stay home and keep house," said the woodman.

0114   "If you stay home to do my work, you'll

0115   have to make butter, carry water from the

0116   well, wash the clothes, clean the house, and

0117   look after the baby," said the wife.

0118   "I can do all that," replied the husband.

0119   "We'll do it tomorrow!"

0201   So the next morning the wife went off to

0202   the forest. The husband stayed home and

0203   began to do his wife's work.

0204   He began to make some butter. As he put

0205   the cream into the churn, he said, "This is

0206   not going to be hard work. All I have to do

0207   is sit here and move this stick up and down.

0208   Soon the cream will turn into butter."

0209   Just then the woodman heard the baby

0210   crying. He looked around, but he could not

0211   see her. She was not in the house. Quickly,

0212   he ran outside to look for her. He found the

0213   baby at the far end of the garden and

0214   brought her back to the house.

0301   In his hurry, the woodman had left the

0302   door open behind him. When he got back to

0303   the house, he saw a big pig inside, with its

0304   nose in the churn. "Get out! Get out!"

0305   shouted the woodman at the top of his voice.

0306   The big pig ran around and around the

0307   room. It bumped into the churn, knocking it

0308   over. The cream splashed all over the room.

0309   Out the door went the pig.

0310   "Now I've got more work to do," said the

0311   man. "I'll have to wash everything in this

0312   room. Perhaps keeping house is harder work

0313   than I thought." He took a bucket and went

0314   to the well for some water. When he came

0315   back, the baby was crying.

0316   "Poor baby, you must be hungry," said the

0317   woodman. "I'll make some porridge for you.

0318   I'll light a fire in the fireplace, and the

0319   porridge will be ready in a few minutes."

0320   Just as the husband was putting the

0321   water into the big pot, he heard the cow

0401   mooing outside the door. "I guess the cow is

0402   hungry, too," he thought. "No one has given

0403   her any grass to eat or any water to drink

0404   today."

0405   The man left the porridge to cook on the

0406   fire and hurried outside. He gave the cow

0407   some water.

0408   "I haven't time to find any grass for you

0409   now," he said to the cow. "I'll put you up

0410   on the roof. You'll find something to eat

0411   up there."

0412   The man put the cow on top of the house.

0413   Then he was afraid that she would fall off

0414   the roof and hurt herself. So he put one

0415   end of a rope around the cow's neck. He

0416   dropped the other end down the chimney.

0501   Then he climbed down from the roof and

0502   went into the house. He pulled the end of the

0503   rope out of the fireplace and put it around

0504   his left leg.

0505   "Now I can finish making this porridge,"

0506   said the woodman, "and the cow will

0507   be safe."

0508   But the man spoke too soon, for just then

0509   the cow fell off the roof. She pulled him up

0510   the chimney by the rope. There he hung,

0511   upside down over the porridge pot. As for the

0512   cow, she hung between the roof and the

0513   ground, and there she had to stay.

0514   It was not very long before the woodman's

0515   wife came home. As she came near the

0516   house, she could hear the cow mooing, the

0601   baby crying, and her husband shouting for

0602   help. She hurried up the path. She cut the

0603   rope from the cow's neck. As she did so,

0604   the cow fell down to the ground, and the

0605   husband dropped head first down the chimney.

0606   When the wife went into the house, she

0607   saw her husband with his legs up the

0608   chimney and his head in the porridge pot.

0609   From that day on, the husband went into

0610   the forest every day to cut wood. The wife

0611   stayed home to keep house and to look

0612   after their child.

0613   Never again did the woodman say to his

0614   wife, "What did you do all day?" Never

0615   again did he tell his wife that he would

0616   stay home and keep house.

No. words   <u>791</u>   (not counting the title)

No. sentences   <u>68</u>

The Man Who Kept House. McInnes, John A. ed. 1962. NY: Abelard-Schumann.

APPENDIX C8: NARRATIVE RETELLING GUIDE: *THE MAN WHO KEPT HOUSE*

Reader: _____   Date: _____

Character Analysis:
(40 points)

Recall (20 points)
9 – Man (husband)
9 – Woman (wife)
2 – Baby

Development (20 points)
Husband
    2 – Woodman
    3 – Thought he worked very hard
    5 – Changed attitude over time
Housewife
    5 – Worked Hard
    5 – Accepted challenges

Events:
(60 points)

Woodman thinks he works very hard. He comes home and asks his wife what she does all day. Wife responds that she keeps house and keeping house is hard work. (10 points)   _____

The husband challenges the wife to change places. The wife agrees and tells husband what he has to do. The husband says they will change places the next day. (10 points)   _____

The wife goes off to the forest and the husband stays home. (5 points)   _____

The husband is involved in a number of events that cause problems: (15 points)   _____

    Butter making.
    Baby cries and woodman goes to find her. He leaves the door open.
    Pig gets into the house, the woodman chases it and the pig spills the cream.
    Woodman starts to clean up the mess.
    The baby cries again and the woodman prepares to feed the baby.

    The cow's mooing interrupts the woodman who realizes that the cow needs to be fed. He puts the cow on the roof to feed. He is afraid the cow might fall off the roof so he throws the rope from the cow's neck down the chimney. When he gets into the house he ties the rope to his own leg.

    As he thinks again about the porridge, the cow falls off the roof pulling the woodman up the chimney. Cow and woodman are hanging, one in the house and one outside.

As the wife returns home she hears the commotion. She cuts the cow down and then finds her husband upside down with his head in the porridge pot. (10 points)   _____

Every day after that the husband goes to his work and the wife to hers. The husband never again asks the wife what she does every day nor says he will do her work. (10 points)   _____

Character Analysis (40)   _____

Events (60)   _____

Total Points   _____

Plot

The woodman believes his work is harder than his wife's. When he trades places with her he discovers her work is more complicated and harder than he thought.

_____

_____

_____

Theme

Things aren't always as easy as they appear to be. Keeping house is demanding work. A woman's job is just as hard as a man's. The grass is always greener on the other side of the fence.

_____

_____

_____

Goodman, Watson, Burke

APPENDIX C9: *THE BEAT OF MY HEART* TYPESCRIPT

Name_____

Date _____ Grade/Age _____

Teacher_____

Reference_____

THE BEAT OF MY HEART

0101   Lub-dup . . .

0102   Lub-dup . . .

0103   Lub-dup . . .

0104   This strange sound

0105   is the sound

0106   of a wonderful machine

0107   inside your body.

0108   It is the sound

0109   of your heart beating.

0110   Your heart is a pump

0111   which will never

0112   stop working

0113   as long as you live,

0114   but it can rest

0115   even while it is working.

0116   Your heart

0117   is a hollow muscle

0118   divided into four parts.

0119   It is about the size

0120   of your fist.

0121   As you grow,

0122   it too will grow in size.

0201   To find out

0202   where your heart is,

0203   put your right hand

0204   in the middle

0205   of the left side of your chest.

0206   Now move your fingers around

0207   until you find

0208   the spot where

0209   the heartbeat is strongest.

0210   Your hand is now

0211   pointing to your heart.

0212   Listen to the heartbeat

0213   of a friend

0214   by putting your ear

0215   to his chest.

0216   To hear the sound even better,

0217   hold an empty mailing tube

0218   or a rolled-up piece

0219   of heavy paper

0220   to your friend's heart.

0221   When the heart goes lub,

0222   it is drawing in blood.

0223   When it goes dup,

0224   it is pushing blood out

0225   to all parts of the body.

0226   Your heart has

0227   this most important job to do —

0228   pumping blood

0229   to all parts of your body.

- -

0301   Blood feeds

0302   all the cells and organs

0303   of your body

0304   so that they can do

0305   their own special work

0306   to keep you physically fit.

0307   Your heart pumps blood

0308   from your head

0309   to your toes,

0310   to your liver

0311   and your lungs.

0312   Just as a wheel

0313   can turn slowly or fast,

0314   your heart can work

0315   at a slow or a fast pace.

0316   If you want to see

0317   how your heart changes quickly

0318   from working at a slow pace

0319   to working at a faster pace,

0320   try this.

0321   First listen

0322   to a friend's heartbeat

0323   and count the number of beats

0324   in a minute.

0325   Now ask your friend

0326   to run fast

0327   for about a minute.

0328   Then listen to his heart again.

0329   How many times a minute

0330   is his heart beating now?

0401   Count his heartbeats again

0402   after he has rested

0403   for a minute.

0404   By comparing the number

0405   of heartbeats

0406   under these different conditions,

0407   you will discover that

0408   the heart is

0409   a sensitive machine

0410   working inside the body.

0501   You can test this fact again

0502   by checking your own heartbeat.

0503   Place three fingertips

0504   of your right hand

0505   on the inside of your left wrist.

0506   You will feel the beat

0507   of your heart.

0508   This is called your pulse.

0509   Count the number of times

0510   your heart beats in a minute.

0601   Now, run for a minute

0602   and count the heartbeats

0603   in your pulse again.

0604   Lie down and rest for a minute,

0605   and then count once more.

0606   See how exercise makes

0607   your heart work

0608   harder and faster?

0609   Exercise helps your heart

0610   to become stronger

0611   and be able

0612   to do its work better.

0613   Your heart beats

0614   as long as you live.

0615   It rests for 1/6 of a second

0616   between every beat.

0617   When you are asleep or resting,

0618   your heart beats

0619   at a slower rate.

0620   This rest gives your heart

0621   a chance to keep

0622   in good working condition

0623   as well as to grow

0624   bigger and stronger.

- -

0701   Since you are becoming

0702   taller and heavier

0703   every school year,

0704   your heart must grow larger, too.

0705   Your bigger body needs

0706   a bigger motor to keep it

0707   in good working order.

0708   There are many ways

0709   to take care of your heart,

0710   but the two best ones are

0711   the easiest to do.

0712   One is to get lots of exercise

0713   by playing vigorous games

0714   out of doors.

0715   Play games that have lots

0716   of running and jumping,

0717   or hitting and kicking balls.

0718   The other way

0719   to take care of your heart

0720   is to be sure you get

0721   at least ten hours of sleep

0722   every night

0723   and do restful things

0724   from time to time

0725   throughout the day.

0726   On and on your heart beats—

0727   year in and year out.

0728   Lub-dup . . .

0729   Lub-dup . . .

0730   Lub-dup . . .

No. words   <u>635</u>   (not counting the title)

No. sentences   <u>46</u>

Vannier, Maryhelen. 1967. In *Sounds of Mystery*. Edited by Bill Martin Jr. New York: Holt, Rinehart and Winston.

APPENDIX C10: EXPOSITORY RETELLING GUIDE: *THE BEAT OF MY HEART*

Reader: _____   Date: _____

**Specific Information
(50 points)** _____

       The Heart (10) _____

Is a pump (Analogy)
Rests even while working
Is a hollow muscle
Divided into four parts
About the size of your fist
Grows as you grow

Blood (8) _____

With one beat blood is drawn in; with the next beat blood is pushed out
Blood feeds cells and organs which is needed for the body to be physically fit
Blood pumps to liver to lungs

Heartbeat (8) _____

The heart can beat slow or fast
Heartbeat felt in your wrist is your pulse
Rests 1/6 second between beats
Beats at a slower rate when asleep or resting

Conditions (8) _____

Exercise helps heart become stronger and do work better.
Two best ways of taking care of heart: vigorous games and at least 10 hours of sleep every night

Experiments Making Use of Specific Information

Find your heart by moving fingers around on the left side of your chest. Find where the beat is strongest. (3) _____

Listen to the heartbeat of a friend by putting your ear to his chest. Listen by using mailing tube or paper roll. (3) _____

Learn how heart changes quickly from slow to fast pace by listening to a friend's heart. Count beats in a minute. Ask friend to run fast for a minute. Count beats in a minute. Count beats again after friend has rested for a minute. Compare number of beats. (6) _____

Check own heartbeat by taking your pulse rate for a minute. Run for a minute and count again. Lie down for a minute and count again. (4) _____

**Generalizations
(25 points)** _____

Heart is a machine inside the body
Heart has an important job to do
Exercise makes heart work harder and faster
Rest gives heart a chance to go slower

**Major Concepts
(25 points)** _____

Is a most important organ for life
There are ways we can find out about our hearts

Retelling

Specific Information _____

Generalizations _____

Major Concepts _____

Total Points _____

Inference

Comments

Goodman, Watson, Burke   © 2005 Richard C. Owen Publishers, Inc.

APPENDIX C11: BURKE READING INTERVIEW (BRI)

Name _____ Age _____ Date _____

Occupation _____ Education Level _____

Sex _____ Interview Setting _____

1. When you are reading and come to something you don't know, what do you do?

   Do you ever do anything else?

2. Who is a good reader you know?

3. What makes _____ a good reader?

4. Do you think _____ ever comes to something she/he doesn't know?

5. "Yes" When _____ does come to something she/he doesn't know, what do you think he/she does?

   "No" Suppose _____ comes to something she/he doesn't know. What would she/he do?

6. How would you help someone having trouble reading?

7. What would a/your teacher do to help that person?

8. How did you learn to read?

9. What would you like to do better as a reader?

10. Do you think you are a good reader? Why?

APPENDIX C12: THE BURKE INTERVIEW MODIFIED FOR OLDER READERS (BIMOR)

1. When you are reading and you come to something that gives you trouble, what do you do? Do you ever do anything else?

2. Who is a good reader you know?

3. What makes _____ a good reader?

4. Do you think _____ ever comes to something that gives him/her trouble when he/she is reading?

5. When _____ does come to something that gives him/her trouble, what do you think he/she does about it?

6. How would you help someone who was having difficulty reading?

Original by Carolyn Burke, adaptations by Watson, Dorothy and Chippendale, Ene-Kaja. 1979. Describing and Improving the Reading Strategies of Elderly Readers. Monograph, Joint Center for Aging Studies, University of Missouri, Columbia, MO. Reprinted by permission.

7. What would a teacher do to help that person?

8. How did you learn to read?

9. Is there anything you would like to change about your reading?

10. Describe yourself as a reader. What kind of reader are you?

11. What do you read routinely, like every day or every week?

12. What do you like most of all to read?

13. Can you remember any special book or the most memorable thing you have ever read?

14. What is the most difficult thing you have to read?

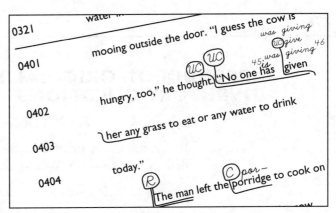

Appendix D
Previous Miscue Analysis Formats

APPENDIX D1: ORIGINAL READING MISCUE INVENTORY QUESTIONS

QUESTION 1: *Dialect.* Is a Dialect Variation Involved in the Miscue?

If a variation is involved, the appropriate box is marked Y for yes. If no dialect variation is involved, the box is left blank.

QUESTION 2: *Intonation.* Is a Shift in Intonation Involved in the Miscue?

If a shift is involved, the appropriate box is marked Y for yes. If there is no variation involved, the box is left blank.

QUESTION 3: *Graphic Similarity.* How Much Does the Miscue Look Like What Was Expected?*

Y—A high degree of graphic similarity exists between the miscue and the text.

P—Some degree of graphic similarity exists between the miscue and the text.

N—A graphic similarity does not exist between the miscue and the text.

QUESTION 4: *Sound Similarity.* How Much Does the Miscue Sound Like What Was Expected?*

Y—A high degree of sound similarity exists between the miscue and what was expected.

P—Some degree of sound similarity exists between the miscue and what was expected.

N—A sound similarity does not exist between the miscue and what was expected.

QUESTION 5: *Grammatical Function.* Is the Grammatical Function of the Miscue the Same as the Grammatical Function of the Word in the Text?*

Y—The grammatical functions of the two are identical.

P—It is not possible to determine the grammatical function.

N—The grammatical functions of the two differ.

QUESTION 6: *Correction.* Is the Miscue Corrected?

Y—The miscue is corrected.

P—There is an unsuccessful attempt at correction. Or a correct response is abandoned.

N—There has been no attempt at correction.

*If the miscue is an omission or insertion, or if the miscue involves more than one word, or if the miscue involves intonation only, this category is not marked.

QUESTION 7: *Grammatical Acceptability.* Does the Miscue Occur in a Structure that is Grammatically Acceptable?

Y—The miscue occurs in a sentence which is grammatically acceptable and is acceptable in relation to prior and subsequent sentences in the text.

P—The miscue occurs in a sentence that is grammatically acceptable but is not acceptable in relation to prior and subsequent sentences in the text. Or the miscue is grammatically acceptable only with the sentence portion that comes before or after it.

N—The miscue occurs in a sentence that is not grammatically acceptable.

QUESTION 8: *Semantic Acceptability.* Does the Miscue Occur in a Structure that is Semantically Acceptable?

Y—The miscue occurs in a sentence that is semantically acceptable and is acceptable in relation to prior and subsequent sentences in the text.

P—The miscue occurs in a sentence that is semantically acceptable but is not acceptable in relation to prior and subsequent sentences in the text. Or the miscue is semantically acceptable only with the sentence portion that comes before or after it.

N—The miscue occurs in a sentence that is not semantically acceptable.

QUESTION 9: *Meaning Change.* Does the Miscue Result in a Change of Meaning?

Y—An extensive change in meaning is involved.

P—A minimal change in meaning is involved.

N—No change in meaning is involved.

APPENDIX D2: GOODMAN TAXONOMY OF READING MISCUES*

Correction

0. No attempt at correction is made.
1. The miscue is corrected.
2. An original correct response is abandoned in favor of an incorrect one.
3. An unsuccessful attempt is made at correcting the miscue.

Dialect

0. Dialect is not involved in the miscue.
1. Dialect is involved in the miscue.
2. Idiolect is involved in the miscue.
3. A supercorrection is involved in the miscue.

*Adapted from Gollasch, F (1982), *The Selected Writings of Kenneth S. Goodman* (Vol. 1). London: Routledge & Kegan Paul.

4. There is a secondary dialect involved in the miscue.

5. A foreign language influence is involved in the miscue.

6. Dialect involvement is doubtful.

Graphic Proximity

0. There is no graphic similarity between ER and the OR.

1. The ER and the OR have a key letter or letters in common.

2. The middle portions of the ER and OR are similar.

3. The end portions of the ER and OR are similar.

4. The beginning portions of the ER and OR are similar.

5. The beginning and middle portions of the ER and OR are similar.

6. The beginning and end portions of the ER and OR are similar.

7. The beginning, middle and end portions of the ER and OR are similar.

8. There is a single grapheme difference between the ER and the OR, or a reversal involving two letters.

9. The ER and the OR are homographs.

Phonemic Proximity

0. There is no phonemic similarity between the ER and the OR.

1. The ER and the OR have a key sound or sounds in common.

2. The middle portion of the ER and the OR are similar.

3. The ER and OR have the end portions in common.

4. The ER and OR have the beginning portion in common.

5. The ER and OR have common beginning and middle portions.

6. The ER and OR have common beginning and end portions.

7. The beginning, middle and end portions of the ER and OR are similar.

8. The ER and OR differ by a single vowel or consonant or vowel cluster.

9. The ER and OR are homophones.

Allologs

0. An allolog is not involved in the miscue.

1. The OR is a contracted form of the ER.

2. The OR is a full form of the ER contraction.

3. The OR is a contraction which is not represented in print.

4. The OR is either a long or short form of the ER.

5. The OR involves a shift to idiomatic form.

6. The OR involves a shift from idiomatic form.

7. The OR involves a misarticulation.

Syntactic Acceptability

0. The miscue results in a structure which is completely syntactically unacceptable.

1. The miscue results in a structure which is syntactically acceptable only with the prior portion of the sentence.

2. The miscue results in a structure which is syntactically acceptable only with the following portion of the sentence.

3. The miscue results in a structure which is syntactically acceptable only within the sentence.

4. The miscue results in a structure which is syntactically acceptable within the total passage.

5. The miscue results in a structure which is syntactically acceptable within the sentence except for other unacceptable miscues.

6. The miscue results in a structure which is syntactically acceptable within the total passage except for other unacceptable miscues in the sentence.

Semantic Acceptability

0. The miscue results in a structure which is completely semantically unacceptable.

1. The miscue results in a structure which is semantically acceptable only with the prior portion of the sentence.

2. The miscue results in a structure which is semantically acceptable only with the following portion of the sentence.

3. The miscue results in a structure which is semantically acceptable only within the sentence.

4. The miscue results in a structure which is semantically acceptable within the total passage.

5. The miscue results in a structure which is semantically acceptable within the sentence except for other unacceptable miscues.

6. The miscue results in a structure which is semantically acceptable within the total passage except for other unacceptable miscues in the sentence.

Transformation

0. A grammatical transformation is not involved.

1. A transformation occurs which involves a difference in deep structure between the ER and OR.

2. A transformation occurs in which the deep structure of the ER and the OR remains the same while the surface structure of the OR is generated by a different set of compulsory rules.

3. A transformation occurs in which the deep structure of the ER and the OR remains the same while the surface structure of the OR is generated by alternate available rules.

4. The deep structure has been lost or garbled.

5. There is some question of whether or not a transformation is involved in the miscue.

Syntactic Change

0. The syntax of the OR and the ER are unrelated.
1. The syntax of the OR and the ER have a single element in common.
2. The syntax of the OR has a key element which retains the syntactic function of the ER.
3. There is a major change in the syntax of the OR.
4. There is a minor change in the syntax of the OR.
5. There is a major change within the structure of the phrase.
6. There is a minor change within the structure of the phrase.
7. There is a change in person, tense, number or gender of the OR.
8. There is a change in choice of function word or another minor shift in the OR.
9. The syntax of the OR is unchanged from the syntax of the ER.

Semantic Change

0. The OR is completely anomalous to the rest of the story.
1. There is a change or loss affecting the plot in a basic sense or creating major anomalies.
2. There is a change or loss involving key aspects of the story or seriously interfering with subplots.
3. There is a change or loss resulting in inconsistency concerning a major incident, major character or major sequence.
4. There is a change or loss resulting in inconsistency concerning a minor incident, minor character or minor aspect of sequence.
5. There is a change or loss of aspect which is significant but does not create inconsistencies within the story.
6. There is a change or loss of an unimportant detail of this story.
7. There is a change in person, tense, number, comparative, etc. which is noncritical to the story.
8. There is a slight change in connotation.
9. No change has occurred involving story meaning.

Intonation

1. An intonation shift within a word is involved.
2. An intonation shift is involved between words within one phrase structure of the sentence.
3. Intonation is involved which is relative to the phrase or clause structure of the sentence.

4. A shift in terminal sentence intonation is involved.

5. The intonation change involves a substitution of a conjunction for terminal punctuation or the reverse.

6. The intonation change involves direct quotes.

Submorphemic Language Level

0. The submorphemic level is not involved.

1. There is a substitution of phonemes.

2. There is an insertion of a phoneme(s).

3. There is an omission of a phoneme(s).

4. There is a reversal of phonemes.

5. There are multiple minor phonemic variations.

Bound and Combined Morpheme Level

1. The miscue involves an inflected suffix.

2. The miscue involves a noninflected form.

3. The miscue involves a contractional suffix.

4. The miscue involves a derivational suffix.

5. The miscue involves a prefix.

6. The miscue crosses affix types.

7. The miscue involves the base. There is some confusion over what constitutes the root word.

Word and Free Morpheme Level

1. The ER and/or the OR involve a multiple morpheme word.

2. The ER and/or the OR involve a single morpheme word.

3. The ER is a single morpheme word and the OR is a multiple morpheme word.

4. The ER is a multiple morpheme word and the OR is a single morpheme word.

5. The miscue involves a free morpheme within a longer word.

6. The miscue involves one or both of the free morphemes in a compound or hyphenated word.

7. The OR is a nonword.

8. The OR is a phonemic or morphophonemic dialect alternate of the ER.

Phrase

1. A substitution is involved at the phrase level.

2. An insertion is involved at the phrase level.

3. An omission is involved at the phrase level.

4. A reversal is involved at the phrase level.

Clause

1. A substitution is involved at the clause level.
2. An insertion is involved at the clause level.
3. An omission is involved at the clause level.
4. A reversal is involved at the clause level.
5. Clause dependency is altered within the sentence. Only one ER sentence should be involved in the miscue.
6. Clause dependency is altered across sentences. Two ER sentences should be involved in the miscue.

Grammatical Category and Surface Structure of Observed Response

1. Noun Category
2. Verb Category
3. Noun Modifier
4. Verb Modifier
5. Function Word Category
6. Indeterminate Category
7. Contraction Category

Observed Response in Visual Periphery

0. The visual periphery is not involved in the miscue.
1. The OR can be found in the near visual periphery.
2. The OR can be found in the extended visual periphery.
3. It is doubtful whether the visual periphery was involved in the miscue.

APPENDIX D3: EXAMPLES OF INQUIRY USING MISCUE ANALYSIS

Grammatical Function

An informative question in miscue analysis has to do with grammatical function.

Is the grammatical function of the miscue the same as the grammatical function of the text?

Words in context of discourse can almost always be assigned a grammatical function, such as noun, verb, preposition, etc. However, since English is a word-ordered language, the syntactically acceptable positions of words are limited. Readers make intuitive use of surrounding structures and grammatical constraints to help them predict appropriate syntax. The degree to which miscues retain the same grammatical function as the ER indicates the reader's knowledge of English sentence structure. Although readers do not always substitute the same grammatical function, at least 75 percent of the time nouns are substituted for nouns, verbs for verbs, adjectives for adjectives, and function words for function words (Flurkey and Xu 2003). The reader's intonation and the use of inflectional endings usually make it possible to assign grammatical function, even for nonwords. Transformed sentences are identical, not identical, or indeterminate. If the miscue disrupts the text to the point that the grammatical function cannot be determined, the miscue is considered *indeterminate*. This disruption seldom occurs. If there is ambiguity, the observer can often clarify the reader's syntax by listening carefully to the recording and then deciding on the grammatical function that is most clearly supported by the reader's intonation.

For most purposes substitutions fall into common categories, such as noun for noun or verb for verb; however, some teachers/researchers want more in-depth investigation and therefore add features, such as common noun for common noun, proper noun for proper noun, transitive verb for transitive verb, intransitive verb for intransitive verb, etc. The Goodman Taxonomy of Miscues (Appendix D) provides a system for comparing more intricate structures.

Peripheral Vision

The role of perception in reading is investigated by studying the reader's use of the peripheral field. To determine the use of peripheral field ask:

To what degree do readers use graphic information in the near or far periphery?

This question can be modified considering the interests of the teacher/researcher and may include: Is the word or phrase that is substituted or inserted:

- Within the near periphery of the ER?
- Within the far periphery of the ER?
- Above, below, or on the same line of the ER?
- On the same line, does it precede or follow the ER?

The Goodman Taxonomy, which includes this category, defines *the near periphery* as the line immediately above or below the miscue, and *the far periphery* as the second or third line above or below the line in which the miscue occurs. In the taxonomy, only a complete word or phrase is considered when examining miscues in the peripheral field.

If parts of words or whole words that are parts of other words in the text are involved, these are not coded as being in the peripheral field. However, if a researcher wants to study this phenomenon, clearly stated questions and definitions need to be established.

Conclusions about peripheral vision resulting from miscue research include:

- Miscues most often in the periphery are function words, such as articles, prepositions, and verb particles.

- In most cases, proficient readers produce more peripheral miscues than less proficient readers.
- Insertion miscues are usually found in the near periphery.

K. Goodman and Burke, 1973; Flurkey and Xu, 2003.

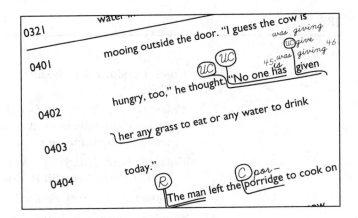

Bibliography and References

REFERENCES

Allen, Roach Van. 1982. *Language Experience Activities*. New York: Houghton Mifflin.

Altwerger, Bess and Kenneth Goodman. 1981. *Studying Text Difficulty Through Miscue Analysis: A Research Report*. Occasional Paper No. 3. Tucson, AZ: University of Arizona, College of Education, Program in Language and Literacy.

Bialostok, Steve. 1992. *Raising Readers: Helping Your Child to Literacy*. Winnipeg, ON: Peguis Publishers.

Brown, Joel, Kenneth Goodman, and Ann Marek. 1996. *Studies in Miscue Analysis: An Annotated Bibliography*. Newark, DE: International Reading Association.

Burke, Carolyn L. 1980. The Reading Interview. In *Reading Comprehension: Resource Guide*. Edited by Beverly P. Farr and Darryl J. Strickler. Bloomington, IN: Indiana University Reading Programs.

Cambourne, Brian and Hazel Brown. 1990. *Read and Retell: A Strategy for the Whole-Language/Natural Learning Classroom*. Portsmouth, NH: Heinemann.

Cambourne, Brian. 2002. Holistic, Integrated Approaches to Reading and Language Arts Instruction: The Constructivist Framework. In *What Research Has to Say about Reading Instruction*, 3rd ed. Edited by Alan Farstrup and S. Jay Samuels. Newark, DE: International Reading Association.

Carpenter, Patricia and Marcel A. Just. 1983. What Your Eyes Do While Your Mind is Reading. In *Eye Movements in Reading: Perceptual and Language Processes*. Edited by Keith Rayner. New York: Academic Press.

Christian, Diane and Walter Wolfram. 1989. *Dialects and Education: Issues and Answers*. Englewood Cliffs, NJ: Prentice Hall Regents.

Christian, Diane, Carolyn Adger, and Walter Wolfram. 1999. *Dialects in Schools and Communities*. Mahwah, NJ: Lawrence Erlbaum Associates.

Coles, Gerald. 1998. *Reading Lessons: The Debate over Literacy.* New York: Hill and Wang.

Coles, Gerald. 1999. Literacy, Emotions and the Brain. In *Reading Online*, the International Reading Association's Electronic Journal, March. www.readingonline.org.

Coles, Richard E. 1981. *The Reading Strategies of Selected Junior High School Students in the Content Areas.* Ph.D. dissertation, University of Arizona.

Collins, Kaye C. 1999. *Foxfire 11.* New York, NY: Anchor Books.

Comber, Barbara and Ann Simpson, eds. 2001. *Negotiating Critical Literacies in Classrooms.* Mahwah, NJ: Lawrence Erlbaum Associates.

Davenport, M. Ruth. 2002. *Miscues Not Mistakes.* Portsmouth, NH: Heinemann.

DeFord, Diane. 1981. Reading, Writing and Other Essentials. *Language Arts,* Volume 58, number 6, pp. 652–658.

Duckett, Peter. 2002. New Insights: Eye Fixations and the Reading Process. *Talking Points.* Volume 13, number 2, April/May, pp. 16–21.

Duckett, Peter. 2003. Envisioning Story: The Eye Movements of Beginning Readers. *Literacy Teaching and Learning.* Volume 7, numbers 1 and 2; pp. 77–89.

Edelsky, Carole and Karen Smith. 1984. Is that Writing—Or Are Those Marks Just a Figment of your Curriculum? *Language Arts.* Volume 61, number 1, pp. 24–32.

Erickson, Fred. 1986. Qualitative Methods in Research on Teaching. In *The Handbook of Research on Teaching,* 3rd ed. Edited by Merlin C. Wittrock. New York, NY: Macmillan.

Ewoldt, Carolyn. 1981. A Psycholinguistic Description of Selected Deaf Children Reading in Sign Language. *Reading Research Quarterly.* Volume 17, number 1, pp. 58–89.

Ewoldt, Carolyn and David Mason. 1996. Whole Language and Deaf Bilingual Bicultural Education—Naturally! *American Annals of the Deaf.* Volume 14, number 14, pp. 293–298.

Flurkey, Alan D. 1998. *A Linguistic Alternative to Fluency.* Occasional Paper No. 26. Tucson, AZ: Program in Language and Literacy, University of Arizona.

Flurkey, Alan D. and Jingguo Xu, eds. 2003. *On the Revolution of Reading: The Selected Writings of Kenneth S. Goodman.* Portsmouth, NH: Heinemann.

Flurkey, Alan D. and Yetta Goodman. 2004. The Role of Genre in a Text: Reading through the Waterworks. *Language Arts.* Volume 81, number 3, pp. 233–244.

Folger, Teresa L. 2001 *Readers' Parallel Text Construction While Talking and Thinking about the Reading Process.* Ph.D. dissertation, University of Missouri–Columbia.

Gee, James Paul. April, 2001. Critical Literacy as Critical Discourse Analysis. In *Critical Perspectives on Literacy: Possibilities and Practices.* Edited by Jerome Harste and P. David Pearson. International Reading Association Pre-convention Institute, New Orleans, LA.

Gollasch, Fred W. 1980. *Readers' Perception in Detecting and Processing Embedded Errors in Meaningful Text.* Ph.D. dissertation, University of Arizona.

Gollasch, Fred W. ed. 1982. *Language and Literacy: The Selected Writings of K. S. Goodman.* London: Routledge and Kegan Paul.

Goodman, Debra. 1999. *The Reading Detective Club.* Portsmouth, NH: Heinemann.

Goodman, Kenneth. 1973. Miscues: Windows on the Reading Process. In *Miscue Analysis: Applications to Reading Instruction.* Edited by Kenneth Goodman. Urbana, IL: ERIC Clearinghouse on Reading and Communication Skills and the National Council of Teachers of English.

Goodman, Kenneth. 1982a. Dialect Barriers to Reading Comprehension. In *Language and Literacy: The Selected Writings of Kenneth S. Goodman.* Edited by Frederick V. Gollasch. Volume 2. London: Routledge and Kegan Paul.

Goodman, Kenneth. 1982b. The Goodman Taxonomy of Reading Miscues. In *Language and Literacy: The Selected Writings of Kenneth S. Goodman.* Edited by Frederick V. Gollasch. Volume 1. London: Routledge and Kegan Paul.

Goodman, Kenneth. 1984. Unity in Reading. In *Becoming Readers in a Complex Society.* Edited by Alan C. Purves and Olive S. Niles. Chicago, IL: University of Chicago Press.

Goodman, Kenneth. 1993. *Phonics Phacts.* Richmond Hill, ON: Scholastic Canada. Published in the United States by Heinemann.

Goodman, Kenneth. 1994. Reading, Writing, and Written Texts: A Transactional Sociopsycholinguistic View. In *Theoretical Models and Processes of Reading,* 4th ed. Edited by Robert B. Ruddell, Martha R. Ruddell, and Harry Singer. Newark, DE: International Reading Association.

Goodman, Kenneth. 1996a. *Ken Goodman on Reading: A Common-Sense Look at the Nature of Language and the Science of Reading.* Portsmouth, NH: Heinemann.

Goodman, Kenneth. 1996b. Principles of Revaluing. In *Retrospective Miscue Analysis: Revaluing Readers and Reading* by Yetta Goodman and Ann Marek. Katonah, NY: Richard C. Owen Publishers, Inc.

Goodman, Kenneth. 2004. Reading, Writing, and Written Texts: A Transactional Sociopyscholinguistic View. In *Theoretical Models and Processes of Reading,* 5th ed. [CD supplementary articles 3.4/1–40]. Edited by Robert B. Ruddell and Norman J. Unrau. Newark, DE: International Reading Association.

Goodman, Kenneth and Catherine Buck. 1982. Dialect Barriers to Reading Comprehension Revisited. In *Language and Literacy: The Selected Writings of Kenneth S. Goodman.* Edited by Frederick V. Gollasch. Volume 2. London: Routledge and Kegan Paul.

Goodman, Kenneth and Carolyn Burke. 1973. *Theoretically Based Studies of Patterns of Miscues in Oral Reading Performance* (Grant No OEG-0-9-320375-4269). Washington, DC: U.S. Department of Health, Education and Welfare.

Goodman, Kenneth and Lois Bridges Bird. 2003. On the Wording of Texts: A Study of Intra-Text Word Frequency. In *On the Revolution of Reading: The Selected Writings of Kenneth S. Goodman.* Edited by Alan D. Flurkey and Jingguo Xu. Portsmouth, NH: Heinemann.

Goodman, Kenneth and Susanne Gespass. 1983. *Text Features as They Relate to Miscue Pronouns* (Occasional Paper No. 7). Tucson, AZ: University of Arizona, College of Education, Program in Language and Literacy.

Goodman, Kenneth, Brooks E. Smith, Robert Meredith, and Yetta Goodman. 1987. *Language and Thinking in School,* 3rd ed. Katonah, NY: Richard C. Owen Publishers, Inc.

Goodman, Yetta. 1996. Retellings of Literature and the Comprehension Process. *Notes from a Kidwatcher: Selected Writings of Yetta M. Goodman.* Edited by Sandra Wilde. Portsmouth, NH: Heinemann.

Goodman, Yetta. 2000. Revaluing Readers While Readers Revalue Themselves: Retrospective Miscue Analysis. In *Distinguished Educators on Reading: Contributions That Have Shaped Effective Literacy Instruction.* Newark, DE: International Reading Association.

Goodman, Yetta. 2003. *Valuing Language Study: Inquiry into Language for Elementary and Middle Schools.* Urbana, IL: National Council of Teachers of English.

Goodman, Yetta and Carolyn Burke. 1972. *Reading Miscue Inventory Manual: Procedures for Diagnosis and Evaluation.* New York: Richard C. Owen Publishers, Inc.

Goodman, Yetta, Dorothy Watson, and Carolyn Burke. 1996. *Reading Strategies: Focus on Comprehension.* Katonah, NY: Richard C. Owen Publishers, Inc.

Goodman, Yetta and Debra Goodman. 2000. I Hate 'Postrophe S: Issues of Dialect and Reading Proficiency. In *Language in Action: New Studies of Language in Society.* Edited by Joy Peyton et al. New Jersey: Hampton Press.

Goodman, Yetta and Ann Marek. 1996. *Retrospective Miscue Analysis: Revaluing Readers and Reading.* Katonah, NY: Richard C. Owen Publishers, Inc.

Guba, Egon G. 1987. What Have We learned About Naturalistic Evaluation? *Evaluation Practice.* Volume 8, number 1, pp. 23–43.

Harris, Theodore and Richard Hodges, eds. 1995. *The Literacy Dictionary: The Vocabulary of Reading and Writing.* Newark: DE: The International Reading Association.

Harste, Jerome and Carolyn Burke. 1977. A New Hypothesis for Reading Teacher Research: Both the Teaching and Learning of Reading Are Theoretically Based. In *Reading: Research, Theory, and Practice: Twenty-sixth Yearbook-NRC.* Edited by Natip, A. Minneapolis, MN: Mason Publishing.

Harste, Jerome C., Vivian Vasquez, Mitzi Lewison, Amy Breau, Christine Leland, and Ann Ociepka. 2000. Supporting Critical Conversations in Classrooms. In *Adventuring with Books,* 12th ed. Edited by Kathryn Mitchell Pierce and Cathy Beck. Urbana, IL: National Council of Teachers of English.

Holdaway, Don. 1979. *Foundations of Literacy.* Sydney, Australia: Ashton Scholastic.

Horn, Ernest. 1929. The Child's Early Experience with Little A. *Journal of Educational Psychology.* Volume 20, number 3, pp. 161–168.

Hoskisson, Kenneth. 1975. The Many Facets of Assisted Reading. *English Teacher.* Volume 52, number 3, March, pp. 312–315.

Hunt, Kellogg. 1965. *Grammatical Structures Written at Three Grade Levels.* Champaign, IL: National Council of Teachers of English.

Irwin, Pi A. and Judy N. Mitchell. 1983. A Procedure for Assessing the Richness of Retellings. *Journal of Reading.* Volume 26, number 5, pp. 391–396.

James, William. 1892. *Psychology.* New York: Holt and Company (abridgement of larger work, *The Principles of Psychology,* 1882).

James, William. 1981. *The Principles of Psychology.* Cambridge, MA: University Press.

Kalmbach, James. 1986. Getting at the Point of Retelling. *Journal of Reading.* Volume 29, number 4, pp. 326–333.

Koshewa, Allen. 1999. *Discipline and Democracy: Teachers on Trial.* Portsmouth, NH: Heinemann.

Lincoln, Yvonna S. 1990. Toward a Categorical Imperative for Qualitative Research. In *Qualitative Inquiry in Education: The Continuing Debate.* Edited by Eliot W. Eisner and Alan Peshkin. New York: Teachers College Press.

Lincoln, Yvonna and Egon G. Guba. 1985. *Naturalistic Inquiry.* Beverly Hills, CA: Sage Publications.

Long, Patricia C. 1985. *The Effectiveness of Reading Miscue Instruments—A Research Report* (Occasional Paper No. 13). Tucson, AZ: University of Arizona, College of Education, Program in Language and Literacy.

Marek, Ann and Carole Edelsky. 1999. *Reflections and Connections: Essays in Honor of Kenneth S. Goodman's Influence on Language Education.* Cresskill, NJ: Hampton Press, Inc.

Meek, Margaret. 1988. *How Texts Teach What Readers Learn.* Great Britain: Thimble Press.

Menosky, Dorothy M. 1971. *A Psycholinguistic Description of Oral Reading Miscues Generated During the Reading of Varying Positions of Text by Selected Readers from Grades Two, Four, Six and Eight.* Ph.D. dissertation, Wayne State University.

Mooney, Margaret E. 2001. *Text Forms and Features: A Resource for Intentional Teaching.* Katonah, NY: Richard C. Owen Publishers, Inc.

Mooney, Margaret E. 2004. *A Book Is a Present: Selecting Text for Intentional Teaching.* Katonah, NY: Richard C. Owen Publishers, Inc.

Moore, Rita and Carol Gilles. 2005. *Reading Conversations: Retrospective Miscue Analysis for Struggling Readers 4–12.* Portsmouth, NH: Heinemann.

Murphy, Sharon. 1998. *Fragile Evidence: A Critique of Reading Assessment.* New Jersey: Lawrence Earlbaum Associates.

Murphy, Sharon. 1999. Validity and Reliability of Miscue Analysis. In *Reflections and Connections: Essays in Honor of Kenneth S. Goodman's Influence on Language Education.* Edited by Ann Marek and Carole Edelsky. Cresskill, NJ: Hampton Press, Inc.

Neisser, Ulric. 1976. *Cognition and Reality: Principles and Implications of Cognitive Psychology.* San Francisco, CA: Freeman and Company.

Owocki, Gretchen and Yetta M. Goodman. 2002. *Kidwatching: Documenting Children's Literacy Development.* Portsmouth, NH: Heinemann.

Paley, Vivian. 2004. *A Child's Work: The Importance of Fantasy Play.* Chicago, IL: University of Chicago Press.

Paulson, Eric. 2002. Are Oral Reading Word Omissions and Substitutions Caused by Careless Eye Movements? *Reading Psychology.* Volume 23, number 1, pp. 45–66.

Paulson, Eric and Ann E. Freeman. 2003. *Insight from the Eyes: The Science of Effective Reading Instruction.* Portsmouth, NH: Heinemann.

Paulson, Eric J. and Kenneth Goodman. 1998. Influential Studies in Eye-Movement Research. In *Reading Online,* the International Reading Association's Electronic Journal, December. www.readingonline.org/research/eyemove.html.

Paulson, Eric and Jeanne Henry. 2002. Does the Degree of Reading Power Assessment Reflect the Reading Process? An Eye-Movement Examination. *Journal of Adolescent and Adult Literacy.* Volume 46, number 3, pp. 234–244.

Peyton, Joy, Peg Griffin, Walter Wolfram, and Ralph W. Fasold. 2000. *Language in Action: New Studies of Language in Society*. Cresskill, NJ: Hampton Press.

Rhodes, Lynn K. 1981. I Can Read! Predictable Books as Resources for Reading and Writing Instruction. *Reading Teacher*. Volume 34, number 5, pp. 511–518.

Rhodes, Lynn K. and Curt Dudley-Marling. 1996. *Readers and Writers with a Difference: A Holistic Approach to Teaching Struggling Readers and Writers*, 2nd ed. Portsmouth, NH: Heinemann.

Rosenblatt, Louise. 1976. *Literature as Exploration*. New York: Noble and Noble.

Rosenblatt, Louise. 1978. *The Reader, the Text, the Poem: The Transactional Theory of the Literary Work*. Carbondale, IL: Southern Illinois University Press.

Rosenblatt, Louise. 1994. *The Reader, the Text, the Poem: The Transactional Theory of the Literary Work*. Carbondale, IL: Southern Illinois University Press.

Sadoski, Mark, Robert F. Carey, and William D. Page. 1999. Empirical Evidence for the Validity and Reliability of Miscue and as a Measure of Reading Comprehension. In *Reflections and Connections: Essays in Honor of Kenneth S. Goodman's Influence on Language Education*. Edited by Ann Marek and Carole Edelsky. Cresskill, NJ: Hampton Press, Inc.

Sampson, Michael, Roach Van Allen, and Mary Beth Sampson. 1990. *Pathways to Literacy: A Meaning Centered Perspective*. New York: Holt, Rinehart and Winston.

Short, Kathy G. and Kathryn Mitchell Pierce. 1998. *Talking about Books: Creating Literate Communities*. Portsmouth, NH: Heinemann.

Siegel, Marjorie. 1999. *Reading as Signification*. New Fetter Lane, London: Falmer Press.

Sims, Rudine. 1972. *A Psycholinguistic Description of Miscues Generated by Selected Young Readers during the Oral Reading of Text Material in Black Dialect and Standard English*. Ph.D. dissertation, Wayne State University.

Smith, Frank. 2004. *Understanding Reading: A Psycholinguistic Analysis of Reading and Learning to Read*. Mahwah, NJ: Lawrence Erlbaum Associates.

Smith, Laura A. and Margaret Lindberg. 1973. Building Instructional Materials. In *Miscue Analysis: Applications to Reading Instruction*. Edited by Kenneth Goodman. Urbana, IL: ERIC Clearinghouse on Reading and Communication Skills and National Council of Teachers of English.

Squires, David. 2001. *The Impact of Elementary Education Majors' Intuitively Held Beliefs on Reading Instruction*. Ph.D. dissertation, Indiana University.

Tierney, Robert J., Connie Ann Bridge, and Mary J. Cera. 1979. The Discourse Processing Operations of Children. *Reading Research Quarterly*. Volume 14, number 4, pp. 539–573.

Trelease, Jim. 2001. *The Read-Aloud Handbook*. New York: Penguin Books.

Vasquez, Vivian. 2000. Building Community through Social Action. *School Talk*. Volume 5, number 4, pp. 2–4.

Watson, Dorothy and Ena-Kaja Chippendale. 1979. *Describing and Improving the Reading Strategies of Elderly Readers*. Columbia, MO: University of Missouri Joint Center for Aging Studies. Monograph.

Watson, Dorothy and Carol Gilles. 1987. E.R.R.Q.: Estimate, Read, Respond, and Question. In *Idea and Insights: Language Arts in the Elementary School*. Edited by Dorothy Watson. Urbana IL: National Council of Teachers of English.

Whitmore, Kathryn and Caryl Crowell. 1994. *Inventing a Classroom: Life in a Bilingual Whole Language Learning Community.* York, ME: Stenhouse Publishers.

Wilde, Sandra. 2000. *Miscue Analysis Made Easy: Building on Student Strengths.* Portsmouth, NH: Heinemann.

Wolfram, Walter. 1998. Linguistic and Sociolinguistic Requisites for Teaching Language. In *Language Study in Middle School, High School and Beyond.* Edited by John S. Simmons and Lawrence Bates. Newark, DE: International Reading Association.

Xu, Jingguo. 1998. *A Study of the Reading Process in Chinese through Detecting Errors in a Meaningful Text.* Ph.D. dissertation, University of Arizona.

Young, Terrell, ed. 2004. *Happily Ever After: Sharing Folk Literature with Elementary and Middle School Students.* Newark, DE: International Reading Association.

BOOKS FOR CHILDREN AND YOUNG ADULTS

Bouchard, David, Henry Ripplinger, et al. 1995. *If You're Not from the Prairie ...* New York, NY: Atheneum Books for Young Readers.

Brumbeau, Jeff. 2001. *The Quilt Maker's Gift.* New York: Scholastic Press.

Byars, Betsy. 1970. *The Summer of the Swans.* New York: Viking Press.

Cooper, Susan. 2002. *Green Boy.* New York: Simon and Schuster Publishing.

Covernton, Jane and Craig Smith. 1988. *Petrifying Poems.* Adelaide, Australia: Scholastic.

Deacon, Alexis. 2002. *Slow Loris.* La Jolla, CA: Kane/Miller Book Publishers.

Di Camillo, Kate. 2003. *The Tale of Despereaux.* Cambridge, MA: Candlewick Press.

The Diary of Anne Frank. 1991. New York: Doubleday, Random House.

Dillon, Leo and Diane Dillon. 2002. *Rap a Tap Tap: Here's Bojangles—Think of That!* New York: Blue Sky Press.

Dunleavy, Deborah. 2004. *The Jumbo Book of Drama.* Toronto: Kids Can Press, Limited.

Evans, Douglas. 2000. *The Elevator Family.* New York: Delacorte Press.

Fitzgerald, John D. 1971. *The Great Brain.* New York: Dell Publishing.

Fox, Mem. 2001. *Boo to a Goose.* New York: Puffin Books.

Gilmore, Kate. 1999. *The Exchange Student.* Boston, MA: Houghton Mifflin Company.

Goodman, Yetta and Carolyn Burke, compiler. 1972. The Old Man, the Son, and the Donkey. In *Reading Miscue Inventory Readings for Tape Procedure for Diagnosis and Evaluation.* New York: Macmillan.

Hamilton, Virginia. 2002. *Time Pieces.* New York: Blue Sky Press.

Kositsky, Lynn. 2004. *The Thought of High Windows.* Tonawanda, NY: Kids Can Press.

Lawrence, Louise. 1994. *The Patchwork People.* Boston, MA: Houghton Mifflin Company.

Lowry, Lois. 1993. *The Giver.* Boston, MA: Houghton Mifflin Company.

Lowry, Lois. 2000. *Gathering Blue.* Boston, MA: Houghton Mifflin Company.

Lowry, Lois. 1989. *Number the Stars.* Boston, MA: Houghton Mifflin Company.

McInnes, John. A., ed. 1962. The Man Who Kept House. In *Magic and Make Believe*. Canada: Thomas Nelson and Sons Limited.

McKee, David. 1973. *The Man Who Was Going to Mind the House*. New York: Abelard-Schumann.

McKissack, Patricia. 2001. *Goin' Someplace Special*. New York: Atheneum Books for Young Readers.

Moore, Lilian. 1965. Freddie Miller, Scientist. In *Adventures Here and There*. Edited by Emmett Betts and Carolyn M. Welch. New York: American Book Co.

Robinson, Sharon. 2004. *Promises to Keep: How Jackie Robinson Changed America*. New York: Scholastic.

Rosen, Michael. 1994. *Poems for the Very Young*. Boston, MA: Kingfisher/Houghton Mifflin.

Sender, Ruth M. 1988. *The Cage*. New York, NY: Simon and Schuster Publishing.

Smith, Doris B. 1973. *A Taste of Blackberries*. New York: Harper Collins's Children's Books.

Thomas, Jane R. 1979. *Elizabeth Catches a Fish*. Boston, MA: Houghton Mifflin Company.

Vannier, Maryhelen. 1967. The Beat of My Heart. In *Sounds of Mystery*. Edited by Bill Martin Jr. New York: Holt, Rinehart and Winston.

Voight, Cynthia. 1981. *Homecoming*. New York: Ballantine Books.

Wiesner, William. 1972. *Turnabout*. New York: The Seabury Press.

Wiles, Deborah. 2001. *Love, Ruby Lavender*. Orlando, FL: Harcourt, Inc.

Woodson, Jacqueline. 2002. *Hush*. New York: G. Putnam's Sons.

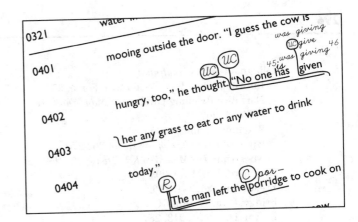

Index